# BLACK INTELLECTUALS

# BLACK INTELLECTUALS,

RACE AND RESPONSIBILITY
IN AMERICAN LIFE

# WILLIAM M. BANKS

W·W·NORTON & COMPANY

NEW YORK · LONDON

Copyright © 1996 by William M. Banks

All rights reserved
Printed in the United States of America
First Edition

For information about permission to reproduce selections from this book write to
Permissions, W. W. Norton & Company, Inc. 500 Fifth Avenue, New York, NY
10110.

The text of this book is composed in Sabon
with the display set in Sabon
Composition and Manufacturing by the Maple-Vail Manufacturing Group.
Book design by Jacques Chazaud
Excerpt from "Black Art" by Amiri Baraka used by permission of Sterling Lord
Literistic. Copyright © 1966 by Amiri Baraka.

Library of Congress Cataloging-in-Publication Data

Banks, William M.
Black intellectuals : race and responsibility in American life /
by William M. Banks.
p.    cm.
Includes bibliographical references and index.
**ISBN 0-393-03989-7**
1. Afro-American intellectuals.   2. Afro-Americans—Intellectual
life.   I. Title.
W185.86.B267   1996
305.896′073—dc20                                        96-6486
                                                        CIP

W. W. Norton & Company, Inc., 500 Fifth Avenue, New York, N.Y. 10110
    http://web.wwnorton.com
W. W. Norton & Company Ltd., 10 Coptic Street, London WC1A 1PU

1 2 3 4 5 6 7 8 9 0

To my father and original homeboy!
W. S. M. Banks II

# CONTENTS

*Illustrations follow page 176*

# FOREWORD

Since World War II there has been a steady increase in the volume and variety of works dealing with African American history. Inspired by the failure of the war to extend its ideals and objectives even to members of an important group that fought in the war, and moved by efforts of civil rights organizations to achieve for black Americans the things that had been denied them since the seventeenth century, articulate African Americans set out to make their own contribution to the struggle. Newspaper editors sought to increase interest in what major organizations, including the government, were and were not doing to improve the positions of African Americans. Essayists and novelists lent their talents to the cause. Historians wrote long treatises surveying the entire sweep of the African American's sojourn in the New World; and they wrote somewhat briefer accounts of one period or one aspect of African American history. The quantity of such writings grew with every passing year.

Clearly lacking was any focus or analysis of what black thinkers were saying and writing. There was no lack of clearly stated views by individual black thinkers. If anything, they were more numerous and more active than during any preceding generation, including the much touted Harlem Renaissance. What was lacking was any critical examination of what the group—historians, novelists, theologians, sociologists, psychologists, and others—were thinking and saying. In other words, how did critical observers evaluate what black intellectuals were saying about the status, condition, and aspirations of African Americans?

This lack of a critical view of what African American intellectuals have been doing in recent years was all the more striking because of an earlier tradition extending far back into the previous century. Members of the Negro conventions, beginning in 1831, played that role both individually and as groups. At the Buffalo Convention of Colored Citizens in 1841, Henry Highland Garnet, activist and commentator, thundered to his listeners, clearly a select group of articulate leaders, "Awake, awake, millions of voices are calling you! Let your motto be resistance; no oppressed people have secured their liberty without resistance." Meanwhile, Garnet's contemporaries such as William Wells Brown, Frederick Douglass, and Samuel Ringgold Ward accepted his challenges by examining and criticizing virtually every aspect of American life and found it wanting. At the end of the nineteenth century and in the early years of the twentieth, the members of the American Negro Academy played a similar role. In 1898, the year following the academy's founding, its first president, Alexander Crummell, declared that its purpose was the "civilization of the Negro race in the United States, by the scientific processes of literature, art, and philosophy." Its members were the scholars and the thinkers "who have secured the vision which penetrates the center of nature, and sweeps the circle of historic enlightenment." He added that true scholars were also "reformers" and "philanthropists" who would challenge the country to live up to its promises.

These earlier groups have seldom been revisited, and in recent years they have received scant attention. Carter G. Woodson considered the earlier period in *The Mind of the Negro as Reflected in Letters during the Crisis, 1830–1860*. Alfred A. Moss Jr. has provided an illuminating account of a later group in *The American Negro Academy: Voice of the Talented Tenth*. Several writers, among them David Levering Lewis and Nathan Huggins, have looked closely at the Harlem Renaissance. As far as I know there has been no examination of the more recent years, nor has there yet appeared a comprehensive, overall history of African American intellectuals.

In this work, William M. Banks has undertaken to fill this void. He has devoted many years to this daunting task, and I am very familiar with the high, rigorous standards he set for himself in the research and the writing. In *Black Intellectuals,* he has nevertheless provided the reader with a historical account of the black intellectual which historians can welcome. His reading of the literature of the long period that he covers is obviously extensive, and his mastery of details can hardly be questioned. He sees clearly the linkages of literature, art, and philosophy, to which Crummell referred in 1898, as critical to the survival and the development of blacks, whether they are intellectuals or simply men and women with good intentions. Indeed, the intellectuals whom Banks sees are not simply those with extensive formal training or high standing among the literary luminaries, although such personages constitute the dominant group. He also sees the purveyors of popular culture as playing significant roles in the intellectual health and well-being of African Americans.

It is difficult enough to deal with the matters raised in this work on terms that are consonant with the subject matter itself. Cultural and philosophical questions challenge their interpreter to come to grips with them, using the concepts and language as they use them. Banks, however, is not satisfied with such a limited universe. If discourse is worthwhile, even in intellectual matters, it should be placed within the reach of all, no matter how limited their training, if they can benefit from such discourse. Thus Banks seeks to engage the nonintellectual as well as the intellectual. He does this not by condescension but by example, not by instruction but by engagement. The result is a very readable account of the entire sweep of African Americans' thought and culture from the eighteenth century to the present, one deserving recognition as the major work that it is.

JOHN HOPE FRANKLIN

# ACKNOWLEDGMENTS

When I reflect on the writing of this book, I cannot help thinking of my parents, who labored to convince me that listening is as valuable a skill as speaking. Since beginning this project, I have spent hundreds of hours listening carefully to many brilliant, and often wise, persons. Some I knew well, others not at all. Not all can be mentioned. Still, it is important that I acknowledge at least some of those who contributed to this book.

Many years ago Robert Carkhuff had a deep intellectual and human impact on me. At the height of the black liberation movement of the sixties, he helped me sort out what I could and could not be. Around the same time, Harry Barnard affected me in ways that he surely does not realize.

The Institute for the Study of Social Change, at the University of California at Berkeley, provided early and generous logistical support for my work. A year at the first-rate facilities of the National Center for the Humanities, in Research Triangle Park, North Carolina, gave me the time to shape the book. Dialogue with such scholars as John Hope Franklin, William Chafe, William Bennett, Mary Clark, David Garrow, Vincent Franklin, Masud Zarvazedeh, Nell Painter, George Reid, and many others led me to discard some of my flightier notions. John Hope and Aureila Franklin helped me weather some difficult times. Their thoughtfulness and generosity reinforced a saying of my maternal grandfather: "Never let your brain outgrow your heart."

A subsequent summer as a fellow at the Center for the Advanced Study of the Social and Behavioral Sciences, in Palo Alto, California, allowed me to rethink the social scientific content in my study. A grant from the Humanities Research Council and the Committee on Research of the Berkeley campus helped fund travel and interview-related expenses. The Undergraduate Research Apprenticeship Program at Berkeley provided two talented undergraduates, Sharon Hasselman and Winston Chiong, who made significant contributions.

Cogent advice and valuable support from Gregg Thomson, Loyce Taylor Lovelace, Stephen Small, Robert Middlekauff, and Leonard Nathan was important as I grappled with my ideas and the manuscript, encountering hurdle after hurdle. Troy Duster, Bob Blauner, Ishmael Reed, Hardy Frye, and Bill Lester read draft chapters. All of them were helpful. Donald Billingsley found a way to disagree with every idea I had about intellectuals.

Russell Schoch and Alix Schwartz provided me with good ideas about how to organize a potentially unwieldy project. The wise mind and red pencil of Amy Einsohn helped me put it all together. All the while Jean Libby assisted me with the voluminous and wide-ranging references.

Tom D'Evelyn, my agent, reflected on the manuscript and suggested even more revisions, and all of them made sense. Tom's sincere belief in the kind of book I wanted to write was rewarding. Conversations with him and my editor, Ed Barber, vice-chairman at W. W. Norton, have girded me for those who may suggest that I should have written a different kind of book.

Stefanie Kelly, Jill Robinson, and Gia White calmly assisted with many details of actual production. Their skills and interest were important assets as I moved ahead.

From beginning to end, the art of Clifford Brown, Pookie Hudson, Miles Davis, Marvin Junior, Dinah Washington, and John Coltrane filled, or helped me fill, many voids.

Lastly, all of my life I have had the advantage of a robust and demanding extended family. They must be acknowledged, especially my mother, Hattie L. Banks, who, early on, gifted me with the idea that I could achieve anything I wanted to achieve. Her grandchildren Troy, Tracey, Trey, and Shane are now the next to take up that loving challenge.

# PREFACE

Discussion of black intellectuals in American life has traditionally fallen under studies of the broader black community or of black political and social leadership. In focusing on black intellectuals, as an entity in themselves, this book explores a number of deeper questions: How did racial discrimination and prejudice shape the emergence and activities of African American intellectuals? How did race define them? How did race influence individual intellectuals' life choices and attitudes? What are the central controversies among black intellectuals and between them and their white counterparts?

The seed for this study was planted in 1968, when I read Harold Cruse's *The Crisis of the Negro Intellectual.* I was stimulated by Cruse's examination of the historical tension between separatist and integrationist impulses in black thought, and particularly by his plea for a critical role for intellectuals. At the time, despite gut sympathies for some of the goals of black activists, I had misgivings about their priorities and their rhetoric. Yet I was not sure whether criticizing these activists would be helpful or proper. Cruse, a nationalist himself, had no doubts. His example convinced me that sharp critical commentary was necessary, and that to fall silent was to be disloyal to the intellectual's mission.

As I began work, the question of defining the term *intellectual* was always on my mind. Because my interest lay with social and cultural matters, I did not want to restrict myself to definitions based on a list of professions or occupations. Nor did I want to work with one that would exclude the earliest African American interpreters of culture, those slaves who re-created the African roles of priests and medicine men. In the literature on intellectuals, the definition that came closest to my conception was the distinction Richard Hofstadter drew between *intellect* and *intelligence:* "Intellect . . . is the critical, creative, and contemplative side of mind. Whereas intelligence seeks to grasp, manipulate, re-order, adjust, intellect examines, ponders, wonders, theorizes, imagines. Intelligence will seize the immediate meaning in a situation and evaluate it. Intellect evaluates, and looks for the meaning of situations as a whole."[1] Thus my conception of intellectuals focuses on individuals who are reflective and critical, who act self-consciously to transmit, modify, and create ideas and culture.

Autobiographies and biographies of black intellectuals were central to my research. All of these works addressed the impact of race on their subjects. My understanding of contemporary issues was aided immeasurably by interviews I conducted during the early 1980s with some twenty men and women of diverse interests and ages; most of them were affiliated with academic institutions, but I also spoke with independent creative artists. Some readers may wonder why I have not mentioned various celebrated persons or provided more biographical detail about others. I can only say that the inclusion or exclusion of any particular individual, or the relative length or brevity of the discussion of an individual, is not meant as an index of his or her accomplishments. The brief biographies at the end of the book provide some details about the lives and work of many persons mentioned in the text. Information about several intellectuals not discussed there is also included in the section. My goal in this volume has not been to present a catalog; rather, I have tried to chart the contours of black intellectual life across American history and to chronicle its fluctuating fortunes.

BLACK INTELLECTUALS

# 1 ⫷

# LAYING
# THE FOUNDATIONS

He [the Master] said I was going on just like my brother
Bige, who had learned to read and was a preacher, and
was raising the devil on the place. So after a little scorn-
ing, I stopped it, and gave up reading until I got to be
19 years old. But the more I read, the more I fought
against slavery.                    —C. H. HALL, ex-slave

And what of the slaves who were skilled? That always
gets left out.                         —RALPH ELLISON

THE AFRICANS WHO came to North America as slaves brought
with them—and tried to preserve—their traditions. In West African villages they had known two intellectual types, priests and medicine men. Priests, considered intermediaries between the gods and
members of the community, assumed the task of interpreting the universe and codifying and rationalizing cultural values. They were
expected to explain natural phenomena such as death, disease, and
drought and to function as a moral and aesthetic compass for life
within the tribe. While their role varied among the thousands of
tribes along Africa's west coast, peoples of the region shared a tradition that looked to a local authority to provide cultural meaning.
During the eighteenth and nineteenth centuries slave preachers in
North America carried on this priestly tradition, one familiar and
important to African-born slaves.

West African medicine men possessed knowledge and insight of
a different kind. They treated illnesses and ailments and passed on

technical information about the physical environment. When the forces of nature threatened the community, villagers turned to medicine men for cures and advice. These highly valued operatives knew the artifacts, potions, or rituals necessary to fend off evil spirits and restore equanimity to tribal life. Unlike the priests, whose status was divinely endorsed, medicine men were trained specialists who learned their craft from older medicine men in the tribe.

As intellectual workers, both groups played key roles in reproducing the cognitive and spiritual codes of their villages. But to Europeans foraging West Africa in search of cargo for slave ships, the often elaborate social organization in African villages was of no concern. All Africans were simply commodities. Because priests and medicine men tended to be older, few were seized by European slavers for transport to the Americas. Instead, slavers picked the strongest of the young men, those who promised to have a long and productive work life.[1] Some African women were seized to perform "woman" work, but many more women slaves ended up in the fields like men.[2]

Of the two types of intellectuals that lingered in the cultural memory of Africans, only the medicine man was compatible with the condition of plantation slavery. The priests were not to be tolerated by slaveholders, for at least two reasons. First, at a pragmatic level, the slaveholding class sought to extract as much work as possible from the Africans. In a social order based on economic definitions of worth, the idea of a reflective and nonlaboring slave was unimaginable. Second, the slaveholders strove to dominate and shape every aspect of a slave's life, and they were understandably intolerant of any authority that might compete for a slave's allegiance. Determined to acculturate Africans to the milieu of slavery, planters reasoned that the symbols and reminders of a previous existence must be eliminated. While the slaveholders could not destroy the Africans' ideas, values, and beliefs, they could neutralize the primary articulators of such thoughts and replace them with European authorities.

In slave society, however, the figure of the African medicine man resurfaced as the "conjurer." Unlike the priest, the medicine man was encouraged in slave society because he (occasionally, she) was seen by masters to be useful. Everyone at one time or another became ill, and the conjurer's knowledge of folk medicine and its applications was respected. Conjurers were technicians who could get things done and resolve concrete problems—of whites as well as blacks. The recollections of a former slave, preserved in the 1930s by a WPA oral history project, show the overlap in the function of the slave conjurers and the African medicine men. "I don't believe in conjurers because I have asked God to show me such things—if they existed— and he said, 'there ain't no such thing as conjurers.' I believe in root doctors because, after all, we must depend upon some form of root or weed to cure the sick."[3] African slaves, recalling their past, thought it unwise to cross conjurers, who were believed capable of condemning people to a life of misfortune. Susan Snow, another former slave, shared with interviewers her apprehensions about conjurers:

> Dey used to say my ma was a cunjer an' dey was all scared of 'er. But my ma was scared o' cunjers too. I don't know nothing about it, cause old folks didn't talk to young folks in dem days an' I didn't use to be scared o' cunjers, but I's scared now, 'cause I had it done to me. I's tellin' de trufe, son, I'm as skeered of a cunjer as you is of a gatlin' gun.[4]

While the conjurer enjoyed respect—even fear—in slave society, he could not satisfy the social need previously fulfilled by the priest in African societies. Distrustful of slaveholder interpretations of their prospects and reality, black slaves longed for one of their own to emerge and provide clues to the moral and spiritual dilemmas that arose in bondage.

For the slaveholders the variety and flexibility of African religious values and the status spiritual leaders enjoyed in the slave community were puzzling and vaguely threatening. To ensure the allegiance of their slaves, planters sought to shape their religious commitments. A favorite tactic was to supplant traditional African religious beliefs with a carefully constructed version of Christianity. New Testament Christianity, with its central theme of redemptive suffering, merged neatly with white material interests. In introducing Christianity to slaves, masters hoped to render them submissive and obedient to temporal powers. By carefully selecting or cultivating black religious leaders, slaveholders erected yet another cultural mechanism to control the minds of the slaves. Slave ministers could operate only with

the permission of masters, and they were usually coerced into publicly parroting a version of Christianity compatible with the slave
order. But underneath lay another worldview.[5] A former slave
preacher understood the designs of his master, yet found opportunity
to frame and manipulate the Christian message differently.

> When I starts preaching I couldn't read or write and had to
> preach what the master told me, and he say tell them niggers
> iffen they obeys the master they goes to Heaven; but I knowed
> there's something better for them, but daren't tell them, 'cept on
> the sly. That I done lot's. I tells 'em iffen they keeps praying the
> Lord will set 'em free.[6]

Slave preachers recognized much in Scripture that supported aspirations for freedom. Yet plantation life allowed for no direct protests, or even appeals on religious grounds. Thus slave preachers
turned to artful ambiguity. Slave congregations, understanding the
limits of expression, developed communal codes and private references, often dismissed by white ears as incoherent. Long after slavery, ambiguity remained a key characteristic of black intellectuals,
inside and outside of the religious community.

## Education and Control

In the seventeenth and eighteenth centuries, West African culture
was propelled by the oral tradition. Cultural knowledge was accu-
mulated and passed on from generation to generation through
priests, respected elders, and storytellers. The socialization process
for young people included sessions with elders who shared the cultural material necessary for life in the tribe. Intellectual continuity
flowed not through the study of great or sacred books but through
recitation, lectures, and dialogue.

Because literacy had not figured in West African village culture
and because reading and writing were not central to their working
lives, the earliest slaves were not preoccupied with it. Nor did plantation owners encourage literacy. On the contrary, most believed that
slaves had no need to read and write: any slave could work well in

the fields without recourse to books. Like the peasants of Europe, slaves were introduced at an early age to the routine of farming, and they were expected to spend their lives doing more or less the same kind of work.

Nonetheless, during the first century of the slave trade, the formal power and authority system of slavery permitted variability in relationships.[7] Through daily contact some masters were drawn to intelligent slaves with engaging personalities, and favored slaves were occasionally taught to read and write. The literate slaves might then be drafted for work close to the master's family. This literacy, and the power it represented, was afforded only to slaves thought to be loyal. But masters often miscalculated. The case of Nat Turner, a trusted and literate slave who led a rebellion in 1831, illustrates how a façade of acquiescence and humility could hide deep resentment and hostility well enough to fool a slaveholder.

Literacy also threatened the control and surveillance network for slaves in the South. Concern about runaways prompted slaveholders to require passes for all slaves traveling unaccompanied off the plantation. Literate slaves, however, could forge the necessary papers and escape to the North (few white patrollers could read well enough to verify the documents). Many slaves who learned to write did indeed achieve freedom by this method. The wanted posters for runaways often mentioned whether the escapee could write. For example, the following advertisement for a runaway slave appeared in the *Maryland Gazette* on February 27, 1755: "He is supposed to be lurking in Charles County near Bryan-town, where a mulatto woman lives, whom he has for some time called his wife; but as he is an artful fellow and can read and write, it is probable that he may endeavor to make his escape out of the Province."[8]

Anxiety about literate bondsmen stimulated South Carolina in 1740 to pass the first law prohibiting the instruction of slaves. By 1780 most southern states had followed suit. However, a growing ambivalence about slavery led to a somewhat lax enforcement of these statutes. Many prominent southerners had begun to express reservations, and several large slaveholders had freed their slaves, maintaining that slavery was incompatible with the lofty ideals of the American Revolution. Moderates like Thomas Jefferson believed that the economic forces making slavery impractical in the North would eventually destabilize slavery in the South.

In such a fluid political milieu, some slaveholders tolerated slave literacy. Others ignored the statutes for economic reasons, realizing that literate slaves could handle record keeping and business transactions, and thus increase the profits and leisure time of the planter class. The prohibitions were also ignored by pious masters who wanted their slaves to read the Bible. And there are numerous accounts of planter children enjoying "playing school" and teaching their slave playmates the rudiments of literacy. Thomas Johnson, a slave in Virginia in the mid-nineteenth century, later explained how he learned to read and write.

> The youngest son of the master had a copy book. When I saw it I decided to have one like it . . . [W]hen I had five cents, I went to a book store and asked for a copy book. I had made up my mind what to say if the bookseller should ask me for whom I wanted it. I intended on telling him it was for my master. I went home and began to learn from this book how to write . . . but another problem presented itself—I could not spell. At night when the young master was getting his lessons, I used to choose some word I wanted to know how to spell, and say, "Master, I'll bet you can't spell 'looking glass.' " He would spell it. I would exclaim, "Lor's o'er me, you can spell nice." Then I would go out and spell the word over and over again. I knew that once it was in my head it would never be got out again.[9]

Johnson eventually escaped to the North and moved to England, where he enrolled in a seminary. He returned to his native Africa as a Baptist missionary. Other accounts of slaves point to benevolent mistresses as witting, and sometimes unwitting, teachers.

It seemed, then, that literacy would inevitably grow within the slave community, but Eli Whitney's invention of the cotton gin in 1783 changed all that. Up to this time, the arduous process of separating cotton fiber from seed had blunted the crop's profitability. With the cotton gin, a crop once marginal to southern agriculture assumed much greater economic significance. A vast, cheap supply of docile laborers became essential if planters were to exploit the market for cotton and reap the profits they envisioned. Consequently many southern moderates began to reassess their moral discomfort with human bondage. Most slaveholders closed ranks against any ideas or practices that would unsettle the labor pool.

In 1831 a group of slaves under the leadership of Nat Turner, who believed himself to be acting on biblical principles, took up arms and killed more than sixty whites in Southampton County, Virginia.[10] News of the uprising sent shock waves through the entire South. Beset by fear and guilt, planters reasoned that if their slaves heard about the Turner rebellion, they might plan similar actions. Measures were quickly taken to limit the information available to all blacks, both slave and free. The citizens of Southampton passed a resolution that read, "Resolved that the Education of persons of Color is inexpedient and improper as it is calculated to cause them to be dissatisfied with their condition and furnishes the slave with the means of absconding from his master."[11]

To counter the abolitionists who mailed antislavery publications to free blacks and moderate whites in the South, southern state legislatures banned such mailings. When federal courts ruled the prohibitions unconstitutional, most southern states drafted laws that made the possession of antislavery literature illegal. South Carolina's law set the tone: "A free Negro . . . was to be fined $1,000 for the first offense, for the second offense fifty lashes and for the third offense death."[12]

Vigilant enforcement of the anti-literacy statutes soon became the norm. The informal education of blacks was repressed to the fullest extent possible, and the "school games" of white youths and their black pupils came to an end. As so often happens, these prohibitions only heightened curiosity about the off-limits world of reading and writing. Other efforts to restrict the social world of slaves included limits on travel between plantations and punishments for any communication between slaves and free blacks: "A gathering of more than a few slaves (usually five) away from home, unattended by a white, was an 'unlawful assembly' regardless of its purpose or orderly decorum."[13]

Meanwhile, although an overwhelming majority of southern blacks in the nineteenth century were slaves, the number of free blacks in the South grew from 32,523 in 1790 to 258,346 in 1860. This population included many mulatto sons and daughters of slaveholders who had been educated on plantations and subsequently freed. Although a few of the wealthier free blacks sent their children North to be educated, most free black children lacked that opportunity. Recognizing the importance of education, a small but determined number of free parents in the larger towns and cities of the early nineteenth-century South often pooled their meager resources and funded small, frequently one-room primary schools.[14] Usually well attended, even crowded, these schools rarely went beyond the basics of reading, writing, and arithmetic. The teachers, some with skills scarcely superior to those of their students, made up in determination for what they lacked in training.

The success of these primary schools drew the fearful attention of white legislators. When the racial climate worsened after Nat Turner's rebellion, free blacks were powerless to defend their hardwon schools. By 1834 most southern states, especially those in the Deep South, had taken steps to shut the black schools down. In 1837 the Virginia legislature went a step further, passing a law barring the return to Virginia of black children schooled out of state. Within a few years the educational opportunities available to free blacks in Virginia had evaporated: "Before 1830 they had by private means provided schooling in every city in the state. By 1839 all the projects had been effectively cut off, and free Negroes were forced to make exiles of their children or themselves if they wanted the children to be educated."[15]

Blacks were the primary, but not the only, victims of the ruling class's denial of literacy. Controlling southerners also saw little value in literacy-based education for the white masses. In 1850 over 20 percent of the South's whites were illiterate, compared with 3 percent in the Middle Atlantic states, and 1 percent in New England.[16] Concern with literacy as a social value had entered the American consciousness, but the South lagged behind the rest of the nation in accepting public education, which would have required higher taxes. For example, Alabama took no steps to establish a statewide public school system for white children until 1854. Far beyond that date, sectional differences in the state worked against evenhanded school funding. Regions dominated by wealthy planters balked at appropriations that would have shifted their education tax payments to poorer Black Belt areas. In the ideological tradition of rugged individualism, the southern yeoman was himself contemptuous of any policies that smacked of charity. Education thus proved to be one of many areas in which less privileged southern white workers and farmers rejected policies beneficial to them in order to preserve the myths generated by the wealthy planter class. Given the general antipathy of the South to public education and the threat that literate blacks were thought to pose, blacks faced formidable odds in their quest for even basic literacy. Meyer Weinberg's phrase "compulsory ignorance" sums up the educational experience of enslaved blacks in the South.[17]

## Learning in the North

From the time of American independence until 1820, most northern states made no provisions for the education of black children. Free blacks were taxed like other citizens, but their children were not allowed to attend public schools. Undaunted, small communities of northern blacks banded together to build and operate their own schools, even while they continued to agitate for public su  ort of black education. Despite the hardship of what was essentially double taxation, and without qualified teachers or adequate books and supplies, the free black communities still managed to maintain some semblance of schooling for their children.

The relative freedom of the northern states did not preclude the racial subordination of blacks. Even small successes in education were often countered by whites who rejected the idea of any education at all for blacks. In Ohio white mobs on several occasions destroyed schools built by blacks. The administrations of white schools that decided to integrate their student bodies and educate all qualified citizens were also stormed by furious whites. When Noyes Academy in Canaan, New Hampshire, announced in 1835 that it would accept black children, a mob of townspeople descended on the school and dragged the building into a swamp.[18] In New England in 1831 a group of black leaders and white abolitionist supporters bought land in New Haven to build a college for blacks. The plan quickly ran into opposition. So incensed were the white residents at the prospect of a black college in their midst that "on September 10, the 'best citizens' of New Haven, led by the Mayor and a number of Yale professors and students, staged riots before the homes of supporters of the college. Many Negroes wished to proceed in the face of this hostility, but some timid white abolitionists withdrew their support and the college was abandoned."[19]

Despite the violence, northern blacks continued to demand support for black education, frequently invoking constitutional principles. Their most persuasive argument was the simple contention that blacks who paid taxes should be allowed access to a publicly supported school system. The hypocrisy of subjecting blacks to the same kind of injustice that sparked the American Revolution did not escape the notice of some northern legislatures, and several states managed grudging concessions. In 1844 the legislature of Ohio decreed that a portion of the taxes paid by African Americans be allocated for the education of their children. A few towns in Massachusetts permitted blacks to attend their public schools; however, segregated schools—separate and unequal—had become the norm for public education in the northern states by 1835. Describing the efforts of northern blacks to build educational institutions in cities, the historian Leonard Curry has concluded, "One of the remarkable accomplishments in American history is the degree to which they [blacks] marshaled their slender financial and human resources, the rapidity with which they strengthened their institutions, and the effectiveness with which they developed educational opportunities adapted to their needs." But successful as northern blacks were in extending education to blacks in the cities, a fundamental barrier to mobility remained intact. In Curry's words, "Except for a handful of individuals—notably ministers, teachers, physicians and editors— access to employment appeared not to be favorably affected by educational advancement"[20]

As northern blacks tried to gain educational opportunities, whites grew more afraid of the impact of free blacks on the northern economy. Abolitionists actively encouraged blacks to leave the South. But northern white workers, fearing economic competition, successfully pressured their state legislatures to pass inhibiting laws. Illinois voters endorsed by a ratio of two to one a statute outlawing the immigration of blacks. More liberal states required blacks to certify their free status or to post a good-behavior bond of up to one thousand dollars.[21]

## Making a Living

Considering how few jobs awaited educated African Americans in the nineteenth century, the rewards of study were largely intrinsic: neither universities nor law firms nor publishing houses hired blacks in professional positions. School teaching, journalism, and the ministry, careers linked to segregated institutions—that was about it.

Reform was slow in coming. In 1849 the Massachusetts supreme court ruled that blacks had no right to attend white public institutions, ensuring that the privately financed black schools would continue to need qualified teachers. In the North black communities and schools offered their teachers considerable status but meager salaries.[22] In the absence of options for any other intellectual work, however, teaching and the ministry long remained havens for learned blacks.

Within the relatively autonomous black churches, preachers enjoyed a type of freedom unavailable in the outside world. John Mercer Langston, probably the first black to attend a theological school (Oberlin College), felt that the black church provided the African American the "opportunity to be himself, to think his own thoughts, express his own convictions, make his own utterances, test his own powers."[23] After earning bachelor's and master's degrees from Oberlin, Langston studied law with a judge and in 1854 became the first black admitted to the Ohio bar. He continued to "test his own powers" after the Civil War, serving as dean of the Howard University law faculty and, later, as president of Virginia State College. When federal reconstruction policies extended the ballot to all citizens, Langston ran for and was elected to the U.S. Congress from Virginia.

Recognizing the need for well-educated and sophisticated leadership, black congregations increasingly insisted on preachers who had some formal training. Fortunately, the seminaries were less hostile to black aspirations than were secular institutions. The intellectual careers of influential men such as Charles Ray, Henry Highland Garnet, and Alexander Crummell were launched in northern seminaries.

Charles Ray studied theology at Wesleyan University and served as minister of New York's Bethesda Congregational Church for twenty years. From his post Ray became an influential figure in the black abolitionist movement and in 1837 was named general agent of the *Colored American* newspaper. Henry Highland Garnet, another activist nineteenth-century leader, completed seminary training at Oneida Theological Institute in New York in 1840. In 1843 he caused a stir at the National Negro Convention by calling for active resistance to slavery, including armed rebellion if necessary.

Not all northern seminaries were receptive to black talent. In 1837 General Theological Seminary in New York City rejected Alexander Crummell's application for admission because of his race. Embittered but undaunted, Crummell studied privately with several white Episcopal theologians in New England and was eventually ordained in Philadelphia in 1844. Although Crummell joined the black intellectual clergy in calling for liberty and rights for blacks, he continued to emphasize the value of individual moral and mental development within the black community.

As the historian Benjamin Quarles says, men of the cloth dominated black leadership in the nineteenth century: "The eight Negroes who were numbered among the founders of the American and Foreign Anti-Slavery Society in May 1840 had one thing in common. They were all clergymen."[24]

In the antebellum period the original emotional revivalism of black worshipers slowly gave way to the optimism and rationalism of nineteenth-century American culture. Conversion experiences and testimonies no longer guaranteed salvation. Believers were called upon to confront social and moral ills, and the black ministry boldly placed slavery on the agenda of the American religious community.

Despite the social standing of teachers and ministers, some educated blacks had no desire to enter those professions. A few resourceful thinkers found other means to communicate their ideas to a broader public. In 1827 Samuel Cornish and John Russwurm, the first black to earn a bachelor's degree at an American university (Bowdoin College, in Maine, in 1826), founded the first black newspaper in the United States, *Freedom's Journal*. Published in New York, the *Journal* for the two years of its existence was a voice in the growing black protest movement in the North. Because the youthful editors were determined to feature material about and of special interest to free blacks, articles extolling the need for self-help and moral uprightness dominated the *Journal*'s pages. Living in the North and being exposed to the growing influence of the press, Cornish and Russwurm hoped that their weekly would counter the vile treatment typically accorded blacks in mainstream newspapers. Confident of their abilities and intellectual perspective, the editors proclaimed, "We wish to plead our own cause. Too long have others spoken for us."[25] Their example was catching. By 1850, black newspapers were on the streets in most large northern cities.

Although all the papers opposed slavery, most editors reasoned that they could better promote political thinking and activity in the black community by concentrating on the problems of local readership. No theme got more space than racial uplift. Having no reason to believe that support or sympathy would be forthcoming from the white world, blacks were urged to accept the challenge of elevating the race themselves. At a time when few other organs of communication were accessible to literate African Americans, these weeklies featured articles, literary pieces, and letters to the editor. Newly literate blacks relished the chance to show off their skills and to stay abreast of current black thought.

Unfortunately, the noble intentions and hard work of the editors could not compensate for a harsh economic reality that soon weakened the black press. Although the number of literate blacks living in northern cities grew steadily until the Civil War, their communities were nonetheless impoverished and thus hard-pressed to sustain black journals. A majority of the papers closed after a few years. Even so, during their brief heyday they did demonstrate a role for independent black journalism and etch the black press on the roster of institutions that could utilize black mental talent and extend the protest tradition.

## Conventions and Literary Societies

The establishment of the black church and weekly newspaper set the stage for voluntary clubs and associations among educated black elites. Full of ideas and opinions about current events and issues, educated black men and women began to congregate and discuss matters that transcended the special interests of their profession or region. Indeed, across the country, blacks often were aware of and responded to the same or similar events and trends. When the black press printed accounts and commentary on John Brown's raid on Harpers Ferry in 1859, thousands of blacks found themselves talking about the significance and appropriateness of the raid.[26]

The most noteworthy form of organized and voluntary association was the convention movement. Excluded from established political parties and processes but determined to protest slavery and racial subordination, educated blacks from five northern states convened in Philadelphia in 1831 to discuss the condition of black America and put forward recommendations. Soon each of the northern states was hosting its own conventions. The following call to delegates of the New York state convention in 1855 illustrates the broad purpose of the convention movement:

> The undersigned, regarding the present as a favorable time for pressing the claims of the colored citizens of this State upon the consideration of our State Government, with a view to the removal of the odious and invidious disabilities imposed therein, and to gain equal political rights, take the liberty to invite their colored fellow-citizens to assemble, in State Convention, in the city of TROY on the FIRST TUESDAY of SEPTEMBER, 1855. There is a sacred obligation resting upon the colored citizens of this State, to give the ear of our Legislature no rest till every legal and political disability, with all its depressing and degrading tendencies, shall be swept from the Empire State.[27]

Delegates to the conventions were recruited from the ranks of learned blacks in cities and towns. For a week each year the orators and pundits of the race held forth, launching blistering attacks on racism, African colonization, and northern discrimination. The conventions enabled eloquent African American speakers to articulate ideas to sympathetic and informed black audiences. Delegates listened intently while the best and the brightest African Americans demonstrated their grasp of American intellectual traditions. A speech by William Lambert of Michigan in 1843, attacking a proposal to deny blacks the right to vote, illustrates just such a mastery of the origins of American political philosophy:

> That this right is a natural right, belonging to man, because he is a person not a thing—an accountable being and not a brute. That government is a trust to be executed for the benefit of all; that its legitimate ends are the preservation of peace, the establishment of justice, the punishment of crime, and the security of rights. These principles declare eternal war against all political injustice. They condemn all Legislation violating the spirit of equality. They are the foundation of a true, and unproscriptive republican form of government and correct guides in all political action.[28]

Because no other venues were available, the conventions usually took on the air of tournaments, where orators competed with one another to enhance their reputations among their peers. The erudite delegates held many different opinions and often locked in bitter debates on the convention floor. Resolutions proposing African colonization split several national and state conventions, as did resolutions calling for slave revolts. However, the gladiatorial character of the conventions did not detract from the delegates' commitment to improve the social and political standing of black Americans.

Black conventions were more an expressive than an instrumental vehicle. Delegates sadly realized that the resolutions, however painstakingly crafted, would be ignored by state and federal authorities. Indeed, at the height of the convention movement, many northern states were moving to disenfranchise blacks. Still, the published proceedings of the conventions reveal no intellectual or spiritual acquiescence in powerlessness. On the contrary, the level of discourse confirmed the extraordinary progress of blacks in fashioning political and intellectual dialogue. If the delegates left the conventions pessimistic about the prospects for state or national legislative action, they must have been impressed with one another and the strides they had made under an oppressive national regime.

Although political and economic liberty were foremost on the agenda, learned blacks also established literary and cultural associations. In the literary societies, which were organized in all major northern cities, small groups of free blacks met weekly to discuss literature and the arts. New York City was home to the Phoenix Society, founded in 1833; Philadelphia had its Minerva Literary Association; and Baltimore's black literary devotees formed the Young Men's Mental Improvement Society for the Discussion of Moral and Philosophical Questions of All Kinds, in 1835. Like similar clubs in white society, black literary groups were committed to the prevailing cultural beliefs about moral uplift and the civilizing power of art and literature. Maria Stewart, a black writer and lecturer, spoke at Boston's Afric-American Female Intelligence Society in 1832 and challenged the audience to demonstrate "that though black your skins as spades of night, your hearts are pure and your souls are white."[29] Reflecting the bias of the period, black societies tended to follow their white counterparts in consigning cultural affairs to women. Thus, for the first time, black women played an important role in institutions for the learned.

The societies also generated a receptive audience for books by black authors. When some club members could not afford to purchase books, the societies took up collections and formed small libraries. A number of urban libraries that have survived into the twentieth century have roots in the early-nineteenth-century literary clubs.

Although limited in scope, the societies served an important function in the embryonic stages of black intellectual history. Their members reasoned that the white critical establishment could not be trusted to make fair aesthetic judgments of black art: they had seen creative works summarily rejected or dismissed as "quaint" because their creators were black. So they established their own agents of criticism, offering assessments grounded in their experiences as African Americans. For black scholars and writers, this discerning, sympathetic audience provided the commentary so necessary in intellectual work. The contention that black art could not get a fair hearing in the councils of white criticism still echoes.

## Early Literary Efforts

In the eighteenth century the market for books written by black authors was quite limited. Blacks either could not read or lacked money for luxuries such as books. For various reasons, some whites may have been interested, but not enough of them existed to create a market.

Nevertheless, a few blacks did become recognized authors. Jupiter Hammon (1711–?), a slave-poet living in New York, is usually credited with being the first published black author; his poem "An Evening Thought: Salvation by Christ, with Penitential Cries" appeared in 1760. Steeped in religious themes, his work rarely included direct comments about his status as a slave. In the sermon "Address to the Negroes in the State of New York" Hammon's most popular work— and the only piece that was reprinted—he was quite reconciled to his status as a slave.

> Now I acknowledge that liberty is a great thing, and worth seeking for, if we can get it honestly; and by our good conduct prevail upon our masters to set us free: though for my own part I do not wish to be free, . . . for many of us who are grown up slaves, and have always had masters to take care of us, should hardly know how to take care of themselves; and it may be for our own comfort to remain as we are.[30]

In the same address he encouraged blacks to learn to read so as to absorb the Bible's wisdom. (The goodwill of masters that allowed Hammon to learn to read and write, and eventually get his work published, did not extend to giving him his liberty.) Hammon's poetry and prose were firmly rooted in the American literary tradition of the period, and his use of black speech cadences in his poems was innovative, but his apologies for slavery diminished his stature among later black authors and critics.

The career of Phillis Wheatley (1753–1784) also reflects the particular predicament of slaves who had to modulate their literary voices. Brought to Massachusetts from Africa as a slave in 1761, Wheatley was sold to a genteel and wealthy New England family. Purchased to be the personal servant of John Wheatley's wife, young Phillis soon impressed the family with her rapid mastery of English. Under the influence of the pious Wheatleys, she absorbed the Calvinist Methodist tradition. Before long she was composing verses that caught the attention of local literati.

Wheatley's poor health and status as a household servant afforded her the leisure to write. After her debut and subsequent acclaim as a poet, John Wheatley arranged for her to accompany his son to England, where, he believed, the climate would be better for her health. In England, in 1773, she received considerable attention as a novelty; despite—or perhaps because of—her slave status, Wheatley was praised by the aristocracy. Her mastery of the form and style of English sentimental verse astounded the local arbiters of culture. "An Elegy Poem on the Death of George Whitefield," her poem on a famous and influential figure of the Great Awakening, had appeared in 1770 and was quickly reprinted in several editions. Her *Poems on Various Subjects, Religious and Moral* was published in 1773. Wheatley's European sojourn was cut short when she returned to New England to care for her ailing mistress.

When her owner died, Wheatley was freed. Soon she married a free black, John Peters. According to one biographer, "her husband was proud and irresponsible, and not only estranged his wife's white friends from her, but also forced poverty upon her and upon the three children she bore him."[31] Cut off from the material security she had enjoyed in the home of a wealthy New England merchant, Wheatley found her new life difficult. Former friends who had subscribed to her books no longer offered assistance, and the growing din of revolution diverted attention from the slave-poet. Among her last works was a tribute to the American Revolution and its concern for liberty. She died at the age of thirty-one in 1784.

Wheatley occasionally referred to herself as African in origin but generally avoided comments about slavery and its effects. Like Hammon and other black authors of the period, she recognized that there were limits to what blacks could say in print. Modern readers have criticized the absence of protest in these early black poets, yet the mere existence of a black poet symbolized a challenge to whites who doubted blacks' creative ability. Moreover, a close and sympathetic reading of the texts of Hammon and Wheatley reveals their clever use of irony and ambiguity to question the morality of slavery. Consider the following lines by Wheatley:

*Should you, my lord, while you peruse my song*
*Wonder from whence my love of freedom sprung,*

*Whence flow these wishes for the common good,*
*By feeling hearts alone best understood,*
*I, young in life, by seeming cruel fate*
*Was snatched from Afric's fancied happy seat.*

Surely, in the words of a critic, " 'Seeming cruel' and 'fancied happy'
give her away as not believing in the cruelty of the fate that had
dragged thousands of her race into bondage in America nor in the
happiness of their former freedom in Africa."[32] Just as the slave
preachers had resorted to ambiguity, Wheatley and Hammon relied
on irony to convey a coded message. As we will see, twentieth-century writers like Zora Hurston, Chester Himes, and Ishmael Reed
would continue to refine the ironic mode as a tool for social criticism.

Other black thinkers were less veiled than Hammon and Wheatley.
Writing in 1788 under the pseudonym Othello, a former slave living
in the North left no doubt about his intentions:

It is neither the vanity of being an author, nor a sudden and
capricious gust of humanity, which has prompted this present
design [writing]. It has long been conceived and long been the
principal subject of my thoughts. Ever since an indulgent master
rewarded my youthful services with freedom and supplied me at
a very early age with the means of acquiring knowledge, I have
laboured to understand the true principles, on which the liberties of mankind are founded, and to possess myself of the language of this country, in order to plead the cause of those who
were once my fellow slaves, and if possible to make my freedom,
in some degree, the instrument of their deliverance.[33]

# 2 ⋘

# BLACK THINKERS
# IN A WHITE
# MOVEMENT

It is not the *ought*-ness of the problem that we have to
consider, but the *is*-ness!          —WILLIAM PICKENS

A s WE HAVE SEEN, early black thinkers developed in all-black institutions—schools, conventions, churches, and literary societies.
Beginning around 1830, however, the abolitionist movement introduced a new and challenging stage for intellectual performance. This
movement was organized and dominated by northern whites who
opposed slavery on religious and moral grounds. To dismantle that
un-Christian system, they undertook to educate influential church
congregations and societies in the North. They hoped to bring about
moral reform and change by appealing to the social elite through
conventions, rallies, lectures, pamphlets, and essays that appeared in
the local press. The movement enlisted prominent Americans such
as Ralph Waldo Emerson, Henry Wadsworth Longfellow, Herman
Melville, and John Greenleaf Whittier. Framed in purely moral
terms, the abolitionist cause was attractive to upper- and middle-
class whites far removed from the economic or political realities of

slavery. The historian Bertram Wyatt-Brown has written that, for the most part, the northern abolitionists

> belonged to the ranks of the professional class—school teachers, ministers and writers. As members of the intelligentsia, they moved within that small band of neighborhood citizens who started lyceums, campaigned for common schools, organized temperance chapters, raised funds for colleges, libraries and asylums, welcomed professors, clergymen, and foreign missionaries to their homes, humble or grand as the case may be.[1]

For many "enlightened" whites, abolition was acceptable as a "cause," but actual African American participation was another matter. For a number of reasons, including racial prejudice, northern abolitionists were slow to enlist northern blacks in the crusade against slavery. As late as 1826, many white-controlled antislavery societies excluded blacks as well as women from membership.[2] Early abolitionists had difficulty transcending their sense of noblesse oblige and embracing a genuine racial equality. Free blacks, sharply attuned to moral asymmetry, pointed out this hypocrisy. The message eventually struck home. Led by William Lloyd Garrison, the foremost proponent of moral suasion as an antislavery weapon, antislavery groups began to accept blacks into their ranks.

Interaction with upper-class whites was very important to the black intellectuals involved with the abolitionist groups. For a while, participation in antislavery societies gave learned blacks a wider audience than the conventions and other all-black associations had provided. Rather than preach to the powerless, they could freely mingle and exchange ideas with figures important in the cultural life of the nation. The experience proved intellectually gratifying and emotionally reassuring. In no other context could Henry Highland Garnet and William Wells Brown, the ex-slave and novelist, have worked alongside upper-class whites such as Lewis Tappan and Harriet Beecher Stowe. For the more thoughtful blacks, however, the euphoria of mere association faded as tensions arose between their agenda and that of their white abolitionist counterparts; once more blacks found themselves fighting—this time for meaningful roles in a movement dedicated to black liberty.

Frequently ex-slaves were recruited to speak at abolitionist meetings. Given their limited occupational options, here was a good living. Among the earliest of these orators was Charles Lenox Remond, first employed by the Massachusetts Anti-Slavery Society in 1838 to arouse northern audiences and elicit moral sympathy for the abolitionist cause. The program of one popular antislavery society called for an ex-slave to stand before white audiences and describe his or her life under plantation slavery. The ex-slave's impassioned accounts of beatings, starvation, family separations, and escape converted many a northerner to the abolitionist cause. The list of blacks who achieved some reputation on the abolitionist circuit included Frederick Douglass and Samuel Ringgold Ward, who also published a slave narrative, *Autobiography of a Fugitive Negro,* in 1855. Douglass recalled how he would be marched out before audiences to detail his suffering and degradation, the floggings, the random cruelties. All analyses and interpretation, he noted, were reserved for the white antislavery speakers who followed. Douglass was at first grateful for the support and friendship extended by these whites, but over time the sterility of the routine came into conflict with his restive and increasingly independent mind:

> It was impossible for me to repeat the same story month after month and keep up my interest in it. It was new to the people, it is true, but it was an old story to me and to go through with it night after night was a task altogether too mechanical for my nature. . . . I could not always follow the injunction, for I was now reading and thinking. New views of the subject were being presented to my mind.[3]

On one occasion Douglass's mentor cautioned him against injecting his own ideas into a speech: "It is not best you seem too learned."[4]

Douglass's predicament illustrates a dilemma of the black intellectual who hoped to develop egalitarian relationships with powerful whites. True collegial relationships within the abolitionist movement were undermined by the whites' sense of racial and social superiority. And blacks could not achieve recognition and legitimacy within northern intellectual circles unless they obtained the approval of influential whites. Without such acknowledgment, black thinkers found themselves on the margins of cultural and political discourse. From the margins they could, of course, engage in critical commentary, but, especially in the area of race relations, black thinkers wanted to enter the mainstream of intellectual and political dialogue.

Black intellectuals were in many ways unprepared for these conflicting currents. Faced with hostility nationwide and needing no more enemies, they sought ways to participate and still to assert their dignity and autonomy. They had to carefully mitigate many racist assumptions and beliefs. Unfortunately, the conflict over the extent and nature of black involvement in abolitionist societies was only one of many tensions that shaped the vision of the black intellectual.

## Disputes about Black Schools

Atop the free black agenda in the North was public support for the schooling of black youth. Through persistent agitation and a number of lawsuits in northern cities, blacks convinced several states that black taxpayers were entitled to this public support.[5] But legislatures balked at permitting blacks to attend the all-white public schools. Publicly subsidized separate facilities would be better for both races, they argued. Given their poverty and their belief in education, most blacks in the nineteenth century welcomed any type of publicly supported schooling. Separate education was better than no education at all. Moreover, they were not eager to push their children into the racist environment of white schools. Many concluded that black children were better served by separate schools with sympathetic black faculty and staff.

Nonetheless, a small but influential group of northern free blacks resisted the principle of separate institutions and insisted that the public schools be integrated. Anticipating later debates, they focused on the inherently inferior nature of segregated education. Charles Reason, a black professor at Central College in McGrawsville, New York—an integrated school—maintained that separate schools would induce a sense of inferiority in black youth.[6] Only through contact and competition with whites, he argued, could black students gain the confidence they needed to achieve their full potential.

The arguments of Robert Purvis, a privileged and educated African American, summarized the case against separate institutions. Purvis, a mulatto, was born free in Charleston in 1810. His father, a successful white businessman, sent his young son to Philadelphia to shelter him from southern repression and provide him with a quality education. When his father died in 1826, young Robert inherited and managed the family cotton-broking firm.[7] Purvis perceived racially separate institutions as a backward step; at black conventions, he attacked those who supported separate schools. He was horrified at the idea of black schools specializing in industrial or manual training. "The Industrial School being necessarily (if not in theory, yet in fact) a complexional institution, must foster distinctions, and help draw more definitely (so far as educational privileges are involved) those lines of demarcation under which we have labored and still are trying to eradicate."[8] A consistent foe of racial exclusiveness, Purvis also advocated modifying the names of organizations and removing any reference to race from their bylaws.

Purvis attracted criticism from prominent black intellectuals. Among others, Frederick Douglass frequently challenged the depth of Purvis's commitment to black freedom, pointing to his privileged background and the wealth he had inherited from a white father. Like many intellectuals of subsequent generations, Douglass held that group commitment was directly related to individual experience. Purvis's universalistic rhetoric confirmed for Douglass his distance from the everyday problems of black Americans.

Other black leaders questioned the rationale for integrated schools. Alexander Crummell, who was to become one of the century's most distinguished black intellectuals, rejected the assumption that white educators could effectively teach poor and disadvantaged black students.[9] James McCune Smith, a physician who earned A.B. and M.D. degrees at the University of Glasgow and published scientific studies attacking racial-inferiority doctrines, joined Crummell in arguing that integrated classrooms guaranteed nothing and that black teachers were more likely to demand superior achievement from black students. Some black teachers opposed integrated schools on economic grounds, fearing the loss of their jobs.

In nineteenth-century America, without doubt, most whites (even abolitionists) wanted no more than rudimentary education for blacks. Private schools established by blacks in the North, though economically pressed, were therefore the only places free to choose objectives and curricula that whites would have considered inappropriate, or at least irrelevant, for blacks.

In the black primary schools, the color, qualifications, and training of teachers varied considerably. Blacks with some college training were, of course, favored by black school organizers, but the small number allowed to matriculate in northern colleges did not satisfy the demand for teachers. In many communities white teachers were hired to staff black schools. This was a controversial solution. In general, black schools preferred less-credentialed black teachers to white teachers, however well trained.

For some black thinkers the problem went beyond complexion and academic training, to the values and assumptions of white teachers. Frederick Douglass believed that white education would alienate a black student from his community, his history, and his personal experience:

> He must either abandon his own state of things which he finds around him, and which he is pledged to change and better or cease to receive culture from such sources, since their whole tendency is to change him, not his condition, to educate him out of his sympathies, for all that is worth to him is his elevation, and the elevation of his people.[10]

While most black intellectuals concentrated on the particulars of black freedom, some joined with whites in the temperance, women's rights, and other social movements. Advocates of all-black organizations reminded the interracialists that most white social reformers were ambivalent in their attitude toward social and political equality. But despite the racism encountered in white abolitionist circles, a significant number of blacks argued against exclusively black organizations. William Whipper, a wealthy businessman and follower of the antislavery moralist William Lloyd Garrison, believed that such organizations reinforced existing schisms between black and white. In 1835 Whipper, Robert Purvis, and others helped found the American Moral Reform Society (AMRS), whose mission was to transcend the confines of race and address such issues as temperance, free speech, and women's rights. The minutes of the AMRS's 1835 convention reveal the new program:

> We have buried in the bosom of Christian benevolence all those national distinctions, complexional variations, geographical lines, and sectional bounds that have hitherto marked the history, character and operations of men; and now boldly plead for the Christian and moral elevations of the human race.[11]

Samuel Cornish, editor of *Colored American,* offered a scornful account of an AMRS meeting he attended in 1835:

> We found Purvis, Whipper and others (of those Christian benevolence and cultured intellect, we have so many and such strong evidences) vague, wild, indefinite, and confused in their view. They created shadows, fought the wind, and bayed at the moon for three full days.[12]

That many blacks were active in other reform issues is important in the history of the black intellectual. Slavery, of course, dominated the agenda, but women's rights, temperance, and moral uplift shared the spotlight. Many of the arguments for the abolition of slavery and the establishment of civil equality for free blacks were consistent with the rationale for women's rights, and many blacks supported women's rights but were concerned about dissipation of energy from the antislavery cause.

## The Lure of Africa

Another issue dividing educated free blacks was the question of emigration to Africa. By 1840 many had concluded that blacks had no viable future in the United States. No doubt this sentiment was shared by a wide cross section of blacks, but for the educated and well-trained few, the lack of appropriate employment was excruciating. As a cofounder, in 1827, of *Freedom's Journal,* John Russwurm had labored on several fronts to abolish slavery and increase liberties for free blacks. Now with Cornish he continued to hope that the wide distribution of reasoned opinion and information would improve the prospects of blacks in America. The two worked together to produce a publication worthy of the public's respect. Two years later, however, Russwurm resigned as editor and offered this bleak assessment:

> In many things it is our duty to experiment until we arrive at the truth; but unless we have reasonable hopes for a favorable issue they are all useless; hence then, we conclude that all efforts to improve the mass of coloured persons must prove abortive; and this conclusion we adopt from the evidence of our own eyes.[13]

Such pessimism was not uncommon among black intellectuals who observed the chains of white supremacy shackling the aspirations of the black community. Furthermore, as individuals they found their progress thwarted in spite of their superior education and achievements.

Frederick Douglass opposed any and all colonization movements, but he did express sympathy for the special plight of educated African Americans. When Harriet Beecher Stowe, the author of *Uncle Tom's Cabin,* wrote to Douglass in 1853 asking how to invest in black interests, he suggested she fund a black college devoted to the mechanical arts. A traditional liberal arts degree, he wrote, only made the black graduate's life more frustrating: "It would seem that education and emigration go together with us, for as soon as a man rises amongst us, capable, by his genius and learning to do us great service, just so soon he finds that he can serve himself better by going elsewhere."[14] He then cited contemporaries—John Russwurm, Henry Highland Garnet, and Alexander Crummell, all outstanding thinkers educated in the North—who, sorely disappointed by what the country would offer them, eventually cast their lot with the emigrationists. Though of proven intellectual competence, they were denied the opportunity to work in areas of their training. Somewhat self-effacingly, Douglass lamented, "I regret their election, but I cannot blame them, for with an equal amount of education and the hard lot that is theirs, I might follow their example."[15]

Most of the plans put forward by pro- and anti-black emigrationist factions alike called for the emigration of free blacks only. Their departure would have satisfied supporters of slavery by eliminating the vanguard of black antislavery agitators. Astute free blacks recognized this but argued, for instance, that the presence of African Americans in West Africa would perhaps mobilize native Africans against further participation in the selling of human beings, thus striking a mighty blow for freedom. Yet why, asked Douglass, would the heads of African villages who had marketed captives for decades be receptive to the emigrationists' antislavery arguments?

Some black emigrationists confessed an attraction to the prospects of commerce and wealth in Africa. Henry Highland Garnet, in particular, ridiculed the anticolonists, pointing out that while blacks were busy vilifying each other's highbrow principles, whites were busy extracting and developing the riches of the African continent to increase their mastery in the world.[16]

Other black intellectuals had political, rather than commercial, aims. Martin Delany was admitted to Harvard Medical School in 1850, but Oliver Wendell Holmes, then dean of the Medical School, yielded to pressure from white students and dismissed Delany after one semester. Thoroughly embittered, Delany looked to Africa for the freedom he believed was impossible for blacks in the United States. Delany and Crummell saw emigration as a stage toward the goal of building and maintaining a powerful black nation,[17] thereby disproving the central tenets of proslavery ideology: that the black race was incapable of self-government and independent moral action; that without the benevolent and paternalistic intervention of whites, blacks would lapse into barbarism and heathenism. Delany was adamant:

> It is time that we had become politicians, we mean, to understand the political economy and domestic policy of nations; that we had become as well as moral theorists, also the practical demonstrators of equal rights and self-government. . . . Have we got now sufficient intelligence among us to understand our true position, to realize our actual condition, and determine for ourselves what is best to be done?[18]

Talented blacks, by settling abroad and building a strong nation, he said, would refute for all time the racist lie.

## The Stigma of Black Inferiority

Of all the ideological roadblocks to equality facing black intellectuals in the nineteenth century, the most challenging was the widely held belief that blacks were mentally inferior to persons of other races. In mobilizing their arguments, black thinkers were at a considerable disadvantage. Because of slavery and their exclusion from schools, most blacks were indeed uneducated. Further, many slaves and free blacks adopted customs and behaviors that violated nineteenth-century standards. In 1833 Maria Stewart wrote of her decision to enter the all-male world of preaching: "Had those men among us, who have had an opportunity, turned their attention as assiduously to mental and moral improvement as they have to gambling and dancing, I might have remained quietly at home and they stood contending in my place."[19] Middle-class blacks, particularly the growing group of educated women, were unsparing in their criticism of drunkenness and vice in the free black community.

Conceding the ignorance and crudity of the black (and white) masses, black thinkers pointed to the social tragedy of slavery as the explanation for the shortcomings of Negroes. The black radical David Walker insisted that the backwardness of blacks was not surprising, considering their isolation in American society. The solution, of course, was to abolish slavery and provide civilizing opportunities for the freedmen. Pressing their case further, black thinkers challenged propagandists for black inferiority to explain the success of those blacks who had not been enslaved. Anyone who doubted the mental capability or moral caliber of the black race had only to note the accomplishments of many free blacks in the North. Sufficient exposure to black "genius," it was assumed, would dissolve racial prejudice and discrimination.

But the "exceptional man" tactic was most likely doomed to fail, as Benjamin Banneker, a free mulatto, had discovered when he tried the approach on Thomas Jefferson. Jefferson, a slaveholder who

opposed slavery, acknowledged blacks to be equal to whites in brav-
ery, tolerance for heat, and emotionality, but considered them "inferior to whites in the endowments of body and mind."[20] In 1791
Banneker sent Secretary of State Jefferson a copy of an almanac he
had written and suggested to him that his feat was evidence of blacks'
mental ability. In his reply Jefferson did not address directly the issue
of blacks' intellectual capacity; instead, he offered platitudes about
his hope for the continued progress of the black race. Jefferson later
expressed doubt that Banneker had actually written the almanac,
suggesting that it may have been the work of a white friend.

Men such as Banneker experienced confusion when dismissed by
whites. Black thinkers identified with Banneker's scientific contribution, believing it vindicated their own claims to intellectual stature
and potential. Surely, the achievements of an essentially self-taught
free black gave evidence of the potential repressed by slavery. Yet
individual examples of merit, however numerous, failed to shake the
beliefs of a racist culture. Like Jefferson, skeptics disingenuously
claimed fraud, charging that the alleged achievements of blacks were
in fact the work of white accomplices. Others attributed the talent of
blacks to the flow of "white blood" in their veins.

# 3 ⋘

# THE BLACK
# INTELLECTUAL
# INFRASTRUCTURE

To me the beast in Du Bois was the lure of leadership,
the lure of being able to marshal people to march across
the green with you. I think he wanted that. Du Bois said,
"I have to choose between being a scholar and a propagandist." A propagandist is but a mediated form of that
other kind of leader who stands up, rants and raves, and
takes the people to storm the gates. I think it was unfortunate that he did that.        —HENRY LOUIS GATES

BETWEEN 1865 AND 1915 a social framework for the development of
a genuine black intellectual group slowly took shape. Education
still led the way. Black parents encouraged their children to value
learning, and black communities frequently made great sacrifices to
establish and fund educational institutions. The early goal of black
education was to extend literacy, but it was soon realized that survival in a complex and changing nation would require more than
that. Up-to-date institutions were necessary if blacks were to be a
viable part of the American future.

## Emancipation and
## the Push for Black Education

Emancipation and the end of the Civil War freed black aspirations
manacled under slavery. Monitored by northern occupying troops,

freed blacks voted, ran for office, filled important posts in state and local governments, and generally pushed their way into postbellum southern political life. But because the world of electoral politics at the local and state levels could accommodate only a few blacks, and because the lack of capital blocked most economic ventures, new citizens turned primarily to education for social advancement. The free black community was remarkably optimistic about the power of schooling to improve the lot of blacks; ex-slaves did not view their poverty as an insurmountable barrier to learning.

The sacrifices that former slaves endured so their children could acquire an education that had been denied the parents are part of a poignant chapter in American history. J. W. Alvord, general superintendent of schools for the Freedmen's Bureau, an agency formed to oversee social programs designed for the ex-slaves, traveled throughout the South between 1865 and 1868 and reported on the efforts to educate newly freed slaves. Impressed by their commitment to education, he wrote, "They have seen power and influence among white people is always coupled with *learning;* it is a sign of the elevation to which they now aspire."[1]

Reconstruction legislation had provided funds for the education of free blacks, but hostile white officials in the southern states were imaginative in their resistance; they withdrew tax funds for schools, for instance, to stall black education. Horace Mann Bond, in his 1939 study of black education in Alabama, noted that from 1869 to 1874, 67 percent of the money appropriated by the state for education was diverted to other purposes.[2] In Louisiana, according to Alvord, the suspension of the general tax for black schools elicited a strong protest.

> The consternation of the colored population was intense. Petitions began to pour in. I saw one from the plantations across the river, at least thirty feet in length, representing ten thousand Negroes. It was affecting to examine it and note the names and marks (x) of such a long list of parents, ignorant themselves but begging that their children might be educated; promising that from beneath their present burdens and out of their extreme poverty they would pay for it.[3]

The federal reconstruction program mandated the establishment of primary, or common, schools throughout the South. Open to all ex-slaves, these schools were designed to provide free blacks with rudimentary literacy skills, knowledge about moral values, and the requirements of citizenship. Because no effective and accountable system of publicly financed education was in place in states like Alabama, ex-slaves had to pay tuition to enroll their children in the "freedmen's" schools. Despite the financial hardship, emancipated blacks flocked to the schools all over the South. Some southern whites doubted whether blacks could learn. Others conceded that the ex-slaves were educable, but held that the prospect of educated blacks was untenable. Peter Dox, a congressman from Alabama, complained that black schooling was creating problems. He said he had to polish his own boots because blacks refused to do it.[4] Clinging to the vestiges of power and privilege, southern whites correctly viewed educated blacks as a threat to the political regime they hoped one day to reconstruct. Northern advocates, however, insisted on educating blacks, arguing that a people so long isolated from mainstream values must be reacculturated and that the freedmen's schools would accomplish this goal.

Freedmen's schools were staffed largely by northern missionaries and the few educated blacks who chose to remain in the South after the war. The missionaries were, for the most part, sincere in their desire to raise the educational and moral standards of free blacks. Against the claim that freedmen were incapable of, or had no interest in, learning, the missionary Pamelia Hand described her experience as a teacher of Arkansas freedmen in 1868: "I expected to find them anxious to learn but after all I confess I was unprepared for the amount of zeal manifested by most of them for an education. I can say as one of old told me, 'The half had not been told.' I am surprised each day by some new proof of their anxiety to learn."[5]

Products of the religious educational system of New England, the Yankee "schoolmarms" placed moral education on an equal footing with literature and mathematics. Recent scholars have criticized northern missionaries and their role in freedmen's education, noting that the values and standards taught by white northerners were those of the dominant and essentially racist society.[6] Indeed, many of the northerners who volunteered to teach in the freedmen's schools saw themselves as civilizers rather than as educators, and consequently they spent more time on affairs of the soul than on matters of the mind.

Accounts of the teaching missionaries often ignore the presence of highly educated black women in the ranks of those who went South to educate former slaves. Many black women, graduates of normal schools and the more liberal colleges like Oberlin, wrote to the American Missionary Association (AMA), which sponsored many schools, expressing their conviction that it was their "duty as a people to spend our lives trying to elevate our own race."[7] Edmonia Highgate graduated with distinction from the public high school in Syracuse, New York. In 1864, while a principal in Binghamton, Highgate asked the AMA to send her to the South. After four years in very trying settings in northern Maryland, New Orleans, and Mississippi, Highgate returned to the North. In a speech before the Massachusetts Anti-Slavery Society in 1870, she warned, "The teachers sent out by the evangelical organizations do little to remove caste prejudice, the twin-sister of slavery. We need Anti-Slavery teachers who will show that it is safe to do right."[8] Few of the white teachers went so far as to accept and teach social equality. Rather, their intention was to instill the "proper" values and habits of mind, and thereby prepare their students to become hardworking, conscientious soldiers of the cross.

The northern missionaries' emphasis on religious instruction attracted the support of many southern conservatives. In 1866 a Baptist association in Alabama reluctantly concluded, "Our first duty is to give religious instruction to the ignorant and destitute at our doors and in our employ."[9]

Despite such limitations, the freedmen's schools did constitute the first black educational network in the South, supplementing the skeletal schools that free southern blacks had established earlier in cities like Norfolk, Baltimore, and New Orleans. Some of those schools had operated underground, carefully changing location to avoid detection by zealous authorities. This became unnecessary during the later stages of the Civil War, when southern army officers considered the enforcement of slave antiliteracy statutes to be a low priority.

After the war, the original black schools had important advantages in the competition for the allegiance of recently freed slaves. Foremost was the reputation the schools had earned during very difficult times. Second, most blacks distrusted whites, even those who professed belief in black freedom. Like Douglass and the black abolitionists of an earlier period, southern blacks saw an imperative to make their own agenda and control their own institutions. Despite the help that flowed from the hearts and purses of white northerners, a sizable percentage of the newly freed population chose to enroll and teach in the black-sponsored schools.[10] Funding from the federal reconstruction authorities, however, favored the schools under white missionary control.

As more and more blacks enrolled in primary schools, it became apparent that the number of teachers that would be needed to work with black pupils far exceeded the supply available in the North. The most obvious source of talent was the freedmen population, and black and white supporters of black education in the South soon founded "normal schools" to train black teachers. Initially intended to meet secondary school standards, a number of these schools were gradually upgraded. By 1900 collegiate programs were in place at institutions like Fort Valley High and Industrial School, in Georgia, and Bishop College, in Texas.[11] The number of students advancing to the collegiate level remained low, reflecting not a lack of interest but the poverty of potential teachers. Most normal-school graduates could not afford the years of additional training and signed up for teaching positions as soon as they were even marginally qualified.

To meet the postbellum demand for education across the country, two types of higher educational institutions evolved: state land grant colleges and private colleges. In 1862 Congress had passed the Morrill Act, which made federal land available to states that wanted to serve important regional and local interests by establishing colleges. Southern states accepted the land and established agricultural and technical colleges, but excluded blacks. In 1892, under pressure from blacks and northern radicals, Congress revised the Morrill Act to make more land and funds available, with the stipulation that a separate system of black colleges be created in the former Confederate states and that the states allocate the funds to black and white colleges according to the state's population mix. This "separate but equal" model satisfied most blacks at first, but their satisfaction was short-lived.

With the eclipse of the reconstruction government, and with no federal presence to monitor their disbursement of funds, the southern states quickly institutionalized inequality:

> In Georgia, the state in 1881–82 appropriated $14,000 for some white colleges and $8,000 for a black one. By 1913–14, the figure for white colleges had risen to $539,000, the black college appropriation was unchanged. . . . After a decade of the second Morrill Act, expenditures on white land grant colleges exceeded those of black ones by a ratio of 26:1.[12]

In addition to public land grant colleges, several private black colleges were established by black and white religious denominations in the North and the South. Black religious bodies such as the African Methodist Episcopal and Baptist churches tried hard to maintain schools like Allen University (South Carolina), Morris Brown College (Atlanta), and Virginia College (Richmond, later renamed Virginia Union). Their financial support, however, usually collected each Sunday in black churches throughout the country and supplemented by white philanthropy, barely kept the campuses open.[13] Born of racial oppression and white paternalism and handicapped by dependency, private black colleges were forced to accommodate their policies to the mandates of agencies external to the schools and the black community.

Far more than white institutions, black colleges were captive to forces struggling to dominate the South economically. Northern capitalists were on the march for new markets and a cheap, reliable work force. The remnants of the southern planter class saw white supremacy as a key element in the restoration of their agrarian power and readily accepted violence as a means to that end. The *Negro Year Book,* published by Tuskegee, reported that 1,914 blacks were lynched between 1892 and 1901.[14] This gruesome figure, however, does not include the various forms of violence short of actual murder that were practiced against blacks. "The number of outrages upon [blacks] between 1868 and 1871 still defies reasonable estimation," one historian has written. "The multitude that were murdered left no accounts. And most who survived were too frightened to report attacks on them to the law."[15]

Caught between an aggressive capitalist class and southern racists, the black community lacked the economic power and political clout to sustain the autonomy of its colleges. The prerogatives of northern industrialists and southern politicians could not be ignored by the administrators of black institutions in southern and border states. Southern officials exerted budgetary pressure to ensure that the publicly supported land grant colleges for blacks remained substandard and uninvolved with pressing political and social debates.

Wealthy patrons had their own agendas at private black colleges. The politically controversial W. E. B. Du Bois resigned from Atlanta University in 1908 when foundations and patrons balked at further funding for the university's conferences he had initiated. Du Bois was particularly riled when a white Mississippi planter with no scholarly credentials received funds from the Carnegie Institution to conduct a historical study of blacks. Du Bois himself had been turned down when he requested funds for a similar study.[16]

Doubting the ability of blacks to rise to the highest levels of scholarship, white philanthropists such as Andrew Carnegie dodged the issue. Carnegie supported the type of quasi-industrial education provided by the Hampton Institute, founded in 1868 by Samuel Armstrong, the son of New England missionaries. Armstrong, classically educated at Williams College, in Massachusetts, thought, like most whites of the time, that a liberal arts curriculum would be wasted on black students:

An elaborate course of study, making them polished scholars, would unfit our graduates for the hog and hominy fare and lowly cabin life that awaits most of the workers in our poor and sparsely settled country. A three or four year course commencing with the rudiments, requiring of the beginners a knowledge of reading and writing and the first rules of arithmetic, and embracing among other things, the elements of grammar, mathematics, science and history, is enough.[17]

Armstrong and the Hampton philosophy found a vocal advocate in Booker T. Washington, an ambitious mulatto from Malden, West Virginia. Born into slavery in 1856, Washington enrolled at Hampton and completed the instructional program in 1875. After teaching in West Virginia for two years, he attended the Wayland School in Washington, D.C., to pursue classical and religious studies. Finding Wayland's classical curriculum too impractical and too distant from the world he knew, he stayed less than a year. In his autobiography, *Up from Slavery,* Washington said that Wayland students were at a disadvantage compared with Hampton graduates: "They knew more about Latin and Greek when they left school, but they seemed to know less about life and its conditions as they would meet it at their homes."[18] Washington conceded that a classical education might be suitable for some people, but he thought the particular circumstances of black southerners required a program of basic educational skills and manual training.

After leaving Wayland, Washington found few occupations open to him. When Principal Armstrong called upon his prize pupil to deliver the May 1879 commencement address at Hampton, Washington jumped at the opportunity. He came to Hampton two months before the scheduled event and spent the time researching and polishing the address. His speech, titled "The Force That Wins," dazzled and reassured both blacks and whites in the audience as he solidly endorsed Armstrong's educational philosophy and implored southern blacks to make the best of their situation. Armstrong, recognizing Washington's gifts and the value of having an articulate southern black committed to the Hampton model, offered him a job as a teacher and study hall assistant.

Two years into Washington's tenure at Hampton, Armstrong recommended him for the principalship of a new school being established in Tuskegee, Alabama. Washington took the job and moved quickly to mold Tuskegee in the image of Hampton, emphasizing discipline, hard work, and manual training.[19]

Tuskegee's program was obviously practical. In addition, Washington likely believed it nonthreatening to northern white benefactors and southern elites. Accommodating whites, rather than confronting their prejudices, would generate more opportunities for the students of Tuskegee—and for himself. The Tuskegee education thus furthered the social aims of Washington and his white benefactors. Horace Mann Bond has observed, "Since the school was an instrument of a social policy, it was difficult to tell where it was primarily an educational institution and where a social device."[20]

The question how best to educate the black masses greatly perplexed the members of the black intelligentsia. They themselves had benefited from rigorous intellectual and creative training. Such training, however, was of little use for the masses of blacks who grappled with subsistence and basic literacy. What kind of educational philosophy and programs, they asked, would best prepare blacks to sustain themselves economically and culturally in a complex and hostile society? While highly educated blacks had no doubts about their own abilities, they knew that slavery and oppression had seriously handicapped the black community. T. Thomas Fortune, a journalist and editor of the *New York Age,* a leading black newspaper from 1884 to 1907, was an outspoken critic of racial discrimination, going so far as to advocate violence against perpetrators of racial crimes. Nevertheless, when Fortune pondered the educational needs of the black South in 1895, he recoiled at the trend toward collegiate and liberal studies. Fortune thought it nonsensical that higher education was being proposed for "a class of persons unprepared in rudimentary education, and whose immediate aim must be that of the mechanic and the farmer." Echoing a tenet of the white powers he frequently attacked, Fortune concluded that blacks "should be instructed for the work to be done."[21]

On the other side of the racial divide, Governor A. D. Candler, of Georgia, testified before the Committee on Industrial Commission in 1901, "The best school I ever saw for the Negro, or the white boy either, was the corn patch to learn the art and science of farming."[22]

W. E. B. Du Bois accepted the need for trained black workers, but he saw no reason to reject liberal and advanced education for the most talented portion of the black population. Du Bois, born in Great Barrington, Massachusetts, in 1868, had earned a B.A. degree from Fisk University, in Nashville, in 1888 and a Ph.D. from Harvard University in 1895. No doubt reflecting his own experience, and a projected role for himself in African American life, Du Bois insisted that the elevation of the black community could not be realized without "providing for the training of broadly cultured men and women to teach its own teachers."[23] By 1916 he had become skeptical about the industrial education offered at places like Hampton. In a letter to Paul Hanus, president of the American Association for the Advancement of Science, Du Bois spoke of Hampton's standards and mission:

> The difficulty of Hampton is that its ideals are low. It is, as it seems to me, deliberately educating a servile class for a servile place. . . . If she was educating white boys and girls parents would quickly bring her to task (and) make her prove the efficiency of her methods. But since she is educating Negroes everybody is willing that she should experiment as long and as freely as she pleases.[24]

For the most part, however, black intellectuals accepted the lesser task. Higher-level programs would have to wait. The first goal was to attain economic self-sufficiency, and that, they maintained, depended on industrial training.

Primary and vocational education ruled the day. Most black college heads chanted the rhetoric of industrial education for blacks. Even so, a number of them cultivated the treasures of liberal arts study for themselves. Booker T. Washington, the foremost proponent of black industrial education, sent his own daughter to Radcliffe and often publicly acknowledged a role for higher learning in the black agenda.[25]

## Higher Education for Black Americans

Into the early twentieth century, black normal schools and colleges remained poorly funded. The school year for blacks in rural areas of the South was typically seven months, not nine; that allowed students to labor in the cotton and tobacco fields. In his autobiography, *Born to Rebel,* Benjamin Mays, a scholar of black religion and the president of Morehouse College, in Atlanta, from 1940 to 1968, discusses the effect of the shortened school year when he was growing up in South Carolina in the 1920s:

> In the seventeen years since I entered the first grade at the age of six, I had spent only seventy-three months in school—the equiv-

alent of eight nine-month years of schooling. Had I been able to complete each year without being taken out for farm work, I would have graduated at fourteen instead of twenty-one. I regret those lost years.[26]

Nevertheless, the abbreviated year that Mays lamented would have been welcomed by blacks in some areas if it had meant they would have a school. Often, white officials simply refused to build and staff black public schools: "In 1911, the entire state of Maryland had a single [black] public high school, in Baltimore. At the time about 200,000 Negroes lived in the state. In 1925, Atlanta's public schools operated forty kindergartens for white children, but none for blacks."[27]

The task of providing secondary-level training thus fell to the economically precarious black private schools. And while they did a remarkable job, given their inadequate resources, many of their graduates headed to college campuses woefully unprepared for truly collegiate work.

The all-black campuses that welcomed these black youth were often sterile, repressive places, tightly monitored by state officials, white corporate philanthropists, or black religious denominations. Indeed, aware of the source of their legitimacy and power, black college administrators tended to be authoritarian. Academic freedom was a problematic ideal. Faculty in the black colleges served at the pleasure of the president, who in turn served at the pleasure of the governing board.

On some campuses the spiritual overwhelmed the secular mission. At religiously sponsored colleges, students and faculty were held to strict moral codes. Smoking, drinking, and other modern vices were forbidden; daily attendance at religious services was required of students and faculty alike.[28] At Tuskegee, Booker T. Washington worried about social interaction between unmarried men and women faculty. On several occasions he formally reprimanded faculty for such contacts. In 1908 John C. Wright, the chair of Tuskegee's English department, was told in a cautionary letter from Washington, "Experience has proven that it is best for the school to pursue the policy of asking its unmarried teachers, to refrain from making the mistake of too frequent association with the same individuals of opposite sex."[29] A year earlier Edgar Penney, Tuskegee's chaplain for many years, had had to resign after a coed accused him of sexual advances. Although the charges were never corroborated and Penney denied any wrongdoing, Washington decided that the gossip and rumors about the incident gave him no choice but to ask for Penney's resignation. Washington "tactfully" took no position on the chaplain's guilt or innocence.[30]

In the South, which still lagged behind the rest of the nation on all measures of educational achievement, blacks with college training were greatly admired by the masses of African Americans and held up as examples of what could be accomplished through perseverance and patience. Many barely literate and socially backward blacks were transformed by black educational institutions. In 1904 Booker T. Washington boasted to a Lincoln's Birthday gathering in Madison Square Garden that "not a single graduate of the Hampton Institute or of the Tuskegee Institute can be found today in any jail or state penitentiary."[31] Combining a disciplined approach to learning with a moral education that embraced the value of service, the institutions survived and launched the careers of many black intellectuals. Horace Mann Bond graduated from Lincoln University in 1923 and returned to the Pennsylvania school as president in 1945. In between, he earned a doctorate at the University of Chicago and wrote *Negro Education in Alabama* and *The Education of the Negro in the American Social Order.*

The vast majority of blacks seeking higher education enrolled in black colleges. By 1900, according to Du Bois, only 390 blacks had graduated from white colleges—128 of them at Oberlin University, in Ohio. No other integrated school had graduated as many as 20 blacks by the turn of the century. Several northern universities admitted blacks but took steps to keep their quotas small. The hostility of white students and alumni and a professed concern for the safety of black students were frequently cited as reasons for the quotas. Those blacks who did enroll at the universities met with social ostracism and rank discrimination.

By comparison, Du Bois reported, in the same year black four-year colleges had graduated 1,941 students.[32] Atlanta University, Howard, Virginia Union, and a few other prestigious colleges competed to hire these graduates, particularly those with advanced degrees. Also, black land grant institutions, such as Morgan State, North Carolina College, and Virginia State, offered important employment opportunities.

Following the lead of private northern colleges, the few private four-year colleges for blacks emphasized Latin and Greek in their requirements. In 1900 Howard University required of graduates four years of Latin and two years of Greek. Fisk, Wilberforce, and Atlanta all required at least two years of the classics for graduation. Still, as Du Bois noted, these requirements fell "from one to two years behind the small New England colleges."[33] The first-year curricula of Fisk and Atlanta mirrored the New England classical tradition at the turn of the century:

### Fisk.

FALL TERM.—Latin: Vergil's Aeneid, four books. Greek: Iliad (Seymour). Mathematics: University Algebra (Wells).

WINTER TERM.—Latin: Latin Prose Composition. Greek: Iliad, first three books completed; Thucydides, Seventh Book (Smith); Peloponnesian War. Mathematics: Spherical Geometry; Trigonometry (Wells).

SPRING TERM.—Latin: Cicero's De Senectute et De Amicitia. Greek: Thucydides. Mathematics: Surveying, including field work with compass, transit, and Y level (Robbins). . . .

### Atlanta.

FALL.—Xenophon's Anabasis-5; Cicero's De Senectute and De Amicitia (Kelsey's)-4; Algebra (Wells)-5; Hebrew History-2; Elocution-1.

WINTER.—Memorabilia (Winians)-5; De Amicitia and Livy (Lord)-4; Algebra-5; Hebrew History-2; English Composition-1.

SPRING.—Odyssey (Merry)-5; Livy-4; Algebra-5; Greek History (Myers)-2; English Composition-1.[34]

As the nineteenth century progressed, higher education everywhere abandoned the classical model. Influenced by European universities, especially those in Germany, American colleges developed programs that prepared students for the emerging industrial order. The labor needs of corporations were usually quite specific, and universities tended to modify curricula and expand electives to keep pace with new technologies and emerging professions. This shift of emphasis, encouraged by corporate philanthropy, met with resistance from classical purists, but the business elite represented the new concentration of power, and institutions conformed to the priorities of big business.

Surveying the occupations of black college graduates at the turn of the century, Du Bois found that 53.4 percent of those responding to his questionnaire were teachers and that 17 percent were preachers.[35] In reporting the data, Du Bois did not distinguish between elementary, secondary, and college instructors, but most of his respondents would have been teaching in primary schools. The need for teachers was so great that students at some black high schools were hired as teachers before they had graduated. Mary Church Terrell, who taught at Washington's M Street School, wrote, "The first class would have graduated in 1875, but the demand for teachers being so much greater than the supply, the first two classes were drawn into the teaching corps before they had completed the prescribed course."[36] The service orientation of newly educated blacks corresponded neatly with the growing need for black teachers. Educated blacks were thus commandeered to implement a grassroots education program meant to bring social benefits to the many rather than the few.

By 1900 the hundreds of blacks who functioned as educational leaders were humbled by their inability to alter their institutions. They had little power and no control over resources. Faced annually with huge debts, black administrators had little choice but to comply with the demands of corporate philanthropists and adopt the Hampton-Tuskegee model. Occasionally, they tried to camouflage the liberal studies component, but philanthropists were not easily duped. They employed agents to inspect the schools for departures from Booker T. Washington's approach. At Fort Valley Normal College, John W. Davison, the president, was removed when Washington loyalists accused him of deviating from the industrial education model.[37]

Although the speeches and writings of the black intelligentsia influenced the thinking of many African Americans, especially the educated, they could provide no endowments. Elected officials had nothing to fear from black newspapers. In fact, some militant black editors made peace with accommodationist ideology in return for financial support. Had the black intelligentsia, as a group, not been wedded to the ideal of service to the race, its powerlessness would have been easier to cope with. But the intellectuals were the "social guides," morally upright and informed citizens, the best! Racial oppression had fostered a strong sense of community among the various social strata in black America, and talented blacks unquestioningly accepted a responsibility to aid or speak on behalf of the unlettered black masses. In 1896 Henry L. Morehouse, a patron of liberal arts study for blacks, coined the term *talented tenth* to refer to a class of highly educated and morally upright African Americans who he hoped would constitute a vanguard for the black masses.[38] In 1905 W. E. B. Du Bois called for a cadre of blacks to be "leaders of thought and missionaries of culture among their people."[39] To describe this group he appropriated Morehouse's term. The "Talented Tenth" came to be a source of pride—and occasionally contempt—in African American life.

Still, powerful white philanthropists and southern politicians could afford to ignore the pleas of the black intelligentsia for broader educational opportunities. Black intellectuals could take some consolation in the fact that their ideas, particularly their opposition to the industrial training emphasis, were influencing other blacks. But the shift to the liberal arts that ultimately occurred at places like Fisk and Clark College had more to do with the preferences of white groups, like the American Missionary Association. The brightest blacks had to bide their time until the black community could muster the power to draw attention to its interests. Only then could they compete for key roles in determining the way blacks would participate in American life.

# 4 ⫷⫷⫷

# SLOWLY MAKING
# THEIR MARK

No man can refuse to raise the platform on which he
himself must stand.            —G. N. GRISHAM

OBSESSED BY GROWTH and materialism, America at the turn of
the century was, on the whole, inhospitable to its writers,
white and black. Very few authors could expect to survive on income
from creative writing alone. For some whites journalism provided an
adequate living in preparation for or alongside a literary life. Stephen
Crane, O. Henry, H. L. Mencken, Carl Sandburg, and Theodore
Dreiser all worked as journalists. Covering social, political, and cultural events broadened their experience, and constantly filing stories
sharpened their writing skills. Other American writers, such as
Henry James and Gertrude Stein, drew on sizable family resources
for support as they experimented in the world of art and literary
culture.

Although black writers were not optimistic about their economic
future as artists, many persisted. Being black in America certainly
provided a bounty of dramatic material. Irony, cultural ambivalence,

pathos, and transcendental themes came together in black life, and several writers accepted the challenge to weave these elements into novels, poems, and short stories. Fiction writers such as Paul Laurence Dunbar and Charles Chesnutt diligently studied the poetry and prose writing of the period and ably reproduced its form and style. This early generation of black fiction writers lacked the confidence to launch bold innovations; they knew of no audience that would endorse experimental literature by blacks. So they tended to follow the literary traditions of the period, hoping to demonstrate their worth through mastery of established forms. Thus while their stories differed in content from those written by whites, their well-crafted fiction kept to mainstream American forms and techniques.

The biographies of Dunbar and Chesnutt reveal the special impact of race. In Dayton, Ohio, the literary gifts of young Paul Laurence Dunbar led his white Central High School classmates to elect him class poet. After graduating in 1890, unable to go on to college, he worked as an elevator boy in a downtown office building. Young Dunbar was humbled by his descent to menial work, but he remained sanguine and continued to write and publish poems in Ohio newspapers. He eventually assembled a collection of his poetry but lacked the $125 needed to print the volume. A white friend advanced him the money, and the collection, *Oak and Ivy,* was published.[1] Dunbar quickly repaid the loan, selling copies of the book to elevator passengers charmed by the idea of a poetry-writing elevator boy. Eventually his poetry was noticed by William Dean Howells, the preeminent literary gatekeeper of the period. Howells considered Dunbar a formidable poet and helped him get a number of poems placed in influential national periodicals, such as Howell's own *Harper's Weekly.* Having received Howells's stamp of approval, Dunbar's career gained momentum, and he became the most popular black poet in America.

Dunbar's reception in literary circles through Howells's sponsorship illustrates a tension between black literary works and the taste of the white public. Dunbar's stories of an idyllic plantation South with characters speaking in dialect matched the perceptions of many whites, north and south. The black dialect, though imaginatively used by Dunbar, reinforced the notion of a simple and naive people, unfit for full citizenship. In the following stanza of "Chrismus on the Plantation," for example, an ex-slave commiserates with his former master about life after Emancipation:

> *Er in othah wo'ds, you wants us to firgit dat you's been kin'*
> *An' ez soon ez you is he'pless, we's to leave you hyeah behin'.*
> *Well, if dat's de way dis freedom ac's on people, white or black,*
> *You kin jes tell Mistah Lincoln fer' to tek his freedom back.*[2]

White supremacy had nothing to fear from the peasant-like men and women who peopled Dunbar's fiction. But many educated blacks recoiled at this one-dimensional portrayal of black life, even as they took pleasure in Dunbar's national attention and praise from whites. The ever-present pull of racial solidarity and self-help ideology led even militant black leaders such as Reverdy Ransom and Frederick Douglass to support Dunbar's career.[3] Few black intellectuals, in fact, chose to criticize him publicly. When, in 1895, Dunbar fell on difficult times in Chicago, Douglass, who was on the staff of the world's fair exposition in that city, hired him as a clerical assistant. Within a few decades, however, when the ranks of educated blacks had increased and diversified, black critics turned on Dunbar and other black writers whose works they judged harmful to the image of the race. Wallace Thurman, an acerbic writer of the Harlem Renaissance, was unimpressed with Dunbar's verses but did credit him with being "the first American Negro poet who did not depend on a Wesleyan hymn-book for inspiration."[4]

Dunbar held strong views on northern racism, particularly when it was directed at educated blacks, but his public statements were tempered by another reality. His literary career had been fostered by the support of influential white patrons who recognized his talent and approved of his portrayal of southern life. It is doubtful whether Dunbar could have remained in the good graces of white patrons and the mainstream literary establishment had he decided to turn to the world around him for new, more realistic themes.

Charles Chesnutt's career paralleled Dunbar's but had a different outcome. Chesnutt, considered by many to be the first important black novelist, wrote during the last decade of the nineteenth century. After an early education in missionary schools in Fayetteville,

North Carolina, Chesnutt attracted the attention of several wealthy whites in the town. A leading citizen gave young Chesnutt access to his private library, where he pored over modern literature, the classics, and theological works. When he was nineteen, he accepted a teaching job in a local normal school. Two years later he was named principal of the state normal school for blacks. Despite his rapid ascent in the educational system, Chesnutt was dissatisfied with his life and prospects as a teacher in North Carolina. He decided to become a writer, one who would write a book that would illuminate the American racial dynamic and persuade persons of goodwill to acknowledge a common humanity and extend full citizenship to all upright and law-abiding peoples:

> Not a fierce indiscriminate onset, not an appeal to force, for this is something that force can but slightly affect, but a moral revolution which must be brought about in a different manner. The subtle, almost indefinable feeling of repulsion toward the Negro, which is common to almost all Americans, cannot be stormed and taken by assault; the garrison will not capitulate, so their position must be mined, and we will find ourselves in their midst before they know it.[5]

Chesnutt knew he could not accomplish this in the racist South, so he resigned the principalship in Fayetteville and moved to Cleveland, Ohio. Having taught himself stenography, he quickly found work in Cleveland. A local judge recognized Chesnutt's formidable abilities and offered to serve as his mentor and prepare him to take the bar examination. Chesnutt got the highest score on the exam.[6]

While preparing for the Ohio bar, Chesnutt wrote several short stories that appeared in McClure publications. Although the literary establishment generally praised Chesnutt's work, it did so in patronizing tones, and the stories did not do well commercially. Dealing with the true condition of black Americans, his early stories seem designed to demonstrate that nobility and intelligence were as liberally distributed among the black population as among other groups. With the short story as his tool, he set out to teach white America to renounce its prejudice against blacks.

Chesnutt never received the acclaim he felt he deserved. He

watched helplessly as the condition of African Americans deterio-
rated. Yet, critics found much to praise in his early, less strident
work, such as *The Conjure Woman and Other Conjure Tales,* a collection of short stories in which race is rarely discussed.[7] One white
editor commented approvingly that *The Conjure Woman* could have
been written by a white man. Chesnutt's later works, which explored
such aspects of the U.S. race problem as black class differences, mis-
cegenation, and the subservient tradition, were dismissed by most
critics as mere propaganda. Fully committed to artistic standards,
Chesnutt could not suppress his moral sensibilities and racial identification. Even so, he wavered as he realized that black intellectuals
were forced to choose between acclaim and truth telling. Fortunately
for him, he could make a living in the legal profession and never
became financially dependent on mainstream publishing. In 1905,
convinced that the kind of reasoned approach he had long advocated
was socially irrelevant, he abandoned creative writing.

Dunbar, Chesnutt, and many of their contemporaries developed
their talents to the fullest extent allowed. Seizing any opportunities
for self-improvement, they aggressively sought the help of white
intellectual gatekeepers. Most black writers did not reject the standards and assumptions of the American literary canon but simply
wanted the rules fairly applied to their own art as well. When white
audiences spurned their work, some self-destructed, some capitu-
lated, and some quit. Accommodation brought Dunbar money and
fame, though Richard Wright later speculated that Dunbar paid a
heavy price:

> Dunbar wrote many novels and poems that had wide sales. But
> there was a fatal conflict in him; he drank heavily to drown it,
> to resolve it, and failed. He tells us but little of what he really
> felt, but we know that he tried to turn his eyes as much as possi-
> ble from that vision of horror that had claimed the exclusive
> attention of so many Negro writers, tried to communicate with
> his country as a man.[8]

Chesnutt, in contrast, did not conform in his fiction; he simply
stopped writing it and turned to nonfiction and politics.

During the last quarter of the century, African Americans moved forward in scholarly writing. In 1880, at the age of twenty-five, George Washington Williams, a veteran of the Union army and a graduate of Newton Theological Institution, near Boston, wrote *History of the Negro Race in America*. Published by G. P. Putnam, the book was the first historical study of American blacks to appear in print. Despite Williams's lack of formal training, the book was favorably reviewed by professional historians and scholars. While some reviewers only marveled that a black American had written the first account of America's blacks, others judged it according to the canons of historical research, to the great satisfaction of the thoroughly confident Williams. Boston's largest newspaper, the *Evening Transcript*, said, "Its style is clear and forcible, and its statements are supported by a large army of authorities, which show that the author gave much time to his task and that his researches were conducted with singular judgment and thoroughness." Criticism of Williams's work mentioned weak organization and arguments that went beyond the evidence. Williams later published *The History of Negro Troops* with Harper and Brothers. This volume, too, drew praise. Williams had interviewed black Civil War veterans about their service, a research method that, notes his biographer, "surely marks Williams as one of the pioneer investigators in the field of oral history."[9]

For educated African American women, the opportunities were few. In 1866 Frances Rollin met Martin R. Delany, the emigrationist, who enlisted her to write his authorized biography. When the book, *Life and Public Services of Martin R. Delany,* was published in 1868, Rollin's publisher claimed that the public would not be receptive to a biography by a black woman, so the author was listed as Frank Rollins, Frank being Frances's family nickname.[10] Several decades later, when Monroe Majors wrote to Frederick Douglass for suggestions about black women who should be included in his book *Noted Negro Women*, Douglass hesitated. Douglass, a veteran proponent of full rights for women, said that in his estimation, no black woman qualified as "famous." Although he was familiar with the minds and works of Mary Church Terrell, Anna J. Cooper, and Ida Wells (all admirers of Douglass), he responded,

We have many estimable women of our variety but not many famous ones. It is not well to claim too much for ourselves before the public. Such extravagance invites contempt rather than approval. I have thus far seen no book of importance written by a negro woman and I know of no one among us who can appropriately be called famous. . . . This is no way a disparagement of the women of our race. . . . Many of the names you have are those of admirable persons, cultivated, refined and ladylike. But it does not follow that they are famous. Let us be true and use language faithfully.[11]

Douglass might have ardently supported women's rights in the abstract, but he resorted to excessive standards in assessing the intellectual stature of individual black women. In this regard he differed little from his nineteenth- (and twentieth-) century male intellectual cohorts.

## The Fourth Estate

In the period following the Civil War, black editors and publishers, like other black Americans, had at first been optimistic and then downcast. A modern reviewer writes, "Of the three thousand black newspapers that have appeared in the US, 1,876 were founded between 1880 and 1915, and only fifteen of those survive."[12] Convinced that the federal government was committed to the extension and protection of the rights of blacks, the black press urged reconciliation and turned its attention to internal conditions of black America.

The protest and self-help tradition of the black press, inaugurated in 1827 by *Freedom's Journal*, persisted as talented blacks found work in the editorial offices of newspapers such as the *Weekly Anglo-African* in New York, the *New National Era* in Washington, D.C., and the *Elevator* in San Francisco.[13] As the black reading audience increased, such papers grew more influential in the black community. Early journalism had concentrated on slavery and local black affairs, but by 1860 black journalists had expanded into foreign affairs, economic developments, and other matters not directly related to race. In addition to the daily news, fiction and nonfiction essays appeared in the *Weekly Anglo-African,* founded in 1859, and other publications. Martin Delany, William Wells Brown, and Frances Ellen Watkins Harper, among others, published fine traditional pieces. Still, racial oppression remained foremost in the minds of African Americans. Darryl Pinckney is clear about the motivation of black journalists: "As long as white newspapers were unwilling or unable to attack 'anti-Negro' forces or to air the views of black reformers, there was a service black newspapers could provide."[14]

White society wholly ignored the ideas and initiatives of the black press, preferring to follow white debates on race. One heated dialogue came in 1888, when George Washington Cable, a white native of New Orleans, published an essay in the *Century Magazine* criticizing racial segregation and discrimination in the South. Compared with the views of most black thinkers, Cable's opinions were moderate, but he received more than one hundred letters from white southerners labeling him a traitor to the region.[15] Henry Grady, the foremost southern political philosopher, wrote a rejoinder, insisting that the inferiority of black people justified their separation from whites. Furthermore, insisted Grady, southern blacks were content with their lot.

Although black intellectuals such as Chesnutt were well equipped to engage white intellectuals in this discourse, they could not penetrate the closed white shop. The irony of white thinkers debating the welfare of African Americans was certainly not lost on black intellectuals. During this period black literacy grew, and many blacks moved to northern cities. The stage was being set for the black press to star in the shaping of black social and political thought.

Booker T. Washington, still principal of Tuskegee in 1905, was the nation's most influential black. Knowing the black press's potential to influence black community opinion, he worked to enlist editors for his accommodationist approach to social and political issues. Backed by wealthy whites, Washington skillfully dangled the lure of financial support before revenue-poor editors and rallied many of the nation's black newspapers such as the *New York Age* and the *Chicago Leader* to his side.

White newspapers were heavily dependent on commercial advertising, whereas the black press relied mainly on individual sales and subscriptions. Large white businesses, disdainful of the black consumer market, spent no money on advertising in black papers. In theory, this circumstance fostered editorial independence; but as times grew harder in black communities, fewer blacks could afford to buy newspapers or magazines.

Booker T. Washington's political and financial clout enabled him to squelch black papers that crossed him. J. Max Barber, the editor in 1904–5 of the weekly *Voice of the Negro,* frequently printed material critical of Washington's accommodationist policies. Determined to silence Barber and his *Voice,* Washington secretly discouraged advertisers and later asked Barber's publishers to remove him as editor. Barber soon lost control of the paper and turned to a career in dentistry.[16]

In 1905 W. E. B. Du Bois, frustrated by Washington's growing influence, charged that black papers in New York, Chicago, Washington, Indianapolis, and Boston, as well as the *Colored American Magazine,* had sold out to the Washington-directed "syndicate."[17] Like Barber, the young Du Bois soon found his publishing plans thwarted by Washington's machinations.

Du Bois had earlier concluded that race should be the subject matter of popular journalism and of international scholarly journals. Recognizing that no black organization had the power or reputation to make itself heard, Du Bois wrote to Richard L. Jones, the editor of the popular *Collier's Weekly,* and suggested a column, which he himself volunteered to write. Jones did not agree to a weekly column, citing space limitations, but in June of 1904 he published Du Bois's "The Color Line Belts the World," a condensation of his views on the impact of race differences in the modern world. A year later the persistent Du Bois wrote to Jacob Schiff, an investment banker with a reputation for supporting liberal causes, proposing that Schiff fund "a high class journal to circulate among the intelligent Negroes, tell them of the deeds of themselves and their neighbors, interpret the news of the world to them and inspire them toward definite ideals."[18] Du Bois offered to edit the magazine. Schiff promised to explore his proposal with persons sympathetic to blacks, but then silently let the idea drop. Du Bois suspected that Schiff had been dissuaded by the anti–Du Bois sentiment of Booker T. Washington's political machine.[19]

Independent-minded black intellectuals who rejected Washington's ideology found few outlets for their articles and books. Occasionally a publication such as *Scribner's* or the *New Republic* would print a piece by an African American, but most black writers had to rely on the small black journals and on self-publishing efforts to get their ideas into circulation. The several black publishing houses that were in business lacked the resources to manufacture and distribute more than a few books a year, especially given the economic hardships of blacks who would have been their readers.

One black self-publisher was Sutton Griggs, who founded the Orion Publishing Company to market his own novels. Griggs had trained for the ministry at Richmond Theological Seminary, and in 1895 he accepted a pastorate in Tennessee. While ministering to Baptist congregations, Griggs published five novels at his own expense, the most notable being *Imperium in Imperio* (1899), a sentimental story that portrayed the worsening condition of blacks in the South. Completely dedicated to his Christian calling, Griggs also wrote and published a number of small pamphlets concerning Christian education. In accord with the self-help impulse of the Talented Tenth, the black National Baptist Convention promised support for Griggs's books, but the support never materialized. So Griggs took to the road selling his books directly to the public. Thanks to such efforts, Griggs was more widely read among rank-and-file blacks than were his critically acclaimed contemporaries Dunbar and Chesnutt.[20]

At the turn of the century, prospects for profits were slim for black commercial publishers. Black educational institutions, with their greater resources and authority in cultural and social matters, were therefore better suited to assume the risks of book publishing. Colleges such as Atlanta University, Howard, Hampton, and Tuskegee Institute all published the Talented Tenth, usually concentrating on subjects related to their schools or on material written by members of their faculty. In the decade beginning in 1896, Atlanta University Press published a series on the condition of blacks in the South, edited by Du Bois, then a faculty member. The series contained such titles as *The College Bred Negro, The Negro Artisan,* and *The Negro Common School,* fine examples of sociological research conducted in the South.

As various institutions stepped up their efforts, one ambitious group of black intellectuals, perhaps taking their cue from the increasing corporatization of American life, launched an organization designed to solidify and legitimate the contributions of the Talented Tenth.

## The American Negro Academy

By the turn of the century, Alexander Crummell had become an influential spokesman for African nationalism and the moral uplift of black Americans. He concluded that an organization of highly educated African Americans could advance the interests of black people.[21] Although black professional organizations existed in the late 1800s, Crummel envisioned an elite group bound by intellectual rather than by occupational ties. In 1897 he drafted a constitution for the American Negro Academy (ANA), "an organization of Colored authors, scholars, and artists" with the following objectives:

a) To promote the publication of literary and scholarly works;

b) To aid youths of genius in the attainment of the higher culture, at home and abroad;

c) To gather into its Archives valuable data, historical or literary works of Negro authors;

d) To aid, by publications, vindication of the race from vicious assaults, in all the lines of learning and truth;

e) To publish, if possible, at least once a year an "Annual" of original articles upon various Literary, Historical, and Philosophical topics, of a racial nature, by selected members; and by these and diverse other means, to raise the standard of intellectual endeavor among American Negroes.[22]

The ANA's membership included some of the preeminent intellectuals of the age, men such as William Scarborough, an Oberlin-trained classicist at Wilberforce University; Carter G. Woodson, who held a Harvard Ph.D. in history; the poet Dunbar; and the erudite and ambitious Du Bois. Despite the liberal predilections of the academy's male members, no women were ever admitted. With such women as Anna Cooper, an Oberlin graduate and principal of the

M Street School, or Ida Wells Barnett, journalist and outspoken advocate of antilynching legislation, or Mary Church Terrell, the club movement leader, fully engaged in intellectual discourse on behalf of black America, the ANA members could hardly claim that no women were qualified.

The academy, based in Washington, D.C., published occasional papers—Scarborough's *The Educated Negro and His Mission* and Du Bois's *The Conservation of Races* among others—and periodically held meetings to discuss the state of black America.[23] But this organization, for all its good work, never boasted more than forty members and never realized the expectations of its founders.

Too many of the crude facts of racism worked against the goals of the academy. Its frequently brilliant papers were ignored by the white intellectual community. Limited resources prevented the broad distribution of publications that could have increased the visibility of black scholars and forced a dialogue about the issues. Even whites sympathetic to the cause of African Americans looked to the white mainstream for ideas and values. Moreover, the academy had an uneasy relationship with average African Americans. A small population of highly educated black thinkers supported the academy, but the working class and the poor found abstract issues irrelevant to their day-to-day existence. To the black masses mired in what has been called the "nadir" of their history, other, more pragmatic leaders seemed to offer greater promise.[24] Nor did the black bourgeoisie support the ANA's work and programs; according to the bourgeoisie's definitions of material success and achievement, the intellectually oriented ANA was superfluous. The ANA's broad thrust also went against the trend toward specialization that held sway during the first decade of the century. Other black organizations, such as the National Bar Association (1894) and the National Medical Association (1895), had been founded in the specialized spirit of the white professional associations, and their focus on much narrower interests probably helped ensure their survival. The ANA disbanded in 1928.

The significance of the American Negro Academy, however, exceeded its limited accomplishments. That a group of privileged thinkers combined intellectualism and a sense of social responsibility reinforced the element of community service in black intellectuals' definition of themselves and their work. The importance of social responsibility to their calling had been underscored earlier and would be again—and again.


## The Ministry and Educated Blacks

The ministry continued to absorb a large number of educated blacks. Ministers often pointed out to their congregations and communities the importance of education and Western literate culture. Indeed, many came perilously close to asserting that true freedom could be attained only through the mastery of "high culture." Paul Robeson's father, an African Methodist Episcopal Zion minister, impressed upon young Paul the value of knowledge in any search for freedom. Robeson wrote of his father,

> He firmly believed that the height of knowledge must be scaled by the freedom-maker. Latin, Greek, philosophy, history, literature—all treasures of learning must be the Negro's heritage as well. So for me in high school there would be four years of Latin. And then, in college four more years of Latin and Greek. Closely my father watched my studies, and was with me page by page through Virgil and Homer and the other classics in which he was well grounded.[25]

But Robeson's father was an exception, for few black ministers were educated at seminaries or universities. More frequently, blacks assumed the role of preacher after having been "called." Such persons claiming divine selection usually had a rudimentary knowledge of the Bible, but their position and mobility in the black church depended more on their ability to evoke religious emotions in the congregations than on their grasp of theological arguments. Untrained preachers came to rest in the pulpits of churches with poor and uneducated congregations.

Young educated blacks with middle-class backgrounds often were repulsed by the emotional character of church services attended by the poor. Horace Cayton, who in the 1940s teamed with St. Clair

Drake to write *Black Metropolis,* a landmark study of black Chicago, had such an experience. The product of a middle-class family in Seattle, Cayton faced social rejection from his white high school classmates. Seeking a niche, he ventured from his pedestal of privilege in the black middle class into the religious world of poor blacks, recently arrived from the South: "I made several attempts to gain entrance to the Negro group, including an unsuccessful attempt to become a member of the Mt. Zion Baptist Church. But the services seemed to me loud and vulgar when I contrasted them with those in the church downtown where I had always gone."[26]

As he grew older, Cayton came to understand that the spirituality of the oppressed took a form quite unlike any familiar to middle-class believers. For those on the bottom, a close relationship between believer and a Supreme Being was the central element in a religious experience. An outpouring of emotion in churches of the poor on Sunday morning provided comfort and hope to these victims of an inimical social order.

Nonetheless, Booker T. Washington and others, true to a rationalist credo, criticized preachers who relied on unbridled emotion to inspire and guide their congregations. Speaking before the white membership of the National Educational Association in Buffalo in 1896, Washington said,

> Now, this emotional side of our nature rather tempts us to spend a good deal of our time preparing in a certain way to live in the next world, which is all right. But I notice you not only prepare for the next world, but you take good pains to prepare for this world also. . . . Our preachers like to preach and sing about living in a great, big, white mansion—that is, these people who live in little log cabins down in this world. They like to think and sing about wearing golden slippers in the next world while they trudge along barefooted in this.[27]

Washington seems to have misunderstood or undervalued the important spiritual function served by expressive religion. Such emotionalism recalled the Great Awakening, by downplaying biblical scholarship and traditional interpretation in favor of individual, personal salvation. A majority of black preachers, as a matter of conviction or convenience, stressed commitment of the heart rather than of the mind.

Black women who aspired to join the ranks of the clergy faced special obstacles. High-status leadership roles were in short supply. In 1849 Jarena Lee of Philadelphia published an account of her call to preach. In the face of theological-based opposition from Richard Allen, founder and leader of the African Methodist Episcopal (AME) denomination, she withdrew. A decade later, however, after the loss of her husband and several other members of her family, Lee again felt the call. Now bishop of the AME church, Allen reversed his earlier stand and supported Lee, who cogently challenged the prevailing beliefs about women preachers: "For as unseemingly as it may appear now-a-days for a woman to preach, it should be remembered that nothing is impossible with God. And why should it be thought impossible, heterodox or improper for a woman to preach? seeing the Savior died for the woman as well as for the man."[28]

From 1865 to 1870 the national debate over the Fourteenth Amendment, which established blacks as citizens, and the Fifteenth, which gave black male citizens the right to vote, pulled educated black women into a political vortex. Many conservative and southern white women feminists opposed the Fifteenth Amendment because it provided for black men a right that white women did not enjoy. When Elizabeth Cady Stanton, a leader of the white feminist movement, was asked in 1869 if she was willing to have black men enfranchised before her, she replied, "I would not trust him with my rights; degraded, oppressed himself, he would be more despotic with the governing power than ever our Saxon rulers are. . . . If women are still to be represented by men, then I say let only the highest type of manhood stand at the helm of state."[29]

Black women felt forced to take a stand for or against an amendment that would enfranchise their brothers but not them. Frances Watkins Harper, a poet and lecturer on the antislavery circuit, firmly supported the amendment despite her rejection of black male privilege. Nor was Watkins convinced that women would exercise the vote in a more humane way than men: "I am not sure that women are naturally so much better than men that they would clear the stream by virtue of their womanhood."[30] She called for not simply "more voters, but better voters," and opposed universal and unrestricted suffrage for men and women.

Perhaps as much as the contest for political rights, the stereotype of the "wanton woman" claimed the attention of middle-class black women thinkers. Mass media and bigoted politicians frequently invoked the prevailing images of the vicious and threatening black male with its female counterpart—the promiscuous black woman.

Race and gender awareness in the 1870s led to complicated dynamics. Sexist mores had led many middle- and upper-class white women to organize around issues like temperance and women's suffrage. The resulting "women's clubs" were not truly revolutionary; rather, they reflected the core Victorian ideology, which regarded women as custodians of traditional morality and transmitters of education and family values. They also left black women out, for the most part. True, black women could join women's clubs in some northern cities, but assertive women like Ida Wells Barnett soon exposed disabling differences in black and white priorities. White women's clubs would not, for instance, take a strong stand in favor of antilynching legislation. Frustrated by this, Ida Wells Barnett, Mary Church Terrell, and Anna J. Cooper spearheaded the development of black women's clubs. In 1896 two such associations, the National Federation of Afro-American Women and the National League of Colored Women, met, merged, and formed the National Association of Colored Women (NACW) and selected Mary Church Terrell as their first president.

Because the black women's clubs were grappling with barriers of race as well as gender, their organizations adopted goals broader than those of their white counterparts. Astute thinkers like Cooper and Terrell forcefully advocated expanded career options for educated women, but they understood that such progress was linked to the general welfare of the black population. Terrell was blunt in exhorting her black peers: "Self-preservation demands that we go among the lowly and even the vicious, to whom they are bound by ties of race and sex . . . to reclaim them."[31]

Decades later a historian pondered the race and gender tension: "Black women had attempted to enlist white women in the struggle against racism by appealing to them as women. But the connections between black and white women as women were not as strong as the white women's allegiance to white society."[32]


## Confronting the "Folk"

Nowhere was the status and welfare of the black community more an issue than on black college campuses. The "race question" dominated the discourse of students and faculty at Fisk and at Atlanta University, where the sons and daughters of newly minted middle-class African-Americans were instilled with twin values—individual mobility and service to the group. James Weldon Johnson, author of the critically acclaimed novel *The Autobiography of an Ex-Colored Man* (1912) and a leader of the NAACP, praised the Atlanta University of the 1890s. Johnson's early years were spent in the black middle-class milieu of Jacksonville, Florida. Since Jacksonville had no public high school open to blacks, his parents sent him to Atlanta University in 1887 for secondary and collegiate education.

> [I]t was in this early period that I received my initiation into the arena of "race." I perceived that education for me meant, fundamentally: preparation to meet the tasks and exigencies of life as a Negro, a realization of the peculiar responsibilities due to my own racial group, and comprehension of the application of American democracy to Negro citizens. . . . This knowledge was no part of classroom instruction—the college course at Atlanta University was practically the old academic course at Yale; it was simply in the spirit of the institution; the atmosphere of the place was charged with it. Students talked "race." It was the subject of essays, orations and debates. Nearly all that was acquired, mental and moral, was destined to be fitted into a particular system of which "race" was the center.[33]

Atlanta University, founded by Edmund Ware and two other white Yale graduates, was one of the few black colleges that had managed to resist Booker T. Washington's model of industrial education. But the classical curriculum so dear to the founders eventually had to confront the realities that intelligent and spirited young African Americans faced in the South. Johnson and his peers accepted their privileged status in the black community and saw it as a vehicle to help the less favored of their race. Keenly aware of rural black poverty, black college students valiantly tried to reach out to its victims.

Although some young middle-class black intellectuals felt alienated from the rural folk culture of poor blacks, others like James Weldon Johnson and W. E. B. Du Bois saw in rural black life qualities of humility, perseverance, religiosity, and humor, which could contribute to the spiritual life of the larger society. Conjectures by Du Bois and others about the special character of African Americans reflected the turn-of-the-century interest in the "American character."

The "American character" debate had begun in the 1830s after Alexis de Tocqueville traveled to America and wrote about the paradoxes and uniqueness of American social thought in his *Democracy in America*. Tocqueville was fascinated by Americans' passion for equality. Unlike European countries, the United States seemed to be committed to an egalitarian society. The prescient Frenchman speculated, however, that an undue emphasis on equality in the United States could stifle individuality and lead to a conformity brought on by the "tyranny of the majority." Although blacks were not a part of the polity he studied, Tocqueville did examine white American attitudes toward blacks and slavery. Noting the impact of slavery on blacks, he argued that the "fact of servitude is most fatally combined with the physical and permanent fact of difference in race. Memories of slavery disgrace the race, and race perpetuates memories of slavery."[34] Recognizing that whites, north and south, believed in the inferiority of blacks, Tocqueville saw little prospect for change: "To induce the whites to abandon the opinion they have conceived of the intellectual and moral inferiority of their former slaves, the Negroes must change, but they can not do so as long as this opinion persists."[35]

Throughout the late nineteenth century, scholars in the United States and Europe searched for traits that would distinguish one race or nation from another. Joining the discussion, black intellectuals sought to define a set of positive traits to counter the negative stereotypes. This was a difficult task. Subordinated by social and economic repression, the black population was, for the most part, still rural, poor, and uneducated. Excluded from the nation's rapidly changing social and economic life, blacks had few opportunities to demonstrate the qualities respected by whites. For many black intellectuals, however, the problem was not so much "black backwardness" as the materialistic mood in the nation as a whole. In *Souls of Black Folk* Du Bois criticized the materialism of American life and held up the example of African Americans as a people still relatively untouched by the soulless priorities of a spiritually bankrupt society.[36] "Will America be poorer if she replace her brutal dyspeptic blundering with light-hearted but determined Negro humility? Or her coarse and cruel wit with loving jovial good-humor? Or her vulgar music with the soul of the Sorrow Songs?" In his view, powerless black people were morally superior to powerful whites. But this romantic notion of black folk as a community of conscience in a crass society did not impress most black thinkers. James Weldon Johnson was like Du Bois—he had met rural black folk at Fisk, and he argued in *The Autobiography of an Ex-Colored Man* that American blacks possessed a distinctive cultural sensibility. But that sensibility had nothing to do with a Christ-like redemptive goodness; rather, it was rooted in the humor and vigor of folk culture. Some educated blacks sympathized with Du Bois but still believed that the national die had been cast—wealth was the measure of a person. Responding anonymously to a Du Bois survey in 1900, a college-educated black criticized the materialistic trend: "Never lose sight of the fact that in the United States the dollar makes the man—although the doctrine is false as Hell."[37] To most black middle-class businessmen and professionals, Du Bois's message seemed naive and idealistic; after all, the black masses had to make a living. Interpretation and cultural criticism they left to the intellectuals.

Black thinkers strongly defended and championed the potential of blacks. They noted the many failings of a people only recently freed from bondage and still oppressed everywhere, but they did not question the race's essential fitness. Their balanced critique made little difference to most white Americans. White racial attitudes blended with a huge popular myth—that the U.S. drive for empire was simply an unfolding of the natural order. Like people of color elsewhere in the world, African Americans were victimized by the myth—and the reality—of empire. Black thinkers pretty well gave up fighting the monolith and redirected most of their attention to racial uplift.

## The Talented Tenth
## and the Idea of Responsibility

As we have seen, Africans and their descendants were not encouraged by their society to be individualistic or independent. Instead, traditional African communal values and group oppression in America combined to shape a collectivist orientation. This perspective encouraged a sharing of resources and a reliance on cohorts, and slaves believed that their personal interests overlapped those of the group. Indeed, the slave experience forged an ethos of interdependence and cooperation among blacks that set the tone for individual decisions. The ablest blacks in Africa, and later those in America, were accorded high community status. But they were expected to use their abilities to help other blacks.

Years after his school days at Fisk, Du Bois reflected on the proper role for mentally superior persons:

> The net worth of the Fisk interlude was to broaden the scope of my life, not essentially to change it; to center it in a group of educated Negroes, who from their knowledge and experience would lead the mass. I never for a moment dreamed that such leadership could ever be for the sake of the educated group itself, but always for the mass.[38]

The hopes of Du Bois notwithstanding, group stratification and individual materialism took a heavy toll on togetherness. After Reconstruction the black populace began to fragment; differences of class developed, and a once sturdy communal ethos declined. Privilege, money, ambition, status—all frayed the ties of racial solidarity.

But this situation would change when enough literate blacks came along to create an audience for black thinkers.

# 5 ⋘

# PROSPERITY, CHANGE, AND MORE OF THE SAME

I was there. I had a swell time while it lasted. But I thought it wouldn't last long. . . . For how long could a large and enthusiastic number of people be crazy about Negroes forever? But some Harlemites thought the millennium had come. They thought the race problem had at last been solved through Art plus Gladys Bentley. They were sure the New Negro would lead a new life from then on in green pastures of tolerance created by Countee Cullen, Ethel Waters, Claude McKay, Duke Ellington, Bojangles, and Alain Locke.

—LANGSTON HUGHES

BLACK INTELLECTUALS, LIKE other people, were dazzled by the paradoxes and changes in American life at the end of World War I. U.S. agrarian and decentralized life was crumbling. The small town, with its traditional values, no longer housed most Americans. Large urban centers with richly blending immigrant cultures dominated the cultural and social landscape. The nation was rushing madly toward prosperity for all its citizens. Women were challenging deeply rooted ideas about their place at home and in the world of work. Life expectancy and literacy rates shot up, and the automobile opened new vistas for millions of working- and middle-class Americans. The Central Powers had been defeated, and African Americans assumed Woodrow Wilson right when he spoke of a world made "safe for democracy."

Thousands of southern blacks packed their belongings and dreams and headed north, hoping to fulfill the American promise.[1] Farming technology and uneven agricultural production had rendered many southern blacks economically expendable. Rampant political repression in the South made deteriorating economic problems even harder to endure. Furthermore, those blacks who had seized educational opportunities in the South lived only marginally better than uneducated blacks. Hardly anything spoke for staying put. Southern blacks concluded that the economic vitality and expanded freedoms of the North were reasons enough to migrate. Most of the migrating black males found work in the coal and iron mines. The automotive and shipbuilding industries absorbed many others, but employment for black women was limited to household domestic work or to the cleaning of offices and factories.

New forms of industrial organization confirmed the obsolescence of Booker T. Washington's educational philosophy, scorned by black intellectuals for years. But the new forms did little to improve economic conditions for black workers. Although large industrial labor unions wielded considerable power, their efforts rarely turned to racial equality in the workplace.[2] Consequently, most black workers had to take the lowest-paying jobs. Capitalists became adept at pitting black workers against white unionists. In places like East St. Louis in 1919, racial conflicts erupted.

As New York, Chicago, and other northern cities became vibrant economic and cultural centers, African Americans were cordoned into neighborhoods that could not expand sufficiently to accommodate the growing housing needs of newcomers. And the vaunted educational opportunities in the North were compromised by discrimination and the underfunding of schools that served large numbers of black students.

\* \* \*

By 1920 the success of black communities and institutions in promoting learning was evident. Schools, newspapers, and churches had never wavered in their commitment to educate the masses and, where possible, had recruited, encouraged, and provided financial support for those blacks intent on attending colleges and graduate schools. Edward Bouchet, the first African American to earn a doctorate from an American university (from Yale, in 1876), had been followed by a slow but steady stream of black academics, who paid an extraordinary price.[3]

Blacks matriculating as undergraduates also had difficulties to deal with. Zelma George, later a scholar of African American music, was admitted to the University of Chicago in 1920 but not allowed to live in the dormitories. Her father, a minister in Kansas, moved to a church in Chicago so that his daughter could live at home while attending the university. Later she tried to join the university choir. When the choir members voted on whether to admit George, potentially the first black member, the result was a tie. The university chaplain, asked to break the tie, voted no. She never did sing in the choir. Meanwhile, she bore other burdens. While studying sociology, she decided to become a lawyer. But, she recalled in 1978,

> my father didn't think it was a womanly kind of vocation, and he pointed to a few women who were in law that he thought had become masculine in their mannerisms and approaches to people in the courtrooms. So he said, "Now if you want it bad enough you can get it when you're earning your own money, but I will not finance it."[4]

George took up musical studies instead.

No matter what degrees they earned, blacks faced restricted prospects. The white academic world was as inhospitable to blacks as were all other sectors of American life. Only black colleges welcomed the ebony talent slowly emerging from historically white institutions.

At white universities black undergraduates had noted the trend toward specialization and new scientific disciplines that pervaded American higher education. Yet blacks clustered around the traditional fields—philosophy, classics, and literature. Although they recognized that modern science propelled the nation's future, they saw few opportunities for themselves in the sciences. Getting funding to support scientific research was one of the hurdles.

Ernest E. Just, an outstanding theoretical biologist of the period, met with frequent refusals as he sought research funds. A biographer of Just has written of the "old boy" network that dominated funding for science and of the attendant predicament of black researchers: "For blacks it was especially difficult. They were new to science and to the sources of support. Their professional opportunities were limited; few jobs, fewer colleagues, and no advanced students. Most donors were unwilling to gamble against such odds."[5] Foundations and other funding sources considered Just's interest in pure science an oddity. They could not envision blacks working in other than "applied" areas of science, such as medicine. This bias prompted Just to tailor his research proposals to include ideas on the practical value of his work, usually in medicine.

The biologist George Washington Carver experienced similar problems. After completing graduate work at Iowa State University, he accepted an invitation from Booker T. Washington to head a new agricultural experiment station at Tuskegee.[6] Not knowing at first that the state legislature had appropriated only $1,500 for the operation of the station—less than one-tenth of what it provided stations at the white universities in Alabama—Carver soon realized that he would have to scale back his research expectations. It further complicated Carver's professional life that Washington showed no appreciation of pure research. He looked askance at investigations that did not pertain directly to the day-to-day problems of Black Belt farmers. This difference led to constant feuding over the direction of agriculture at Tuskegee and over the available resources. However, Carver persevered and eventually developed new soil conservation techniques that helped restore the fertility of the region's soil, which was being exhausted by one-crop (cotton) planting.

Kelly Miller of Howard, trained as a mathematician at Johns Hopkins, concluded that mathematics was too remote from the problems facing black people. Miller turned to sociology and from 1895 to 1907 served as professor of mathematics and sociology at Howard.[7] Mindful of the tradition of service established in the nineteenth century, he and other black intellectuals saw the newly emerging social sciences as more utilitarian, and far more accessible.

Sociology, anthropology, and economics were still in their formative stages, and their newness created important openings for black scholars. That human behavior might yield to social scientific understanding was an alluring idea for those in the Talented Tenth. For years they had argued that many problems facing blacks were rooted in systemic discrimination rather than in deficiencies peculiar to the race. Now, employing the framework of social science, black thinkers convincingly asserted that their interpretations of data and their conclusions were at least as rational and legitimate as those of the

apologists for white supremacy.[8] They had long observed how the
mere speculations of learned whites had acquired the status of
"truth" when they reflected dominant viewpoints.

Frederick Hoffman, a white statistician with Prudential Insurance,
received support from the American Economics Association to produce a volume, *Race Traits and Tendencies of the American Negro*
(1896), which purported to demonstrate the genetic inferiority of
blacks.[9] Kelly Miller's critique of Hoffman's work, published as an
occasional paper of the American Negro Academy, offered new
interpretations based on census data. Although Miller's work was
cavalierly dismissed as propaganda and largely ignored, the new disciplines of social science promised to elevate such debates to a more
objective plane. Increasingly, propositions about human behavior
would be scrutinized and validated or disproved by careful empirical testing.

Of particular importance to black intellectuals was the dethroning
of Social Darwinian theories, such as those of the social philosopher
Herbert Spencer. Spencer posited a highly individualistic and com-
petitive social world in which the subordinate position of blacks, for
instance, simply reflected immutable laws of nature.[10] For him the
best social policy was one that let the forces of "natural dominance"
run their course. Du Bois and Miller criticized, in black publications,
the theories of Spencer and other racist social scientists, but their
arguments were ignored by the broader intellectual community.
Black social scientists would eventually prove Spencer wrong by
showing the disadvantaged status of blacks to be a product of human
calculation, rather than an inevitable outcome of sociobiological evolution.

Du Bois had earlier found a venue where he could challenge the
"pseudo-science" of the Spencer camp. In 1896 Du Bois was hired
by the University of Pennsylvania to conduct a survey of Philadelphia's black community. With meager financial backing, he designed
and conducted research that resulted in the book *The Philadelphia
Negro*.[11] This project allowed him to apply his scientific training to
concrete problems. In concept and methodology his work was as
sophisticated as other sociological studies of the period. Although
the explicit goal of the project was not policy formulation, Du Bois
hoped that his meticulous findings would persuade white officials

to provide greater economic opportunities for Philadelphia's black residents. After completing the survey, he proposed a bold and expansive longitudinal study of blacks in the United States. *The Philadelphia Negro* was later considered a milestone in the field, but it had no impact on conditions in Philadelphia and other northern cities.[12] The interests served by economic and political discrimination were too entrenched to be dislodged by any evidence, scientific or otherwise.

The migration of southern blacks to urban centers in the North following World War I created new roles and opportunities for black intellectuals with training in the social sciences. Before the great migration northerners had been able largely to ignore blacks, considering them a southern problem. Even northerners who regarded themselves as sympathetic to the rights of blacks knew nothing about blacks beyond the discourse about slavery. From time to time, black protests in the North forced local and state governments to address specific grievances, such as the lack of public schools for blacks. But the small black population had not gained enough power to compel northern power brokers to address the black community's vital issues.

As more blacks moved north, however, and violent clashes between whites and blacks erupted in northern cities like Chicago, Detroit, and Tulsa, the white establishment frequently commissioned studies of the "Negro problem," and the researchers would usually at least consult black intellectuals about conditions in black communities. The city of Chicago went a step further, hiring the black sociologist Charles Johnson, who had studied with the pioneering race relations theorist Robert Park, a white professor at the University of Chicago, to identify the sources of the restlessness and discontent in black ghettos. Johnson had come to the University of Chicago from Virginia in 1917 after completing studies at Wayland Seminary (the school Booker T. Washington left because of its liberal curriculum) and earning a B.A. from Virginia Union University. Johnson, in keeping with racial protocol, served officially as "associated executive secretary" to Graham Taylor, the white director of the Chicago commission. Yet Johnson did the bulk of the commission's research. The final report identified a number of grievances—employment discrimination, poor housing, unequal law enforcement—and suggested reforms that would improve the quality of life for black Chicagoans and reduce racial animosity.[13] Like Du Bois's equally thoughtful work on black Philadelphia two decades earlier, Johnson's report found its way into the libraries but not into the councils of power. Still, the chance to function as adviser or expert on black affairs was welcomed by black intellectuals, and in the decades that followed that role would become, in effect, institutionalized in American political culture. The effectiveness of the role, however, has been mixed.

Although the new social sciences were attractive to black intellectuals, early-twentieth-century literature allowed even greater freedom and creativity. Literary traditions remained in force, but modernism had broadened the concept of excellence, giving creative persons considerable leeway. Moreover, no formal credentials or training was required of aspiring authors. The creeping credentialism of intellectual and professional life that characterized the period never permeated the field of creative writing. Once talented blacks learned to read and gained access to books, they could teach themselves literary techniques, needing only pencils or pens and paper. Charles Chesnutt, for one, never received any formal literary training beyond high school.

Reaching print, however, was a different matter. Mass-audience periodicals such as *McClure's* and *Collier's,* which dominated the market, rarely published articles by black authors. The intellectual and activist Mary Church Terrell, frustrated by rejection slips from white editors, concluded,

There are few things more difficult than inducing an editor of the average magazine to publish an article on the Race Problem, unless it sets forth the point of view which is popularly and generally accepted. Nobody wants to know a colored woman's opinion about her own status or that of her group. When she dares express it, no matter how tactful it may be, it is called "propaganda." . . . And it seemed to me the only kind of article which found favor with the editors was one that emphasized the Colored American's vices and defects, or held him up to ridicule and scorn.[14]

The emergence of the "little magazines" in New York and other eastern centers confirmed that a market existed, albeit small, for non-mainstream cultural work. Unburdened by the profit motive, "little magazines" like the *Masses* and the *Little Review* appealed to those dissatisfied with American culture. But even their editors largely ignored black intellectuals.[15]

Black journals similar in concept to the "little magazines" appeared intermittently during the first decade of the twentieth century. Idealistic editors eager to infuse new ideas into public debate, and writers searching for outlets, tried to locate audiences for the new journals. Many black intellectuals were as contemptuous of the materialism and acquisitiveness of middle-class culture as were their white counterparts in Greenwich Village. Blacks, however, found it even harder than the white literary avant-garde to gain financial support and loyal readers. Because the audience for innovative black journals was small, financial hardship was the norm; such experimental ventures as *Horizon* and *Moon* were short-lived. Despite their financial failings, the appearance of these periodicals signified a growing self-confidence within the small black intellectual community, which could console itself with the knowledge that funding, not talent or material, was the problem.

Among the intellectually sophisticated black journals that survived for decades were *Crisis: A Record of the Darker Races,* which first appeared in 1910, and *Opportunity: Journal of Negro Life,* first published in 1923. Their longevity is perhaps explained by the fact that they were not exclusively literary or intellectual organs, but were linked to viable organizations in the black community.[16] The *Crisis,* the brainchild of W. E. B. Du Bois, was conceived as the house organ for the National Association for the Advancement of Colored People, which was formed in 1909. Du Bois had spent many years campaigning for a national journal that would communicate the thoughts and works of black intellectuals to a wider audience. The NAACP finally granted him his wish. Starting with a small but regular subsidy from the parent organization, Du Bois guided the magazine to financial solvency and autonomy within five years.[17] Following the lead of editors of earlier black magazines such as the *Colored American,* Du Bois was expansive and eclectic in his selection of material for the journal. A typical number included book reviews, poetry, essays, and his own incisive commentary on a range of political and cultural issues. Few developments affecting the welfare of black Americans escaped the scrutiny of the young editor. At a time when discrimination and racist violence stilled the voices of some blacks, a Du Bois editorial in a 1913 *Crisis* opposed any compromise with racist oppression: "If the United States is to be a Land of Law, we would live humbly and peaceably in it—working, singing, learning and dreaming to make it and ourselves nobler and better; if it is to be a Land of Mobs and Lynchers, we might as well die today as tomorrow."[18] His learned commentary on social questions informed and influenced a generation of budding writers and scholars whose intellectual lives were inextricably linked to the social realities of blacks. For instance, Richard Greener, the first African American to graduate from Harvard, took to Du Bois's book about the abolitionist John Brown and wrote to express his admiration: "I have just finished reading your 'John Brown' and cry out *Macte Virtute! . . .* At any rate thanks for the telling blows you have struck. Long may you be able to wield so trenchant a blade."[19] This growing cadre of assertive black writers and scholars in turn became a reliable source for quality fiction and opinion for the pages of the *Crisis*.

Like the *Crisis,Opportunity* was housed within a black social welfare organization. In 1922, impressed by Du Bois's success, the National Urban League allocated funds to publish an organization journal and chose as its editor Charles Johnson, who had left Chicago to work for the league's New York office as director of research and investigation. In the first issue of *Opportunity,* the head of the Urban League, Eugene Kinckle Jones, aligned the journal's fate with the currents of science and dispassionate reason. He wrote that the journal would "set down interestingly but without sugarcoating or generalization the findings of careful scientific surveys and like facts gathered from research, undertaken not to prove preconceived notions but to lay bare Negro life as it is."[20] Soon after taking the helm of *Opportunity,* and with little fanfare, Johnson began to include creative writing in its pages. Over the years many influential African American writers and intellectuals—for example, Countee Cullen, Zora Neale Hurston, and E. Franklin Frazier—published in the Urban League and NAACP house organs.

In 1925 Du Bois initiated an annual *Crisis* literary competition.
Black writers were urged to submit essays, poems, and short stories
to compete for cash awards. *Opportunity* later launched a similar
contest. Du Bois and Johnson, mindful of the need to put on the best
possible face and to challenge negative ideas about the creative work
of blacks, carefully selected judges who demanded respect; Sinclair
Lewis, Charles Chesnutt, H. G. Wells, and James Weldon Johnson,
all served on panels that evaluated submissions. National publicity,
including annual award banquets, was another benefit of the contests. Winning entries appeared in one of the two sponsoring journals. Other periodical editors searched the submissions for talent
deserving of wider recognition. Young aspiring writers like Langston
Hughes, Countee Cullen, Zora Neale Hurston, and E. Franklin Frazier won awards during the twenties and went on to achieve success
in the world of letters.[21]

These annual competitions served a noteworthy role in the matu-
ration of the black intellectual. They took black writers and artists
seriously. They also thrust black intellectuals into the dialectic of criticism and debates about the objectivity of cultural standards. In
much of their early reaction to the work of blacks, white intellectuals
had been patronizing. Frequently, their reviews had suggested surprise that blacks could create at all. Other critics, as Mary Church
Terrell noted, had summarily dismissed black creative artists as "propagandists."[22] The critical acclaim that accompanied winning works
helped make the case that blacks were able literary artists. Elsewhere
in black America, groups of intellectuals responded to the precedent
of the New York–based *Crisis* and *Opportunity*. In Boston the former editor of *Colored American Magazine*, Pauline Hopkins, started
*New Era* and editorially opposed the powerful Booker T. Washington machine. On the campus of Howard University in 1916, Alain
Locke, the first black Rhodes Scholar and a Harvard Ph.D. in philosophy, helped launch *Stylus,* a student-faculty literary magazine.

Although the proliferation of black magazines outside of New York
City proved that not all of the nation's black intellectuals resided in
Harlem, many of the new entries folded after a few issues. *Stylus*
was an exception, surviving into the 1980s. Beginning with its editor
Locke, the magazine was able to draw on talented faculty and stu-
dent support from Howard, America's largest black university.

Although Locke's leadership and the creative and intellectual contributions of Howard students were crucial to the magazine's success, perhaps its longevity owes more to Howard's financial support. While subscription-supported literary journals like Hopkins's *New Era* foundered during the Great Depression, Howard's *Stylus* hung on, publishing new voices in the black literary chorus.

Publications that lacked the support of an existing organization had a difficult time. Chandler Owen and A. Philip Randolph, both radical activists, tested the waters for the *Messenger*, a New York–based magazine that embraced socialist ideology. Owen had graduated from Virginia Union in 1913, and moved to New York for graduate study. Soon after arriving he met Randolph, who hailed from Jackonsville, Florida, and was struggling to earn a living and attend City College of New York. The two like-minded young men decided that socialism represented the future and founded the *Messenger* in 1917. The *Messenger* spurned the cautious and conciliatory posture of journals like *Opportunity* and the *Crisis* in favor of a combatitive approach to political questions. In their first issue, Owen and Randolph boasted that theirs was "the only Magazine of 'Scientific Radicalism' in the World published by Negroes." Government officials apparently took the *Messenger* at its word: A New York state legislative committee named to investigate potentially seditious publications called the *Messenger* "by far the most dangerous of the Negro publications."[23] Randolph's radical opposition to the American political apparatus fired the controversy in the magazine's platform. But Randolph went after black political leadership as well, particularly the Du Bois branch.

Du Bois had argued in a 1921 *Crisis* editorial that there was no need for a revolution in the United States, and expressed doubts about groups that thought of blacks as members of a revolutionary proletariat class. There could be no class unity, he insisted, because white workers did not recognize any common interests with black workers.[24] The next month Chandler Owen argued in the pages of the *Messenger* that revolution had "gone on steadily in social systems" and was a permanent dynamic in science and culture. Owen went for Du Bois's jugular when he wrote,

> Du Bois after making a veritably superficial scholar of himself
> on the revolution argument proceeds to make himself more

ridiculous in trying to rule out the Negro from the proletariat class. His reason is that we are not a part of the white proletariat because we are not recognized by that proletariat to any great extent. This is about as asinine as saying we are not human beings or men because in the South we are largely not so recognized. Is manhood dependent upon recognition? Is proletariat a product of recognition or is it a state of economic position of human beings?[25]

Elsewhere in the essay Owen drew additional blood in referring to Du Bois's "much overrated mentality." Such hard-hitting analyses guaranteed him the hostility of potential supporters in middle-class black America.

Lacking institutional support, the *Messenger* constantly struggled for funds. In 1925 it became the organ of Randolph's union, the Brotherhood of Sleeping Car Porters. Subsidized by the union, the *Messenger* survived until 1928.

Original work published in the *Crisis* and *Opportunity* convinced many skeptical white critics that blacks could be successful and occasionally innovative literary figures. Such an acknowledgment delighted some black intellectuals, who hailed their acceptance by critics like Van Wyck Brooks as proof that black intellectuals had arrived. Wallace Thurman and others were not so sure.

Thurman, one of the more talented and independent-minded writers in Harlem during the twenties, grew up in the Midwest and attended the University of Southern California. Attracted by the literary ferment in Harlem, and not finding any comparable excitement on the West Coast, Thurman moved to New York and quickly fell in with a coterie of ambitious black writers and poets. He published articles in the *New Republic* and the *Bookman* and yet was tormented by self-doubt about his ability to produce great literature. He was also very skeptical about the writing of his Harlem literary peers. Thurman's legendary consumption of gin did little to calm his fear that black artists had not yet transcended the reproductive stage of intellectual work. Their demonstrated ability to comprehend and appropriate the language and symbols of traditional "high culture" was a necessary first step, but truly great art, Thurman believed, required venturing beyond the familiar and the accepted. In particular, Thurman and Langston Hughes feared that most black artists, seeking acceptance by mainstream white intellectuals, had abandoned the fertile cultural soil of African American life.[26]

Indeed, the creative work of many black authors in the 1920s revealed their sure grasp of the literary conventions of the period. Poets such as Countee Cullen, who graduated Phi Beta Kappa from New York University, had closely studied Western literary forms and crafted masterly poetry within that tradition. The imagery of "To a Brown Boy" sets up tension between a sensuous Africanity and sterile white Christianity: "And lips know better how to kiss / Than how to raise white hymns."[27]

Jean Toomer was another accomplished literary craftsman.[28] Born in 1894 in Washington, D.C., Toomer graduated from Paul Laurence Dunbar High School and studied law at the University of Wisconsin and at City College of New York. After abandoning his hopes for a career in law, Toomer met Alain Locke in Washington, and Locke later introduced him to several black writers in Harlem. During the twenties, however, Toomer—who boasted of having "at least seven" types of blood coursing through his veins—refused to think of himself as black or white. Rather, he insisted that he was an *American*. His *Cane,* an experimental, genre-defying literary work, first published in 1923, poses questions about the search for identity that occupied the more self-consciously black writers of the Harlem Renaissance.[29] Toomer insisted on a transcendent identification for himself, and in 1926 protested his inclusion in the famous anthology *The New Negro,* edited by Alain Locke.[30] Assessing the stories, poems, and rhythms of *Cane,* the literary critic Darwin Turner has written, "In them he questioned and suggested more often than he taught; he adumbrated messages. The components of *Cane* resembled an artist's sketches rather than a reformer's sermons."[31] The poetic realism and form of Toomer's *Cane,* Turner thought, left little doubt that the African American mind was equal to any challenge the Western tradition put forward.

Several paradoxes complicated the quest for status. Although life on the fringes of the cultural establishment proved unrewarding, proud and brilliant artists disliked seeking validation from cultural arbiters who reinforced white supremacy. Black writers felt entitled to fame consistent with their talent, but what were the consequences, they asked themselves, of embracing the values and aesthetics of a culture that marginalized black people? They observed that many of the more creative American thinkers had despaired of the nation's provincial cultural landscape and sought refuge and invigoration in Europe, where they hoped to live the good and creative life. Sons and daughters of American privilege such as Edmund Wilson, F. Scott Fitzgerald, Gertrude Stein, and John Dos Passos had mastered the cultural standards of the United States but found them shallow. As Malcolm Cowley put it, "Life in this country is joyless and colorless, universally standardized, tawdry, uncreative, given over to the worship of wealth and machinery."[32] A generation of disillusioned white intellectuals doubted that anything promising could be achieved on American soil. Those who remained in the United States searched feverishly for ideas, cultural themes, and expressions both original and, in their opinion, liberating.

Some black artists, such as Claude McKay, less attached to the American cultural system and its rewards, operated with a freedom envied by white intellectuals. Relegated to the margins of mainstream cultural institutions, most black intellectuals expressed little of the general frustration articulated by the Lost Generation. Not yet having reached the promised land, few were prepared to abandon it. And many creative artists saw in black cultural life the vitality they craved.

The widely reported forays of white avant-garde artists and intellectuals into the nightlife of Renaissance-era Harlem suggests that many enjoyed the genius and creative spirit of black culture. But the Lost Generation could not have gained insight into black culture as a whole merely by marveling on weekends at the music of Duke Ellington and the musical comedies of Eubie Blake and Noble Sissle. They did not bother to examine thoughtfully the everyday lives of ordinary blacks. Nor were those whites who ventured beyond music into the poetry and prose of Zora Hurston, Sterling Brown, and Langston Hughes able to understand the cultural criticism implicit in African American folk thought.[33] Too often, they viewed this work as quaint and clever but sophomoric.

Some black intellectuals could challenge how whites interpreted what they saw in black communities. Most, however, chose not to explain the rich and complex traditions that informed Hurston's work; nor did they bother to correct the simplistic picture of black

folk culture proffered by white aficionados such as DuBose Heyward, author of the folk opera *Porgy and Bess*.[34] Black intellectuals,
so long excluded from the possibility of any reward or acclaim, were
reluctant to undermine any platforms that afforded even limited
access to the advantages of American high culture.

## Paradoxes of the Harlem Renaissance

America's history of racial subordination put black creative artists
in a dilemma. Defensive, but eager to engage the American cultural
establishment, writers and other artists leapt at chances to escape
the marginal status to which they had been relegated. Black cultural
institutions lacked credibility in the white world, and, in any case,
few of these could adequately support artists and their work. The
Talented Tenth needed patronage, opportunities to publish, to perform, to earn a livelihood. But who was in a position to help, and
what would these benefactors require of their beneficiaries?

During the Harlem Renaissance (roughly 1920–31), a number of
wealthy individuals and philanthropic foundations supported black
artists, enabling them to work practically full-time at their art. A few
of the patrons were black—such as Madame C. J. Walker, whose
hair-processing products for blacks made her a millionaire, and
Caspar Holstein, a chieftain in Harlem's numbers racket—but most
were white. The black community could better support musicians.
Jazz musicians could as a rule work regularly in locales like the Kentucky Club, the Savoy Ballroom, and Roseland.[35] In his social history
of the period, *When Harlem Was in Vogue*, David Levering Lewis
acknowledges black institutions that supported art but contends that
the role of white patronage during the period was crucial: "The
scores of unknown painters, sculptors, and writers poured into Harlem—there would have been no emergency loans and temporary
beds, professional advice and Downtown contacts, prizes and publicity without the patient assemblage and management by a handful of
Harlem notables of a substantial white patronage."[36]

Lewis describes one such patron, Charlotte Osgood Mason, as "a
dowager of wealth and influence" who had considerable interest in
art but little artistic or critical ability, and who apparently fell hard

for African American "primitivism." For her, black aesthetics and the pulse of Africa promised liberation from the sterile and decadent ideals of Western civilization. As word of her largesse and interest spread, black writers, some of whom shared her belief in the potential of a distinctly African American culture, and some of whom simply needed money, made the pilgrimage to her penthouse at 399 Park Avenue. As it turned out, Mason's generosity to struggling artists was not unqualified. Through Alain Locke, a genteel intermediary, who had in 1925 been dismissed from his faculty position at Howard University, she let it be known that she favored art that reflected or examined the primitive and "untainted" qualities of black life.[37]

Some artists balked at Mason's cultural prescriptions. The painter Aaron Douglas at first accepted money from her but later broke with her to pursue his concept of blending abstract elements with socially conscious figurations of the black experience. Langston Hughes was a Mason favorite for years but finally left her entourage because of her insistence that he write as if the "rhythms of the primitive" were surging through him. Genuinely fond of his elderly patron, Hughes lamented the end of their relationship but was philosophical about the breakup: "I was not what she wanted me to be. So, in the end it all came back very near to the old impasse of white and Negro again, white and Negro—as do most relationships in America."[38]

Charlotte Mason also took Zora Neale Hurston under her wing, apparently after Alain Locke brought the earthy and vibrant young folklore collector to her attention. Soon, through her stories, personality, and guile, Hurston had endeared herself to Mason, and in December 1927 they signed a one-year employment contract. For $200 a month, Hurston would act as Mason's "independent agent," collecting black folk material, to which Mason would retain all proprietary rights. Furthermore, Hurston might not discuss or share her findings with anyone else—perhaps because, as Hurston's biographer has speculated, Mason "felt arrogantly that Zora Neale Hurston could not be trusted to know best what to do with it."[39]

Buoyed by the novelty of such support for a project dear to her heart, Hurston roamed the South gathering volumes of folk material. Although impressed with Hurston's work, Mason blocked her efforts to use the material she had collected in her own writing. Projects frowned upon by Mason had to be abandoned, or pursued secretly.

The patron also discouraged Hurston's association with Otto Klineberg, a prominent white social scientist who was directing a major project on racial anthropology in the United States.[40] Their professional association would have enhanced Hurston's reputation in scholarly circles, but Hurston reasoned that Mason could not accept the idea of an intellectually independent African American.

Mason's patronage may also have contributed to the breakup of Hurston's close friendship with Langston Hughes. A biographer speaks of Hurston's fear that Louise Thompson, an intimate of both Hurston and Hughes, would supplant her in Mason's coterie. Hurston, no stranger to poverty and the life of a destitute scholar, was not about to let another writer usurp her station. According to her biographer, Hurston harbored suspicions about Hughes and Thompson that led her to accuse Hughes of plagiarism and unethical conduct in connection with a play on which they were collaborating.[41]

Although nearly stifled by Mason's patronage, young Hurston could not have pursued her work without it. No university or foundation would have subsidized a young black woman intellectual. So, Hurston seized her offer and negotiated as best she could the contrary interests of her patron and her own intellect. Her contemporaries, some jealous of her relationship with Mason, others genuinely concerned about the corrosive influence of white patrons on African American art, were skeptical. In his autobiography, *The Big Sea,* Hughes offers his version of Hurston's plight:

> Only to reach a wider audience, need she ever write books— because she is a perfect book of entertainment in herself. In her youth she was always getting scholarships and things from wealthy white people, some of whom simply paid her just to sit around and represent the Negro race for them, she did it in such a racy fashion. She was full of side-splitting anecdotes, humorous tales, and tragicomic stories, remembered out of her life in the South as the daughter of a travelling minister of God. . . . To many of her white friends, no doubt, she was a perfect "darkie," in the nice meaning they give the term—that is a naïve, childlike, sweet, humorous, and highly colored Negro.[42]

Strong cases have been made that Hurston was a highly independent thinker and that her "performances" were simply that—performances. Yet her role-playing took a toll; her artistic imagination was diverted into roles that distorted her creativity, and her artistic personality became absorbed by the mask.

The folklore Hurston retrieved from southern blacks informed several of her novels in the thirties. But by 1940 her fiction and essays had come to reflect a keen sense of publishers' tastes, often at the expense of her own integrity and imagination. As she candidly told an *Amsterdam News* interviewer in 1944, "Rather than get across all of the things which you want to say you must compromise and work within the limitations [of those people] who have the final authority in deciding whether or not a book shall be printed."[43] The once combative artist, it seems, had accepted a hard lesson—black intellectuals could best make their mark by accepting the constraints imposed by the world of white power and privilege.

At her death in 1960, Zora Hurston lived in a nursing home for indigents in Saint Lucie County, Florida. Her four novels, two folklore collections, autobiography, and numerous essays had brought no measure of financial security. Whatever her personal foibles, Hurston's artistic and financial decline was inextricably linked to the predicament of black thinkers in American life. Reflecting on Hurston's career, especially the final years, Alice Walker has written, "Being broke made all the difference. Without money of one's own in a capitalist society, there is no such thing as independence. This is one of the clearest lessons of Zora's life, and why I consider the telling of her life a 'cautionary tale.' We must learn from it what we can."[44]

Although Mason and other wealthy patrons wielded strong influence, their control over the work of their protégés was not absolute. Black artists could dissemble their motives and impress patrons with conversations and ideas designed to fit a patron's sense of what was appropriate for black folks. Alain Locke titled his complex Harvard dissertation "The Problem of Classification in Theory of Value." Without doubt, his ideas about culture had little in common with Charlotte Mason's notions of African primitivism. Nevertheless, Locke stayed with Mason because he needed a patron willing to subsidize African American artists.[45]

Other financially strapped black writers also did what they had to. Dorothy West, another Harlem Renaissance writer and, in the thirties, editor of the short-lived *Challenge* magazine, had a wealthy white friend named Elizabeth Marbury. One day Marbury asked to meet some of West's black writer friends, and West introduced Marbury to Wallace Thurman. Decades later, in 1978, she recalled with embarrassment, "Wallace Thurman had met her once, had written her [Marbury] the next day to ask her for five hundred dollars, and she gave him the five hundred dollars. . . . I never forgave him for that."[46]

The demands of myopic patrons and the white mainstream audience frustrated black creative writers, who could turn only to each other. An audience more sympathetic to their visions was slowly growing, but the pervasive influence of mainstream thought still worked against a productive artist-audience synergy. The small black critical audience could not yet muster the cultural authority to validate novel forms of art.


## Book Publishing and Markets

Many a slave narrative published at the height of nineteenth-century abolitionist sentiment had enjoyed brisk sales. Harriet Beecher Stowe's well-meaning but maudlin *Uncle Tom's Cabin* sold over 300,000 copies in 1852, its first year of publication.[47]

During the 1920s commercial book publishers, nearly all of them white, discovered that books catering to white readers' latest fantasies about black life sold well. Novels such as *Home to Harlem* (1935), by the Jamaican immigrant Claude McKay, and the controversial *Nigger Heaven* (1926), by the white socialite Carl Van Vechten, successfully tapped the market of Americans curious about the rhythms, sounds, and textures of black America. Eager to duplicate the commercial success of *Nigger Heaven,* several black writers produced manuscripts showing black culture as exotic, earthy, and decadent. The white cultural avant-garde of the Roaring Twenties saw— or thought it saw—much in black life that confirmed Freud's theories that less suppression of the id produced less neurotic individuals. Books such as *Home to Harlem,* Rudolph Fisher's *Walls of Jericho* (1928), and Nella Larsen's imaginative but sentimental *Quicksand* (1928) were published in the twenties. Langston Hughes, with characteristic irony, noted, "It was a period when white writers wrote about Negroes more successfully (commercially speaking) than Negroes did about themselves."[48]

Most black intellectuals were in some measure touched by the "example for your race" syndrome and thus rejected art that emphasized the folkways of the unrefined black masses. For the Talented Tenth, mastery of elite cultural standards was the ultimate measure of achievement. Until the twenties members of the black intelligentsia did not question the primacy of Western aesthetic and cultural standards; rather, they were unhappy that their efforts to produce work reflecting those standards were disregarded. The first writers who slowly made their way into print during the early years of the Harlem Renaissance were staunchly bourgeois in their orientation, believing that art should amplify the more respectable elements and features of African American life. Their criterion of respectability mirrored the values of the dominant culture. Writers such as Countee Cullen and Nella Larsen labored to duplicate the tried, true, and proper.

But there were important exceptions. The talented and eccentric author Wallace Thurman championed a literature that explored the authentic and unique qualities of black life.[49] He urged black writers to turn to the folk tradition for their material, for he saw little artistic merit in books that attempted to celebrate the black bourgeoisie. Dismayed by the penchant of middle-class blacks to enshrine Western concepts of respectability and righteousness, Thurman, Langston Hughes, and a few others encouraged the shift of focus to the unlettered masses. They believed that the most vital cultural themes were expressed in the folkways of common black people rather than in the parlors and literary cliques of the Talented Tenth.

Pithy cultural arguments occupied black thinkers throughout the 1920s. Issue after issue of the *Crisis* and *Opportunity* contained sharp and impassioned rhetoric from proponents of both perspectives. The question of literary merit, however, could not be divorced from practical concerns. Writing that did not appeal to the tastes of a white audience had little chance of being successful, even if it reached print.

A well-recorded incident of censorship involved the novel *The Fire in the Flint*, by Walter White, a politically active black writer. The book portrays in unflinching terms the story of a middle-class professional in the Booker T. Washington vein, encountering bigotry and violence at the hands of white southerners. Though quite melodramatic in its indictment of racial bigotry, the story rang true. White's publisher Doran and Company, was at first enthusiastic about the project but then backpedaled, fearing opposition from white south-erners. White fought against suggested revisions, arguing that the portrayals of the South and southern characters were authentic and represented a corrective to the numerous books by white southerners that vilified or patronized blacks. White also enlisted white liberals such as Arthur Springarn and Will Alexander (himself a southerner) to plead his case. But Doran and Company held firm and refused to release the book. Alfred A. Knopf, on the advice of H. L. Mencken, eventually published *Fire in the Flint,* which sold well, largely because White promoted its controversial aspects to a bigoted but curious South.[50] For black authors, however, the episode highlighted one of Du Bois's complaints: "The white public today demands from its artists, literary and pictorial, racial pre-judgment which deliber-ately distorts Truth and Justice, as far as colored races are concerned, and it will pay for no other."[51]

The size of the market for books by black authors has always been directly linked to white interest in African American culture at the time. As it does today, the cage of racial perceptions prevented most white readers in the twenties from appreciating the universalism of themes developed by black writers, with black characters, in black settings. No matter how self-consciously universalistic black writers tried to be—no matter that black characters acted passionately, hero-ically, treacherously—their work, in the minds of most white readers, remained all about black people. If one accepts the premise that nov-elists, poets, and playwrights should write about what they know best, it follows that black authors will do their finest work when they draw on their own experience. But as was true during the Harlem Renaissance, when they do, their works are viewed as representing "the black experience" rather than the *human* experience.

Wallace Thurman's novel *Infants of the Spring* dissects many of the cultural pretensions of black intellectual life in Harlem in the 1920s. Through his protagonist Raymond, Thurman reflects on two unfortunate characteristics of black writing: "He was tired of Negro writers who had nothing to say, and who wrote because they were literate and felt they should apprise white humanity of the better classes among Negro humanity."[52] Thurman had little patience with Alain Locke, who functioned as a cheerleader for better-educated and financially better-off black citizens. Writers should explore the panorama of black life, Thurman said, including those aspects that the black middle class preferred to ignore. Furthermore, he was critical of black writers who veered into the muddled world of racial politics. Again, even the venerable Du Bois attracted his gibes: "Du Bois is a potentially great writer gone wrong, and the rest are mere chicken feed, pushed into prominence because of expediency."[53]

Believing that whites' fascination with black folk would be short-lived, and cynical about the motives of the white literary establishment, Thurman feared that no truly important art would be created during the Renaissance and a golden opportunity would be lost. He exhorted black writers to seize the moment: "For the time being the Negro was more in evidence in the high places than ever before in his American career, but unless, or so it seemed to [those] of the group who had climbed aboard the bandwagon, they actually began to do something worthwhile, there would be little chance of their being permanently established."[54] Apart from Toomer's *Cane,* Thurman's sharp eye saw little of lasting value in the work of his Bohemian fellow travelers. Nathan Huggins, sensitive to Thurman's perception, wrote in 1971, "Thurman was critical of the renaissance because it was naive, innocent, optimistic and engaged in the promotion of art. After all the talking was over, Thurman knew that it would take a lot of hard work and skill to write good novels and short stories and poems."[55]

Most black writers ignored Thurman's plea and accepted the cultural norms of the only country they knew—America. The frustration of black middle-class writers with political and economic restrictions had yet to evolve into a broader cultural critique of American society. Even Marcus Garvey's mass-based black nationalist movement, like the white mainstream, was entranced by the idea of wealth and empire. It gnawed at black writers that, despite their achievements and capabilities, they were discriminated against and not taken seriously as artists. The more ambitious writers reasoned, or at least hoped, that a growing black reading audience—that is to say, more affluent—would support new literary directions.

Wary as usual, Du Bois observed that many literate blacks had come under the spell of dominant cultural beliefs. He thought that a symbiotic relation between culturally liberated African American artists and an equally open black audience could generate truly great art. These black intellectuals would understand the landscape of Western civilization and the infrastructure of African American life, and they would pursue goals other than respectability and recognition. But he doubted the readiness of black audiences for work that challenged conventions:

> The young and slowly growing black public still wants its prophets almost equally unfree. We are bound by all sorts of customs that have come down as second-hand soul clothes of white patrons. We are ashamed of sex and we lower our eyes when people will talk of it. Our religion holds us in superstition. Our worst side has been so shamelessly emphasized that we are denying we have or ever had a worst side. In all sorts of ways we are hemmed in and our young artists have got to fight their way to freedom.[56]

Du Bois acknowledged the importance of the fight against discrimination and injustice, yet he challenged the black middle class to look beyond those immediate concerns and ponder what values and assumptions it was trying to appropriate:

> When gradually the vista widens and you begin to see the world at your feet and the far horizon, then it is time to know more precisely whither you are going and what you really want. . . . We want to be Americans, full-fledged Americans, with all the rights of other American citizens. But is that all? Do we want simply to be Americans? Once in a while through all of us there flashes some clairvoyance, some clear idea, of what America is. We who are dark can see America in a way that white Americans can not. And seeing our country thus, are we satisfied with its present goals and ideals?[57]

Decades later, Harold Cruse bemoaned what he considers a serious failing of Langston Hughes and the black middle class:

> They all saw things they refused to write about, all of them. The fact that Langston got a medal says what? That he didn't criticize the black middle-class bourgeoisie! That was the forte of a

really powerful critic like Ibsen. The Norwegian bourgeoisie gave him hell. He showed the fraudulence, the emptiness of their existence. But Hughes and others did not want to alienate themselves from the black middle class.[58]

Hughes and other writers hesitated to attack the black middle class and its supporters who wielded financial power and maintained useful social networks. Where else could black writers and artists turn for support? Proud men and women who believed in their work could not afford to alienate the small group of well-to-do and literate blacks. Surely accommodating middle-class blacks was less compromising than appealing to the white purse, so often allied with the nation's white supremacist institutions.

# 6 ⋘

# BEYOND INCUBATION: A TALENTED BUT TRAPPED TENTH

It is only during the last few years that the cracker *intelligentsia* have begun to sniff suspiciously at the old Anglo-Saxon slogans and concepts of justice, democracy, chivalry, honor, fair play, and so forth. The Negro has always been skeptical about them, knowing that they were conditioned by skin color, social position, and economic wealth. —GEORGE SCHUYLER

T HE FIRST QUARTER of the twentieth century was a hard time for blacks seeking careers in white academic institutions. Traditional departments had few positions for them, and many blacks with advanced degrees turned to writing fiction and drama as a means of self-expression and intellectual fulfillment. Rudolph Fisher, a Harlem physician who had earned Phi Beta Kappa honors at Brown University, published novels about urban black folk life.[1] Jessie Fauset resigned her teaching post at M Street School in Washington to work as literary editor of the *Crisis*. Nella Larsen left nursing and a position as a children's librarian to write professionally. During the thirties, however, as the Great Depression settled in, black intellectuals dared not stake their economic survival on writing careers. They had to find more stable and financially rewarding occupations.

By the mid-1930s their perseverance in pursuit of higher education had begun to pay dividends. The number of blacks earning doctoral degrees in American universities had increased significantly. In 1925 only 17 African Americans held doctorates; fourteen years later 109 did.[2] Most were being trained in northern schools such as the University of Chicago and Harvard.[3] And young Ph.D.'s were aggressively recruited by black colleges eager to enhance their prestige by employing graduates of northern universities.

## Black Colleges and
## the Training of Intellectuals

Black people in towns such as Richmond, Knoxville, and Fort Valley, Georgia, where black colleges were located, understood the schools' value. Black townspeople believed that the well-dressed young men and women who attended schools were on their way to success. Young people living in or near black college towns observed role models that seemed attractive and accessible. Horace Mann Bond found that two-thirds of the black doctorate holders between 1922 and 1962 had started in black colleges.[4]

This marked an important change. During their first decades the future of black colleges had hardly seemed promising. Most southern whites fought the idea of black public secondary schools in their midst, seeing little need for education beyond the primary level for the white masses, and certainly no more for blacks. White officials who controlled the black schools adopted lower standards for teachers—and for principals—of black students than for those who taught whites. In one case "a county superintendent, after being nursed through a terrific illness by a faithful Negro retainer, promptly appointed his bodyguard as principal of the Negro county training school as a reward for his services."[5]

More than one-third of the black public school teachers employed in fifteen southern states in 1930 had not completed high school. A study of black teachers in 1931 reported that "a typical Jefferson County, Alabama, Negro teacher shows an educational achievement equivalent to a middle-eighth-grade class."[6] Because the standards for black teachers were low, the candidate pool was large and the pay meager—often half that of white teachers.

Southern state legislatures passed budgets that reflected the views of their constituents. Only 10 percent of the funding for black colleges was provided by the states. The balance came from philanthropists and churches. Despite the obstacles faced by black educational institutions, the literacy rate of southern blacks increased 94 percent between 1890 and 1930 (that of southern whites increased 32 percent), and the demand for more advanced training surged. Not surprisingly, the number of students graduating from the southern black colleges rose dramatically.[7]

By 1930, African Americans from other parts of the country were enrolling in the black colleges of the South. Typical studious and ambitious northern black high school graduates reasoned that they would be better off traveling south to Hampton or Atlanta University than battling discrimination at local white universities. The education obtained at black colleges would prepare them for privileged roles in the largely segregated black world. However, the positive symbolism and economic mobility that black colleges provided was undermined by the reality that the education students received was not the best that the country, or even the South, had to offer. Because educated blacks could enter only a few professional occupations, most black college officials saw no need to develop a comprehensive curriculum. Black college graduates could be assured a place of respect in the segregated black South, but they were not encouraged, or in some instances even allowed, to compete with whites. Consequently, blacks who finished at black colleges in the 1930s were rarely exposed to intellectual challenges. Perhaps predictably, they came to be criticized for not knowing what they had no opportunity to learn.

Black colleges, both public and private, survived as institutions through the good graces of local and state officials. With few exceptions, black college presidents were expected to maintain order and direct the energies of faculty and students away from politics. Despite their predilections, black faculty members trained in the more liberal northern universities did not resist the restrictive guidelines governing the social and political content in both teaching and publication. Discipline was even stricter at colleges affiliated with churches. Everywhere ideas and practices that ran counter to local and conventional wisdom were nipped in the bud. J. Saunders Redding, who taught at several black colleges, was categorical in his denunciation:

Negro colleges have tended to breed fascism—I would say a mild form of it, except that fascism is organically hysterical and there is no mild form of it—and I have met Negro college presidents whose notions are provocative of suspicious wonder and who, by the way they run "their" institutions, seem to be convinced that the methods of democracy are weak and decadent.[8]

Horace Cayton, a black sociologist who graduated from the University of Chicago and joined the faculty of Tuskegee Institute in the 1940s, scorned his colleagues, characterizing them as "second-rate scholars who were not even interested in their work, and more disturbing was their attitude toward their students. There was a strict caste line between students and faculty; the faculty looked down on the students as ignorant sharecroppers."[9] It seemed to Cayton that his colleagues, terrorized by deans and presidents and unable to leave for better jobs, vented their frustrations on their students. Black faculty members recognized that they had no place else to go. The white northerners who came south to teach in private church-related schools shared some of the restrictive ideas about young black students. St. Clair Drake, a student at Hampton and son of a Baptist minister who became a Garveyite, recalled the attitudes of the missionary teachers from the North:

At Hampton you weren't allowed to dance. We had a big strike one year after they punished guys for holding their girlfriends' hands in the movies. What was the reason for this? Most of the white missionaries who came down from the North believed that blacks could learn anything anybody else could learn. They were trying to get you ready for Harvard or Yale. But they believed that blacks had a predisposition for sexuality, needed strict rules to keep boys away from girls, so that the brain could express itself.[10]

Slowly, the increasing sophistication of black families who sent their children south to college created problems for autocratic presidents. By the 1920s a few colleges (Fisk, Howard, and Atlanta) had developed a sizable clientele in the black middle class. The sons and daughters of black privilege came to these schools with an acute sense of their rights and obligations. And they demonstrated. Fisk, in Nashville, and Howard, in Washington D.C., saw significant student protests during the 1920s.

At Fisk students protested actions taken by the college's white president, Fayette McKenzie. To impress potential northern benefactors, McKenzie had abolished the student government, closed the student paper, and forbade all dissent on campus. Middle-class students who shared their fellow alumnus Du Bois's belief in an assertive black leadership class were offended by McKenzie's paternalism. Their protests were eventually joined by Fisk alumni. McKenzie resigned.[11]

At Howard compulsory ROTC helped spark demonstrations. Strongly opposed to the white president, James Stanley Durkee, and his autocratic style, students shut down the campus for eight days in May 1925. Durkee also clashed with many of Howard's star black scholars, with Carter Woodson, Alain Locke, and Kelly Miller. The students' demand that Durkee resign was supported by the alumni and eventually by the board of regents. Durkee stepped down in 1925, and the Howard community made it known that it preferred a black president. In 1926 the regents named Mordecai Johnson, a dynamic Baptist preacher, the first black president in the school's history.[12]

While Fisk, Howard, and Atlanta drew many of their students from the middle class, most other black colleges enrolled students from poor homes who had passed through weak black educational systems in the southern and border states. Lacking the self-confidence of Fisk's and Howard's relatively privileged students, and less aware of W. E. B. Du Bois's ethic of assertive moral consciousness, students at campuses such as Virginia State and Alcorn, in Mississippi, rarely confronted oppressive college administrators.

In the stronger black institutions, blacks with graduate-level training were forced to compete with each other (and with whites) for positions:

By 1936 a sizable group of black Ph.D.'s was available for employment, but fully 80% of them taught in just three institutions, Atlanta, Fisk and Howard. During the decade beginning with 1937, 279 black students received Ph.D. degrees. In 1940–

41, a national survey found no Negroes holding tenured positions in any American university.[13]

As a result, the black colleges and academically superior high schools (such as Paul Laurence Dunbar in Washington, D.C.) had their pick of black master's and doctorate holders.

Howard, then considered the best of the black colleges, was no oasis, however, especially for black scholars intent on expanding knowledge through research. A biographer writes of the research biologist Ernest E. Just's predicament: "The pressures were harrowing. Teaching and committee work kept him on campus up to fourteen hours a day. His research was suffering. To continue effectively he had to leave Howard. But no white institution in America would hire him."[14]

Some black scholars, such as Benjamin Quarles and E. Franklin Frazier, persevered despite the pressures and lack of recognition. They conducted research, wrote, and enriched their fields. Quarles, from the campuses of Shaw, in Raleigh, North Carolina, and Dillard, in New Orleans, contributed important historical scholarship. Quarles's work on Frederick Douglass and abolitionism appeared in the *Journal of Negro History*.[15] Frazier, another Ph.D. from the University of Chicago, made the round of elite black colleges, teaching at Atlanta University (1922–27) and Fisk University (1929–34) and ending up as chairman of the Department of Sociology at Howard in 1934. In spite of heavy teaching and administrative loads, Frazier published dozens of articles and several books and contributed regularly to black newsweeklies such as the *Baltimore Afro-American*. In 1939 his *Negro Family in the United States* received the Anisfield-Wolf Award for that year's best book on race relations.

But many other equally talented scholars ceased to labor for rewards they understandably assumed would never be theirs. Looking back, Harold Cruse, a chronicler of black intellectual life, expresses his disappointment about what happened to talented thinkers of the preceding generation:

I assess their role similar to the way I assess the career of Hugh Gloster, who is now [1985] the president of Morehouse. In the forties Gloster wrote what was to me at the time the definitive

study of black literature, *Negro Voices in American Fiction*. In
my view that was one of the best assessments of black literature
written by a black literary critic. He wrote that one book and
stopped. Gloster got immersed in the black academic world of
Atlanta University, which as far as I know does not teach the
literary values that he once espoused.[16]

Other black scholars, along with some of their counterparts in the
white academic world, resorted to pedantry and platitudes. Algernon
Jackson found many of his black scholarly colleagues lacking in
integrity. In 1933 Jackson wrote, "Few dare to be original. Many
fear to strike at tradition and custom. . . . I have seen and heard
many of the learned Doctors of Philosophy in their class rooms,
whom in spite of a bitter struggle between my natural charitableness
and sense of humor I have christened Doctors of Phraseology
instead."[17]

Beginning in 1935 a growing number of blacks, backed by the
NAACP, brought suit against the educational systems of the South,
charging that the lack of adequate programs for graduate education
violated their constitutional rights. Donald Murray, a black graduate
of Amherst and resident of Maryland, sued the University of Maryland after he was denied admission to its graduate school. Maryland
courts found for the plaintiff and ordered the university to admit
him.[18] Under the "separate but equal" doctrine, states were allowed
to maintain a dual educational system, but opportunities available to
whites had to be available (in some form) to blacks as well. In a show
of compliance with the "equal protection" clause in the Constitution,
some southern states offered to subsidize out-of-state graduate or
professional education for black residents.

In 1936 Lloyd Gaines sued the University of Missouri for denying
him admission to its law school. The Missouri courts ruled that since
the state was willing to provide Gaines a scholarship for study elsewhere, his rights had not been violated. The NAACP apppealed the
case to the Supreme Court, which in 1938 ruled that the state's offer
to Gaines was not equal to what it provided white candidates and
that he had been excluded from the campus because of race.

Hoping to forestall court-ordered integration decrees, southern
legislatures rushed to allocate more funds to black colleges and

pushed them to establish graduate and professional schools. Since the courts had not outlawed segregation, but merely decided that equal facilities were not available to Gaines, southern states aimed to satisfy the *Plessy* v. *Ferguson* "equal facilities" condition by providing hastily devised parallel programs in black colleges. In the period 1942–50 graduate and professional schools were established at black state colleges in Alabama, Florida, Louisiana, Missouri, North Carolina, Tennessee, and Virginia.

Ever pragmatic, black colleges quickly absorbed available monies and expanded. At midcentury enrollment in black colleges doubled, rising from 37,203 in 1940 to 74,526 in 1950. By contrast, college enrollment of whites in the South increased by only 18 percent during the same period.[19] As the colleges grew and consolidated their position in the South, their economic impact on local communities became obvious to all. More important, their graduates provided staff for the schools and professions open to blacks. As the hubs of intellectual activity in the black South, colleges shaped much of the intellectual climate. Looking back on black colleges of the period, the political sociologist Doug McAdam concluded, "By mid-century the poorly supported, inadequately staffed black colleges of thirty years earlier had been transformed into some of the strongest and most influential institutions within the black community."[20]

As protest organizations like the NAACP expanded their activities, black colleges became a source of political leadership. The NAACP's legal arm viewed the early emphasis on breaking barriers to graduate and professional education in a tactical light. Its officers hoped to increase the number of highly educated black leaders in the South. Inheritors of the Talented Tenth tradition, they reasoned that as the number of black college graduates increased, the more talented would need more advanced training. While such northern schools as Harvard, Columbia, and the University of Chicago had extended some graduate opportunities to blacks, their offerings fell well short of what the times demanded. Black intellectual leaders like Howard's Rayford Logan looked ahead: "Today the colored graduate schools would be a farce, if you insist. But what of tomorrow? Are we building for today or for future generations?"[21]

Some strong voices, however, among them E. Franklin Frazier's, spoke out against this proliferation. Although granting the tactical rationale for offering graduate degrees, Frazier insisted that most black colleges did not have enough high-caliber faculty members to mount a respectable graduate program. To initiate second-rate graduate programs simply because blacks were not being admitted to white graduate schools was indefensible, he maintained. Instead, schools should continue to concentrate on their undergraduate programs until their faculties were strong enough to offer advanced-degree programs.[22]

Opportunities that met the standards associated with Frazier's own training were rarely within the reach of even superior black college students. Black southerners could not enroll in the white graduate schools in their states, and for most the cost of attending northern universities was prohibitive. African American teachers undertook graduate work in summer school on northern campuses, a slow and disjointed process. During the Great Depression even summer study ceased to be an option.

## The Lure of Marxism

The Russian revolution marked a watershed for American intellectuals during the twenties. As we have seen, many writers and scholars had become disenchanted with the unchecked U.S. passion for growth and materialism, and Marxism held out the promise of a more humane social order. Revolutionary Russia seemed a mecca of greater social equality. Through publications such as the *New Masses,* the Left encouraged experimentation in literature and attacked many of the bulwarks of the Western tradition. The spirit of rebellion was typified by the intellectual cadre in New York's Greenwich Village. Supported by a community of creative and tolerant people, artists such as Mabel Dodge and Lincoln Steffens waged war against tradition and American canons of taste.

During the 1920s Marxist ideology influenced all the social sciences. Exchanges between black intellectuals and white leftists centered on the distinctiveness and value of black cultural expressions. But the focus of debate shifted dramatically during the Great Depression. Now the important questions for the Left concerned the most effective means of mobilizing all workers, white and black, to exercise collective power. Some Marxists maintained that appeals to cultural groups only caused divisiveness and reinforced the security of the ruling class. Others, especially the Communists after the Sixth Congress of the Communist International in 1928, accepted the right of national groups to self-determination.[23]

Black intellectuals were drawn to a leftist ideology that rejected racism. The turn-of-the-century fascination with the notion of racially inherent characteristics had waned. Socialism as an ideal rejected race as a meaningful social category and elevated social class or the relation of people to the means of production as the pivotal determinant of cultural and political reality. Finally, the scale of the Russian revolution and the popular uprisings in central and western Europe seemed to support the Marxist formulation that focused on class rather than on color. To blacks long stigmatized and oppressed because of their race, the idea that color *should* be irrelevant in society seemed too good to be true.

Several black intellectuals, including Frazier and later Richard Wright, saw little in black American culture worth preserving. Frazier welcomed the appeal to class interests rather than to ethnic features. The cultural traits of black folk, urban and rural, had been shaped by racist social and economic institutions, and the elimination of those constraints would lead to a new and improved way of life for them and all people.[24] Marxists claimed that once free of the capitalist economic order, American workers would create new cultural forms and a more humane social world. But first the matter of an oppressive economic and political regime had to be addressed.

In 1916 young A. Philip Randolph envisioned a social struggle in which blacks were but one element in a broad popular coalition. Socialism would eliminate all racial oppression in the United States, for discrimination was incompatible with the goal of social equality. Of course, Booker T. Washington had earlier observed that racial discrimination was in theory inimical to capitalism: a rational economic system based on individual achievement and the quest for wealth would dismiss distinctions like race as irrelevant. Nonetheless, the American brand of capitalism had coexisted comfortably with racism, and social critics such as Du Bois and William Patterson, a Harlem attorney, maintained that racial subordination was useful—if not essential—for American capitalist development. The absence of American-style racial discrimination in the Soviet Union spoke well for socialism (or so Randolph thought). The idea of equal opportunity and participation—for more than a century, the demand of the Talented Tenth—was finally being endorsed by the American Left.

During the twenties the white Left divided on the issue of race. To doctrinaire leftists the black community was simply one component of a proletariat class long exploited by wealth and privilege. After 1928, though, some Communists considered blacks a national group and acknowledged their right to develop on the basis of their own historical experience. In fact, the Communist Party in the Northeast was dominated by European-American immigrant cells. But white Communist and Socialist intellectuals had little contact with their black counterparts at the time and rarely explored the condition of any subordinated racial groups.

One black intellectual known by the white Left was Claude McKay. In 1921–22 McKay worked in the offices of the *Liberator* in New York. Max Eastman, its influential editor, had recruited McKay for his editorial staff and, for a while, guided his literary career.[25] Eastman did not limit McKay, a native West Indian, to commentary on black affairs. The cosmopolitan McKay developed warm and rich relationships with white radicals who haunted the offices of the *Liberator*. He also maintained close ties to the maids and sporting characters who enlivened Harlem at the time. He identi-fied with the political predicament of black folk but saw no contra-diction, at least intellectually, between working with downtown white radicals and partying with his Harlem brethren.

> I did not come to the knowing of Negro workers in an academic way, by talking to black crowds at meetings, nor in a bohemian way, by talking about them in cafes. . . . I lived in the same quar-ters and we drank and caroused together in bars and at rent parties. So when I came to write about the low-down Negro, I did not have to compose him from an outside view.[26]

He did, however, express discomfort with the pretentiousness of Harlem's social elite:

> I have never wanted to lie about life, like the preaching black prudes wrapped up in the borrowed robes of hypocritical white

respectability. . . . I haven't arrived at that high degree of civilized culture where I can make a success of producing writing carefully divorced from reality.[27]

Prodded by the Soviet-dominated Communist International, the American Communist Party courted African Americans during the late twenties. The party hoped to establish a foothold in Harlem, where poverty should have prepared the black masses for revolt.[28] But the task of mobilizing blacks was not as simple as Communist theorists thought it would be. Long-established middle-class churches and politicians opposed the politics of the Communist organizers. And a third group arrived on the scene to compete with Communists for the allegiance of Harlemites.

The Universal Negro Improvement Association (UNIA) led by Marcus Garvey captured the imagination of the black masses in New York. Garvey urged blacks to look within their own communities for answers to their needs. His organization criticized appeals to the government, on the grounds that whites would always protect their racial interests. Encouraging black emigration, Garvey argued that Africa should be developed as a source of black power internationally.[29] Garvey's appeals to racial solidarity made more sense to the average Harlem resident than the call for unity with a white working class that daily demonstrated its hostility to blacks. Pragmatic Communists, seeking a way to influence or co-opt the enormous social energy of the UNIA, turned their attention to black intellectuals close to the Garvey movement.

After several awkward attempts, the Communists in Harlem were able to recruit credible black nationalist intellectuals. Cyril Briggs, an early Garvey supporter, viewed the party as a potential ally, one whose anti-imperialistic rhetoric resonated with his own politics. Briggs had long embraced the UNIA's racial-pride agenda, but he deplored Garvey's acceptance of capitalism as an economic model. The breach proved too wide, and the ideologically rigid Briggs eventually abandoned the Garvey movement, first to join the ranks of vocal UNIA detractors and then, in 1921, to join the Communist Party. For several years Briggs labored to give the party credibility in a period when most black people in Harlem felt they already had too many strikes against them to run the added risk of membership in the unpopular Communist Party.[30] Cedric Robinson, a scholar of the period, attributes much of the party's gain in black membership to leftist leaders in black nationalist organizations in the 1920s who "established the political and ideological preconditions for the Party's policies and its success."[31]

Several other talented black intellectuals joined the Communist Party. William Patterson, a 1919 Boalt Hall Law School graduate, signed on with the party and moved from a successful law practice in Harlem to the vanguard of the New York Communist Party. Like other promising black recruits, he was carefully indoctrinated. In 1927 he was sent to Russia to study the proper way to interpret economic and social phenomena. More important, he learned there that black intellectuals received in Russia the respect they longed for in the United States. Herein lay perhaps the Communist Party's principal appeal: "Black communists imbibed a sense of the power of the international movement that made their weakness in American life seem easier to bear."[32] Within the next two decades Claude McKay, Langston Hughes, and Paul Robeson would travel to Russia and return impressed, at least for a while.

Sophisticated leftist social theory seemed to address the condition of African Americans. Since most blacks were workers, the Marxist faith in the working class meshed neatly with black community values. However, most white workers rejected the Left's vision of a raceless society. In the uncertain economic climate, white workers believed that their interests would be better served by the continued subordination of blacks. Organized labor, especially the craft unions, sought to insulate white workers from job competition with blacks or to limit blacks to low-status jobs. The overwhelming majority of the white working class endorsed, tacitly or actively, discrimination in education, employment, and housing. The eloquent appeals of some leftists notwithstanding, white workers, ostensible allies with the black masses in the long march toward socialism, rejected or ignored the call for social, political, and economic equality for blacks. Subjected daily to race-based oppression, black workers were not inclined to minimize the effect of racial discrimination in their lives.

With the onset of economic depression in 1929, whites' flirtation with black artists and culture ended abruptly. The few black writers who had once enjoyed some celebrity and success now retreated to the backwoods of American cultural life. After 1930 no one bothered with the highly individualized voices of the Harlem Renaissance. With more than ten million Americans out of work, novels describing the angst of fair-skinned blacks passing for white seemed unworthy of much attention. Nor did the masses of Americans understand the Lost Generation's ruminations about the emptiness of their lives. The America of the thirties listened most to those intellectuals who had turned to the state to preserve the economic well-being of Americans, mostly white Americans.

Meanwhile identification with a nonracial approach to American social reality was easier for black intellectuals than for workers, but still difficult. Some constructed analyses and critiques that focused on class relations rather than race, but these constructs, they knew, betrayed their own experience. The American intellectual community still was not color-blind: graduate schools limited black enrollment; the faculties of major American universities remained all-white; professional organizations prohibited or restricted the participation of black professionals. However longingly middle-class black intellectuals might look at more expansive settings, they were in effect limited to black middle-class enclaves like Strivers Row in Harlem and its equivalents elsewhere in the urban United States. In close proximity to the black masses and the bourgeoisie, they could not help observing the everyday lives of everyday people. In the world of letters, black intellectuals thrived to an extent: they issued thoughtful commentary about black life and culture; but their ideas were never transformed into real social power. Paradoxically, the popularity of black culture and art among white intellectuals in the 1920s gave many black intellectuals a distorted sense of their own importance in the affairs of the ordinary African Americans who could not afford to live on Strivers Row—or even buy a copy of the *Crisis* magazine.

W. E. B. Du Bois had been receptive, at least since 1900, to Marxist analyses of history. In 1907 he wrote,

> In the socialistic trend thus indicated lies the one great hope of the Negro American. We have been thrown by strange historic reasons into the hands of the capitalists hitherto. . . . We have been made tools of oppression against the workingman's cause—the puppets and playthings of the idle rich. . . . Our nat-

ural friends are not the rich but the poor, not the great but the masses, not the employers but the employees.[33]

For the first twenty years of the century, Du Bois had cautiously endorsed many socialist platforms and positions. However, surveying the state of the black nation in 1935, he judged that the supposed coalition of black and white workers committed to progressive change did not exist, and he saw no prospects for such unity in his lifetime. Organized labor, the ally, in theory, of the black working class, had proved disloyal. While maintaining an intellectual commitment to a color-blind society with a socialist orientation, Du Bois the politician awoke to the harsh realities of the depression and urged blacks temporarily to accept segregated institutions and to form separate black economic cooperatives to further their interests.[34]

This recommendation by a venerable guide in the push for black equality confused many of his contemporaries. After blacks had pursued the integrationist ideal for decades, one of its more eloquent proponents was now encouraging "separate development." Other than Claude McKay, few black intellectuals had endorsed that path. Paradoxically, Du Bois's valiant effort to achieve justice for blacks may have contributed to the nationalist social vision he advanced in the thirties. For decades he had championed advancement through racial integration, but the worsening economic predicament of black folk in depression America and the scant support in the centers of power for integrated institutions convinced him that the black community should look increasingly to itself for sustenance and development.

The neo-Marxist assumptions of Ralph Bunche, E. Franklin Frazier, Abram Harris, and many other young academics in the thirties put them at odds with the older generation of black intellectuals. Ralph Bunche was just three years old when Du Bois endorsed the hope of socialism; as a young graduate of UCLA and Harvard, Bunche surely detested racial discrimination, but the liberal mythology of places such as Harvard—and the pride of belonging to the elite—diverted attention from the failure of white workers to embrace black workers. Bunche wrote of African Americans as having "little appetite for social theories and limited ability to digest social forces," confidently asserting his preference for grander, bolder analyses of American social life. His criticism of black parochialism—"The Negro is an American citizen, but his thinking is more Negro than American"—reflected his concentration on social class rather than on race.[35] Because most blacks were workers, Bunche reasoned, a commitment to working-class interests held more promise for blacks than "race loyalty" did. Race as a scientific concept was undermined by the anthropological work of Franz Boas and Ashley Montagu, so the preoccupation of blacks such as Du Bois with "race barriers" was anachronistic and shortsighted.

While Du Bois, Bunche, and Frazier debated, the lives of the black masses grew bleaker. Black workers were everywhere locked into the lowest-paying jobs. In the South, employers, with the approval of white organized labor, usually imposed a wage differential for black and white workers performing the same job. The American Federation of Labor (AFL), the largest organization of trade unions, refused to prohibit discrimination in member locals. Although industrial unions like the International Ladies Garment Workers Union and the United Mine Workers had become more supportive of black participation after several industrial union strikes failed when blacks crossed the picket lines, even in industrial unions discrimination was the norm.[36] Southern legislators, unchecked by black voters, exercised disproportionate political power in Congress, where antilynching legislation faced consistently strong opposition. Conscious of such facts, and willing to be politically involved, critics of Du Bois, such as Bunche and John Davis, helped launch the National Negro Congress (NNC) in 1935. Their intention was to galvanize black leaders around broad economic rather than racial objectives.[37]

It must have amused Du Bois to see critics of his race-oriented approach forming an organization devoted to black problems. Ralph Bunche, A. Philip Randolph, John Davis, and other founders of the NNC grudgingly agreed that, more than any other appeal, racial unity could attract a broad cross section of the black community. Their devotion to a "color-blind" society notwithstanding, intellectuals such as Bunche could not deny that race meant more than class in restricting the opportunities of blacks. Fifty years later William J. Wilson would rekindle this debate and gain broad support for his view that class standing was becoming more significant than race in the life chances of black Americans.[38] In 1935, however, Bunche's class-based arguments appealed primarily to other middle-class black intellectuals and their white fellow travelers. Marxism flourished on college campuses. In the 1980s St. Clair Drake reminisced, "By 1932 I didn't know any black social scientist who privately or publicly didn't claim to be some kind of Marxist." Regarding the role of educated blacks and scholars during the depression, Drake observed, "The Black Bourgeoisie wasn't going to change society, and we scholars weren't going to change society either. But you had a responsibility to tell the other black people who they should ally themselves with to bring about social change."[39]

## Black Writers in the Depression

One effect of the Great Depression was to rob the more fortunate black writers of their wealthy white patrons. Philanthropists turned elsewhere as Harlem fell out of vogue. The black reading audience, though growing steadily, was still too small to support black creative writers. Fortunately, the federal government intervened. In 1935 President Franklin Roosevelt established the Federal Writers' Project. Jerre Mangione, national coordinating editor of the project, has written that the Roosevelt administration worried about the growing radicalism of writers and intellectuals and hoped that an income from the state would dampen their revolutionary ardor.[40] The administration's concern was not unfounded. Writers who had in the twenties exposed the materialism and spiritual emptiness of American culture saw in the Great Depression a powerful vindication of their views. The bleakness and oppression of the thirties revealed capitalism to be inimical to the welfare of the people and stifling to artistic expression and creativity.

The official goal of the Federal Writers' Project was the publication of historical, cultural, and geographical guides to the forty-eight states. Writers were hired to do research, library work, interviews, and surveys in all the states. Motivated more by the need to get people on the payroll than by valid artistic considerations, the government defined *writers* quite broadly. Both fiction and nonfiction writers were eligible, as were "would-be writers." Some of the black recruits had published, but a number managed to qualify in the "would-be" category—among them Ralph Ellison, who later wrote *Invisible Man*.

The project was administered centrally by the federal government. Judging from other New Deal programs in the South, state control would have greatly curtailed black participation in the southern and border states. Had Virginia had its way, it would not have authorized *The Negro in Virginia*, compiled by a staff under the direction of Sterling Brown, an Amherst-educated black intellectual and poet.[41]

The Chicago and New York projects were notable for their success in launching and supporting black writers. In Chicago, Margaret Walker, Willard Motley, Katherine Dunham, and Richard Wright, among others, discussed writing with published authors such as Nelson Algren, Arna Bontemps, and Jack Conroy. New York and Harlem, capitals of the two Americas, harnessed the energies of many promising and accomplished black intellectuals, including Claude McKay and Ted Poston. Volumes of material about African Americans in New York were gathered under the auspices of the state historical guide programs. This material formed the core of two later works, *New World A-Coming* and *The Negro in New York: An Informal Social History*, both by Roi Ottley. The financial help and relative freedom provided by the federal programs also nourished works such as *Native Son*, by Richard Wright, *Knock on Any Door*, by Willard Motley, and *Invisible Man*. Nelson Algren candidly assessed the Chicago project's impact on Richard Wright:

> The writer whom the Illinois Writers' Project helped most was Dick Wright. He was more alert to its advantages and more diligent than most of us. He used the time it gave him to write *Big Boy Leaves Home* and *Native Son*. Whether he would have been able to write *Native Son* if he had had to go on working at the post office is problematical. Surely it would have been a much harder grind.[42]

Ralph Ellison, who had migrated to New York after several years at Tuskegee Institute, in Alabama, impressed fellow project members with his work habits. Ellison and Wright, both knowing of the precarious situation of black creative artists, were determined to seize this rare opportunity. As Jerre Mangione has put it,

Perhaps the greatest beneficiaries of the Project were its black employees. . . .

The emergence of Richard Wright as a top rank novelist, while still a member of the Project, was the clearest testimony of how the Project could provide a young writer with the economic means and the psychic stamina he needed to test his talent.[43]

There is no evidence that government support compromised project writers or caused them to moderate their criticism of society. Wright, Ellison, and McKay continued to criticize American culture. Richard Wright and others spoke out against capitalism and the federal government's response to the economic crisis. In time their views changed, but for reasons that seem unrelated to the Federal Writers' Project. The national administration's continuing anxiety about the impact of politically alienated artists and writers on the population was understandable. John Steinbeck's *The Grapes of Wrath* and Clifford Odets's play *Golden Boy* were attracting large audiences. The Left invited socially committed artists to join the movement for radical social change.

### Scientific Racism and Equality

As early as 1844, black intellectuals had questioned the myth of racial superiority. That year, James McCune Smith, a physician trained at the University of Glasgow, published results that exposed the fraud. Smith found no differences in intelligence attributable to race.[44] Other learned blacks marshaled philosophical and religious arguments for the equality of the races. Still, American society in the nineteenth century supported racism. Treatises from black intellectuals, however sound, were dismissed. The accomplishments of certain blacks were attributed to white ancestors in their blood lines.

During the first two decades of the twentieth century, immigration, particularly from southern and eastern Europe, intensified the debate over racial and group traits. The new disciplines of psychology and anthropology contributed a number of studies based on "intelligence" tests that showed the mental inferiority of such non-Anglo-Saxon groups as Jews, Italians, and, of course, blacks.[45] By the thirties, however, black intellectuals had gained influential allies. Rather than rank cultures and groups as superior or inferior, modern anthropologists and social scientists like Franz Boas, Otto Klineberg, Ruth Benedict, and Melville Herskovits analyzed them according to the concept of "cultural relativity." No one culture or group was genetically superior to another; rather, this theory held, traits developed in response to the social and physical environment. Environment, not genetics, became the focal point for studies of intelligence. Klineberg reexamined patterns of intelligence-test scores and demonstrated how they related to the educational opportunities and socioeconomic backgrounds of students, white and black.[46] Herman Canady published findings showing that the scores of black children tested by white examiners were likely to be inaccurate because of the lack of rapport between white tester and black subject.[47] In 1935 the psychologist Martin Jenkins, later president of Morgan State College, in Baltimore, found that groups of black and white youths with comparable social and educational opportunities contained the same proportion of gifted individuals.[48] In the 1930s dozens of articles in the *Journal of Negro Education* presented evidence for the idea that environment rather than biology determined mental ability.

The environmental thesis fit the agenda of black intellectuals pushing the government to provide educational opportunities for blacks. But public policy lagged far behind the emerging consensus about the effects of social environment. Policies based on racial equality would have effected profound changes in a wide array of institutions. Ending white privilege in employment would have surely provoked retaliation at the polls. A serious attack on residential segregation would have sparked massive resistance. Political leaders were absorbed in the difficult task of rebuilding the country's economy. Although the racial theory was gradually being eroded in the scholarly community, society at large remained organized along racial lines. The black intellectual had to solicit help in changing public opinion on the validity of scientific racism.

The intellectual campaign in the United States against biological racism gained momentum in the 1930s after Adolf Hitler's ideology relegated blacks, Jews, and other non-Aryan groups to the ranks of the mentally inferior. Jewish scholars fled eastern Europe in the face of rabid anti-Semitism, and America was their chosen destination.

This influential community of refugee scholars, all personally affected by racialism, denounced biological racism.[49] Forever searching for allies to their own cause, black intellectuals crafted their anti-racist arguments to highlight the implications of racist thought for other groups. Confronted with the rhetoric of Aryan superiority, many Americans who had ignored the earlier warnings of black intellectuals now heeded them. Germany was not the only new focal point in this debate. The invasion of Ethiopia by Mussolini's Italy in 1935 dramatized for African Americans the racism inherent in European fascism. More than nine thousand blacks attended a 1935 rally to hear W. E. B. Du Bois link racism to fascism and condemn both.[50]

When the United States entered World War II, black intellectuals heartily endorsed the war effort and called upon blacks to support the struggle against fascism. They were of course aware of similar calls for unity with whites during World War I, and they had witnessed the harsh betrayal of black aspirations following the war. A. Philip Randolph and Du Bois agreed with the perception of the horrors of Nazism but, not to be co-opted, led a campaign demanding liberty and freedom on the home front as well.

The wartime rhetoric of freedom provided an excellent context for black political thinkers to push for civil rights legislation (including antilynching laws), the integration of the armed forces, and better employment for blacks in the war industries. Black intellectuals sought to shape the dialogue so that injustice at home would call to mind the atrocities of Hitler. When white mobs in Detroit, angered by the decision of the Packard automobile plant to hire blacks, rioted and murdered thirty blacks, Walter White wrote that the black community looked like "burned-out victims of Nazi terror in Europe."[51] In a special issue of the *Journal of Negro Education* devoted to the role and status of blacks in the war effort, contributors linked blacks' participation with the elimination of racial injustice within American borders.[52] Black thinkers frequently used the term *reconstruction* to signify the importance of including freedom for blacks in the political and economic design of the postwar nation.

Despite the support of the war effort by leading black intellectuals, many rank-and-file blacks were unenthusiastic about marching lock-step to fight for something abroad that they had never enjoyed at home. Elijah Muhammad, a leader of the black nationalist Nation of Islam, argued that blacks had more in common with the Japanese than with American whites. He was promptly arrested in Washington, D.C., and charged with urging citizens to resist the draft and with sedition. The government convicted Muhammad of encouraging draft resistance and sentenced him to five years in a federal prison in Michigan. His arrest and sentencing provoked hardly a stir in black intellectual circles.[53]

But the military and political establishment remained nervous about the black community. Extensive public-relations campaigns were launched to correct blacks' ambivalence about the war effort. Even though blacks as a group never resisted the idea of fighting for the freedom of Europeans, individual blacks agonized over national loyalty in the face of American racism.

In 1940 a draft-age John Hope Franklin volunteered for an office assignment with the Navy Department. Considering himself a pacifist, but willing to contribute to the antifascist fight, he sought a way to support the war effort. Despite his academic training and clerical skills, he was rejected. He was told that he was "lacking in one qualification, and that was color." Franklin then applied to the War Department. A group of academics had been assigned to chronicle the history of the war. Again, Franklin's doctorate in history from Harvard meant nothing to the recruiters, who never responded to his application. "The United States," he later wrote, "however much it was devoted to protecting the freedoms of Europeans, had no respect for me, no interest in my well-being, and not even a desire to use my services." The military no doubt would have welcomed his contributions as an infantryman, or supply worker, but officials in 1940 did not believe that blacks could function as mental workers. His national loyalty strained, Franklin concluded, "The United States did not need me and did not deserve me. Consequently, I spent the remainder of the war years successfully, and with malice aforethought, outwitting my draft board and the entire Selective Service establishment."[54]

Many black intellectuals had urged blacks to support the country during World War I, when conditions for African Americans had been even worse. One of them, William H. Hastie, dean of Howard University Law School, reasoned (or hoped) that the black participation in World War II would lead to greater equality for black citizens. In 1940 Hastie took a leave from academic life at Howard to accept a position with the secretary of war. He hoped that his "insider" role would enable him to move the administration to provide more opportunity for African Americans in the military mobilization. But in 1943 he resigned to protest the continued segregation of air force and army training facilities.[55]

### Enlisted by White Power

Responding to the depression's social stresses, President Roosevelt turned to the campuses, law firms, and professions for policy and administrative talent. The growing political voice of black Americans, especially in urban centers, prompted the Roosevelt administration to include some black thinkers among those called to Washington to plan and implement the New Deal. The "service" ideal, long the cornerstone of black intellectual life, fit well with the ethos of New Deal planners. The bleak terrain of American life and the possibility of contributing to the broader good had loosened the grip of the "detachment" ideal on intellectuals. The political scientist Raymond Moley and economist Rexford Tugwell, both influenced by the pragmatist ideals of John Dewey, cheerfully applied their talents to the reconstruction of society.

The worsening economic environment and the election of Roosevelt had sparked renewed dialogue among black thinkers about the special problems of blacks. Ralph Bunche and Abram Harris called for an economic program to address the circumstances of the vast black working class. The NAACP was sensitive to the charge that stalwarts like Walter White and Roy Wilkins and the civil rights approach of the association were out of touch with the needs of the black masses. Thirty-three young intellectuals and others responded to an invitation from Joel Springarn, president of the NAACP, to meet at his Amenia, New York, estate and discuss possible programs and tactics. In August of 1933 Bunche, Harris, the Howard law professor Charles Houston, historian Rayford Logan, poet Sterling Brown, and others met to exchange views and craft a program that would address the new conditions.[56]

This diverse group of intellectuals reached no consensus on goals or tactics. But differences had been aired, and the NAACP leadership had witnessed the alienation of some of the younger thinkers. Bunche, Harris, and Frazier urged the NAACP to pay more attention to broad-based coalitions and economic reorganization. Not surprisingly, they agreed that black advisers should be appointed to all the national agencies and boards that directly affected the black masses.

Edwin Embree, the white president of the Julius Rosenwald Fund and a close adviser to President Roosevelt, understood the value of appointing a black thinker to guide and represent the national administration on matters affecting blacks—"a generalissimo of Negro welfare," as he put it.[57] Yet, in the minds of Embree and other Roosevelt advisers, the racial climate made it impossible for a black person to function in such a role. Embree argued that only a white man could fight effectively in Congress and in the administration. Ignoring the protests of Wilkins and the NAACP, the administration named Clark Foreman, a white liberal and Rosenwald Fund official from Georgia, to the "Negro adviser" post. Foreman quickly selected Robert Weaver, a black Harvard-trained economist, to assist him.

Although the top posts in the New Deal were beyond the reach of black intellectuals, certain black appointees were expected to "represent" black interests. With few exceptions, they were fairly acquiescent people. True independence for black intellectuals, particularly in matters affecting racial policies, was rare. In effect, many blacks were chosen to lend black legitimacy to policies that others had already elaborated.

In 1934, when the administration needed a black to serve on a Federal Emergency Relief Administration advisory board, Will Alexander, a southern white liberal, recommended Forrester Washington, dean of Atlanta University School of Social Work, for the post:

> First, so far as I have been able to see, he belongs to no particular clique of reaction of Negro opinion. Second, the whole situation in America makes it impossible for a Negro, however well educated, not to "think black." To a surprising degree, Washington seems to be able to view the problems of Negroes with the minimum of racial feelings.[58]

Alexander's distrust of black intellectuals and his recommendation of Washington illustrate the reasoning that guided the selection of black intellectuals for policy-making agencies: Washington was chosen because he was black, and this satisfied the need for symbolic representation. Valued for his ability to "view the problems of Negroes with a minimum of feeling," Washington resigned seven months later. He had become convinced that New Deal programs did not address the social and economic reality of black life.[59]

In 1934 Foreman and Weaver helped establish an interagency advisory group that would monitor "Negro Affairs." The group was led by Robert Vann, editor of the popular black weekly newspaper the *Pittsburgh Courier* and an assistant to the U.S. attorney general. Vann's group included Eugene Jones, formerly with the Urban League, and Henry A. Hunt, president of Fort Valley State College. In most respects this formal group of highly educated blacks was eclipsed by the informal black cabinet or "brain trust" led by Mary McCleod Bethune, president of Bethune-Cookman College, in Florida, and director of the Negro division of the New Deal's National Youth Administration.

Bethune was certainly the most influential black woman in the administration and possibly the most influential black, period.[60] Her influence stemmed not so much from her administrative position or intellectual standing as from her personal friendship with Eleanor and Franklin Roosevelt. Bucking the sexism that checked the progress of most educated black women, Bethune held sway in the black cabinet over her more erudite colleagues Robert Weaver, William Hastie, and Robert Vann. One observer of black influence and power during the depression assessed the standing of Roosevelt's black brain trust as follows:

> By and large they are cut from the same college-bred cloth, and although temperamentally, sharply vivid differences exist among them, as to objectives, they are as close as white on rice. They do their thinking and talking together. Studies are initiated by them, Negro sentiment tested frequently, abstractions harnessed, and eventually mature programs formulated.[61]

The black cabinet was largely symbolic. Despite splashy publicity in the black popular press, it functioned more as a sop to black indignation than as a body for shaping policies pertinent to black people.

Bethune stayed in the administration from 1936 to 1943, during which time she persistently called for more black representation on the staffs and boards of New Deal agencies. After the National Youth Administration folded in 1944, Mrs. Roosevelt arranged to have her old friend paid to head the National Council of Negro Women, a group Bethune had founded before coming to work in Washington.

* * *

Throughout the depression black intellectuals configured and reconfigured themselves around a range of social issues. The fluid political climate of the 1930s mocked rigid ideological thinking. But no matter what the social or intellectual issue, anxiety about racial subordination was invariably a subtext.

Charles Houston, a Howard Law School professor and member of the NAACP's legal vanguard, won a number of important civil rights cases during the thirties, but he was skeptical about the legal system's ability to foster racial justice in the United States.[62]

Differences about the prospects for racial justice continued to divide black intellectuals, just as they had divided the small group of educated blacks a century earlier at the national and state conventions. Universities, arts and letters, and government service all offered the proverbial "half a loaf" to black intellectuals. While they now enjoyed somewhat greater access to the intellectual establishment than before the war, they resented the limitations still imposed on them. Resolutely, they directed their talents to the segregated world of black life, venturing forth occasionally to shake white America from its complacency regarding racial inequality.

# 7 ⋘

# NOT A LULL,
# NOT A STORM

There is a tremor in the middle of the iceberg—from a
stone that the builders neglected.     —ROBERT MOSES

AFTER 1945 WHITE MAINSTREAM intellectuals were preoccupied
with the social and cultural implications of the modern industrial society taking shape in the United States and Western Europe.
Books like *The Lonely Crowd* (1950), by David Riesman, *The Organization Man* (1956), by William F. Whyte, and *The Power Elite*
(1959), by C. Wright Mills, raised questions about the fate of imagination and individual autonomy in the postwar period. Such thinkers
were uncertain about the meaning and extent of freedom in "mass
society"; to them, America's material abundance generated as many
problems as it solved. When postwar intellectuals turned their attention from the country's poor to the growing but fragile middle class,
they saw widespread frustration and spiritual emptiness. A regular
paycheck did not alleviate the boredom of work in factories and large
bureaucracies. Residents of the new mass-produced suburban villages were prey to a consumerism promoted by the mass media.
Arthur Miller's play *Death of a Salesman* (1949) exposed the ten-

sions between the middle class's quest for things and the character development of individuals. Beyond U.S. shores, Stalinism and Soviet expansionism raised unsettling questions. As they learned of the repression sponsored by totalitarian regimes, many Americans formerly sympathetic to Soviet communism became vocal critics.[1]

Concern about the Soviet state and Stalin's global intentions led to a national paranoia skillfully fanned by President Harry Truman and several right-wing legislators. Senator Joseph McCarthy, the pugnacious anti-Communist from Wisconsin, used the Senate Permanent Sub-Committee on Investigations as a platform, forcing many liberal and radical intellectuals to take public positions on issues of cultural and political freedom. He bullied many into disavowing support for unorthodox thought or political dissent.

Dissident black intellectuals, although not at the center of this vortex, did not go unnoticed. The actor and singer Paul Robeson had by 1948 become a spokesman of the American Left. The House Un-American Affairs Committee (HUAC) accused Robeson of saying that blacks would not join the armed services to fight against the Soviet Union. The committee went so far as to call Jackie Robinson, who had recently broken the color bar in major league baseball, to testify against Robeson's views about the loyalty of African Americans. When the State Department canceled Robeson's passport, he did not turn to compromise or negotiation. Instead, he escalated his attack on injustice in the United States. His wife, Eslanda, was hauled before Congress, and startled the committee with a forceful defense of her husband's civil rights.[2]

Robeson's militancy in the face of economic, artistic, and political pressure contrasts with the actions of the venerable Langston Hughes. Since the twenties Hughes had associated with progressive leaders and organizations whose stances ranged from antifascist to antilynching. He had written a number of short stories and poems spotlighting the hypocrisy of America's attitudes toward race.

Ostensibly concerned about the effect of Hughes's writings in overseas libraries, McCarthy called Hughes to Washington in March of 1953 to answer questions about his associations with leftist groups and to explain certain poems that cold warriors like Roy Cohn, the committee counsel, considered anti-American. The hearing was not Hughes's noblest moment. Under interrogation he disavowed much of his earlier literary work, claiming that "a complete reorientation of [his] thinking and feelings occurred roughly four or five years ago."[3] Reflecting on Hughes's sympathies and the political realities of his situation, his biographer has pointed out that Hughes depended on writing for a living, and concluded that he was "an artist who loved the left but dared not speak, out of fear that his tongue might be cut out altogether."[4] Acknowledging that the poet's cooperation with McCarthy was not "a victory of the spirit," Rampersad has summarized as follows the dilemma that faced Hughes, as a black artist, when summoned by the McCarthy committee:

> Hughes had come to his decision by recognizing that his choice was between two imperfections. He could defy the body and destroy much of his effectiveness in the black world. Or he could cooperate, draw the disapproval of the white Left, but keep more or less intact the special place he had painstakingly carved out within the black community.[5]

W. E. B. Du Bois was another intellectual considered subversive by the right wing. In February 1951 a Washington, D.C., grand jury indicted the eighty-three-year-old scholar for "failing to cause" the Peace Information Center, a leftist organization, to register as an agent of a "foreign principal." After five days of hearings, in which Du Bois was ably represented by a team of black lawyers from Washington (with links to Howard University Law School), the federal judge halted the proceedings when the government conceded that it could not establish a link between the Peace Information Center and the Soviet Union. The financial costs and public attacks sustained by Du Bois were, however, considerable. Still, one scholar of the period has concluded that "Du Bois was far from being intimidated by the indictment and trial. It did not cause him to tack his sails to the prevailing winds."[6]

The sociologist C. Wright Mills spoke out against this harassment and attacked the passivity of American intellectuals in the face of conformist pressures. For Mills the intellectual's role was first and foremost that of a social critic who would expose the shallow and self-serving thinking of business and government heads, a group he labeled "the power elite."[7] Mills believed that intellectuals must

't and critique the growing concentration of power in the
ꞈes.

Mills's discontent remained deeper than that of his contemporaries. Liberal thinkers like Lionel Trilling, Reinhold Niebuhr, and Daniel Bell had moderated their earlier criticism of capitalist America. They might still bemoan the unequal division of wealth and the concentration of power, but on the whole they considered these problems solvable by more efficient administration; they saw no need to overhaul the economic order. And unlike Mills, they deemed the threat of Soviet expansion sufficient to warrant a tempering of domestic criticism. They framed their discourse in bipolar terms: Soviet tyranny versus American liberty. This framing enabled many to embrace an optimistic attitude about America. In a period of postwar prosperity and economic growth, most liberal white intellectuals, along with most Americans, were prepared to accept flaws in the American dream, especially the all but invisible flaws that touched powerless groups like black Americans.

## Cautious Optimists

If white establishment intellectuals saw bright prospects, black leaders saw at best a hazy sunrise. On the whole, black intellectuals were less willing to join the chorus of conformists and optimists during the postwar decade. The global Soviet threat and the cultural implications of mass society were not their central concerns. They continued to focus on the lack of liberty and opportunity for black people. They observed that scholars from white ethnic groups were slowly penetrating the major intellectual institutions. In 1951 Lionel Trilling became the first Jewish professor in the English department at Columbia. Oscar Handlin, also Jewish, affirmed his American dream when the history department at Harvard appointed him full professor.[8] Meanwhile, black scholars heard Robert M. Hutchins and William Ogburn, both renowned scholars, publicly oppose the hiring of blacks for the faculty at the University of Chicago.[9]

To ensure domestic tranquillity during the war years, the Roosevelt and Truman administrations had made a number of promises and taken some steps calculated to placate black Americans. After the war many of these promises went unfulfilled. Agencies like the Fair Employment Practices Committee (FEPC), ostensibly established to safeguard the rights of blacks, languished.[10] To be sure, economic growth and the military-industrial complex did improve the general welfare of the black community, but neither the federal nor the state governments rushed to remedy the inequities of American racism. Black activist organizations grew stronger. NAACP membership rose from 50,000 in 1940 to 350,000 in 1945.[11] The example of nonwhite peoples in Africa and Asia wresting control of their countries from colonial powers excited blacks and forced them to think about their own status in democratic America.

*  *  *

One tenet of the black intellectual never changed—without improved education, especially in advanced academic and professional fields, black people would be left behind. The NAACP and other civil rights groups sought to guide the political discontent of black Americans and concentrate on legal battles that would expand opportunity.[12] Their strategy had merit and was to some extent successful: the federal court system rendered decision after decision supporting the principle of equal access and opportunity. Backed by the NAACP, black plaintiffs sued and won the right to attend graduate and professional schools in border states like Kentucky and Oklahoma. Such legal victories were achieved at a time when blacks were voting in larger numbers and becoming active on the urban political front. Many northern political figures, with an eye to winning over black voters in northern cities, endorsed expanded educational opportunities and antidiscrimination laws.

The court decisions that culminated in *Brown* v. *Board of Education,* which prohibited segregation in public education, seemed to herald the coming of a new and glorious age. The legal victories over state-sanctioned segregation delighted whole generations of black scholars and artists. Black intellectuals who had spent their professional lives fighting discrimination and bigotry were buoyant with hope. Ralph Bunche praised *Brown* v. *Board of Education* as a "historic event in the annals of American democracy."[13] Thurgood Marshall, who argued the case before the Supreme Court, predicted fully desegregated public schools within five years.

Weary of the battle against bigotry, and grateful for the legal victories, black middle-class intellectuals began to champion the inevitability and virtue of social and cultural integration. Implicit in their optimism was the belief that increased access to educational institutions and middle-class occupations would eventually improve the welfare of the broader black community. But whereas integrated education and access to white-collar employment were high priorities for the black middle class, the blacks who labored in factories, mines, and fields of the United States were more interested in expanded blue-collar employment and affordable housing. For the time being, however, the priorities of the black middle class and its intellectuals prevailed. Black families hastened to prepare their children for the expected opportunities.

## Recruitment for Intellectual Work

The marginal economic status of most black families in the nineteenth and early twentieth centuries had encouraged this view of education. Blacks knew that superior schooling led the lucky few to prized careers as doctors, lawyers, and ministers in the segregated black community. While others might extol the intrinsic worth of learning, blacks had developed an intensely pragmatic approach. J. Saunders Redding had marveled at "the sharp ambition" of the young black men who were his classmates at Lincoln University in the 1920s:

> They seemed to have a brazen, articulated cunning. They thought of education exclusively in terms of prestige value. They wanted to be doctors and lawyers—doctors mostly—professions that they referred to as "rackets"—they studied textbooks to that end. Almost none of them did any reading beyond the requirements of courses.[14]

The slow but steady erosion, after 1940, of racial barriers to advanced intellectual training buoyed the spirits of most blacks. Whether or not they could precisely articulate their concern about education and the world of ideas, black families knew that good preparation in the lower grades and high school brought important advantages, and many poor families sacrificed to improve the prospects for their children. Clayborne Carson, an American historian and editor of the Martin Luther King Papers, recalls his working-class family's efforts in postwar New Mexico:

> When I look back at my childhood, even though we didn't have a great many books in the house and my parents were by no means intellectually oriented, they did take an interest in their kids' getting some kind of exposure to knowledge. They made a big point of buying an encyclopedia when I was growing up, and that was a very big purchase.[15]

Fortunately, many of the all-black public schools, especially in the southern and border states, had improved to the extent that their graduating students were academically prepared for four-year institutions. All-black secondary schools like McDonough 35 in New Orleans, Frederick Douglass in Baltimore, and Booker T. Washington in Atlanta had well-trained faculties committed to high academic standards.[16] Parents who enrolled their children in such schools accepted the challenge and joined the teachers in encouraging exemplary performance. While few all-black schools were the equal of McDonough 35 or Frederick Douglass, each major town boasted a high school that could advance the best and the brightest of the race. The prospect of racial integration allowed black high school graduates to look beyond the historically black colleges. For a community committed to advancement through education, the prospect of desegregated universities was welcome.

Despite the obstacles, some black families had, over time, established a tradition of academic and intellectual values. Henry Louis Gates Jr. explains the "reinforcement" of intellectual standards in his own family when he was a boy:

> Everywhere I looked there was that sort of positive reinforcement. A lot of people in my family had gone to college or had professional degrees for at least seventy-five years. My whole environment reinforced the fact that in selecting to be an intellectual, to do well in school, if I can put it in that light, was the most important thing I could do. Playing baseball was nice. I

mean, my family loved it, but there was nothing like going to college and being a doctor or a lawyer.[17]

In such families intellectual work was deemed to have both intrinsic and practical value. Intellectual occupations seemed within reach, and black families in the fifties were hopeful about their children's career prospects.

Committed to seeing their children advance by means of a solid education, many families had to weigh economic considerations carefully. Janice Willis, a professor of philosophy at Wesleyan University, describes a difficult time with her parents in a small southern town in the 1950s:

> When I was eight, I got put in fifth grade. They wouldn't let me go in at five, so I got in at six. I turned seven, then the school skipped me through the third and fourth. I came home and said, "Principal Jackson took me in so-and-so's class, and I did so-and-so." My papa blew up. I was too young to know, he was thinking, my sister who was just a year and a half older than me, I'm about to catch up with her, how is it possible to send us to college ... even then they were thinking about it. But all I knew is that she got mad with me, and it had something to do with school, and I didn't know what it meant. I was just describing events to them.[18]

Frequently, talented black students whose families preached academic excellence felt estranged from their classmates. Douglas Daniels, an urban historian and author of *Pioneer Urbanites,* reflects,

> I was the kind of student who was an embarrassment to other students because I always did my homework, I always knew my lessons, I worried about my studies, and I tried to be first. My father stressed the importance of being the best, of being the first, and that was somehow connected to the family name. My older sisters had set up models for me to try and meet, whether I wanted to or not. The teachers always seemed to say that the first day of school, "Oh, are you related to so-and-so? Well, I expect you're as good as they were."[19]

Quite often, precocious youths were caught between the demands of school authorities who wanted to display their talents, and their own wish to be seen as "regular." An amusing account by Janice Willis reveals the social and psychological crosscurrents that bright students frequently faced.

> Teachers would put me on show. One day the superintendent, who was white, visited our all-black school. He came to my class. "Okay," he'd ask, "who knows so-and-so and such-and-such?" I said to myself, "Uh-huh, I'll *never* say anything, because all these folks are going to be on me, people that I want to be friends with." He asked, "What layer of atmosphere is beyond the stratosphere? I wonder if any of you know." The teacher didn't even know; she was just putting on a show for this white superintendent. I finally stood up and said, "Ionosphere," and sat down and thought, "Oh shit, lost again for the day." When he left, the teacher said, "What was that you said? Can you spell it?" Shit, I was messed up all the time, it was hard.[20]

In schools where nonintellectual values held sway, academically motivated black youths, like some of their white contemporaries, frequently had to cope with the resentment of their peers. William Russell Ellis, a sociologist and vice-chancellor of undergraduate affairs at Berkeley, recalls that in the fifties he had to be careful at Compton High School, an integrated and academically oriented school in southern California. The other black students had different values, and Ellis often felt vulnerable:

> I learned in high school how to protect myself from some of the rougher aspects of life. I was weighing in at eighty-nine pounds. The potential of real pain kept me out of the urban male game. I didn't grin, so I wasn't in. I started bringing some attention to the school through my running track. That gave me some status, . . . but in the classroom there was always that standard tension that blacks have a monopoly on. If I pronounced the French words really well, or if the teacher paid attention to me, I'd have to pay verbal dues. And if I tried to fat-mouth back, I'd have to

fight. Well, going to college was like heaven. I was free to talk my talk, and no matter how hot the arguments got, they never wound up in a fistfight. I couldn't believe it![21]

Faced with similar pressures, Ishmael Reed accepted the differences between himself and his classmates and retreated.

Writing and reading were things I enjoyed doing. I was a kind of loner. Nobody would choose me for their basketball teams. Sports was a big thing and I was good at sports up to a point, but I wasn't interested in sports anymore. I got along with kids, but I didn't belong to their clubs, I didn't see myself as being anybody exceptional. I just liked to be alone. Although I'm still friends with many of them, I never socialized. A lot of stuff they were talking about was foreign to what I was going through. I did straight things like go to the YMCA.[22]

For the young Reed, social isolation was compounded by never-ending run-ins with the high school administration, which demanded that he stop challenging his teachers. Unable or unwilling to abide by the nonintellectual norms of his school, Reed dropped out and took a job in a library, where he became what he called a "minor league intellectual." Eventually he returned to school and continued to confound white teachers, who could not conceive of a working-class black youth doing anything other than factory work. Reed, of course, would later make his mark as a highly acclaimed novelist.

The quest for asylum in books and libraries is a common theme in the life stories of black intellectuals. Reading carried them to imaginative terrains far from their second-class citizenship in the United States. For the talented, the curious, and the alienated, the world of books was exhilarating. Richard Yarborough, an English professor, made a connection between social alienation and his passion for reading: "Reading seemed to be one of the few available outlets where I didn't have to depend on others for acceptance, so my love for reading thus reinforced my introspective personality."[23]

Gwendolyn Brooks, growing up in Chicago and feeling estranged from her adolescent peers, found a form of salvation when she learned that other people shared her passion for the written word and agonized over some of the same problems that concerned her: "When I was thirteen I met, somehow, *Writer's Digest*. Why there were oodles of other writers! They, too, suffered and had suffered."[24] The values and perspectives of this new reference group counterbalanced the indifference and anti-intellectualism of her classmates. Once she knew that there were others, black and white, fascinated with words and ideas, she was determined to continue writing and become part of this new community.

Like most other intellectually gifted young people, black students approached college with a mixture of anticipation and fear. For students from provincial backgrounds, the college campuses were excitingly complex and more than a bit intimidating. Troy Duster, a sociologist, recalls wistfully the transition from the supportive and manageable academic environment of his youth to the realities of matriculating at Northwestern University in the 1950s:

> My high school had been 99.9 percent black, but the university I attended was 99 percent white. I was the valedictorian in my high school class of 260. Some of the students nicknamed me "brains" because of my grades. I was way out there on the GPA continuum, 3.9 or something. I say this to indicate that I had really been accustomed to seeing myself apart from the general circumstances in which I found myself, but I had no sense of my own "smarts" when I was in high school. My mother kept saying to me, "You know the reason you are doing well is because you read a lot; but you go out into the world, and you're going to find people who can read as a matter of course. So don't think you're smart, son." She used to drum that into me and never let me get a big head about my achievements. She said, "It is context." Of course, she was right; as soon as I got into college, I was up against all kinds of valedictorians.[25]

The demanding standards of elite universities created problems for students who came from academically undistinguished high schools, but the hurdles were not insurmountable. Duster reflects,

> I thought I was all on the verge of embarrassing myself and my family. In the first six months I remember taking exams and

feeling grateful when I got the grades back. I got all A's and B's. I didn't get a C until the last quarter of my senior year. . . . But the subjective experience of it was toil and turmoil. I was forever huffing and puffing.[26]

A decade later, family expectations and self-confidence helped Henry Louis Gates adjust to the Yale campus. Now an accomplished scholar and recipient of a MacArthur grant, he did not feel comfortable at college until he had demonstrated to himself the same level of success he had been accustomed to in his small-town high school.

I had two weeks of anxiety. I missed my girlfriend, my parents, my home. I wondered if the school had made a mistake in admitting me, if I was really good enough. . . . And then I got my first paper back and I got an "honors." Someone explained that in this class they graded on a curve and if I got an "honors," everybody else got something lower. I figured, "Damn, that was pretty good." After that I just took off, and I did extremely well.[27]

For students who had never lived away from home, the diversity and variety of college life were exciting. Encounters with a large number of thoughtful students and faculty prompted a greater appreciation for ideas and mental processes apart from their immediate practical value. Joseph Himes, who overcame the burden of blindness and earned a Ph.D. in sociology from Ohio State University in 1953, describes his gradual immersion in the intellectual life of Oberlin College as an undergraduate: "I learned to be interested in toying with ideas and playing with them. I learned also to like words and to like to write. In all of these, I learned something about how to organize ideas, how to manipulate them, to manipulate words and make them do what you want them to do."[28]

## From Preparation to Professions

The expanding educational opportunities would not have guaranteed intellectual standing for blacks if occupational role models and appropriate employment had not also been available. Slowly, the black intelligentsia began to look beyond the constricted job options. As exclusionary practices on the basis of race abated in the North, under the pressure of legal and political challenges, more young blacks were able to enter careers other than public school teaching and the ministry. Aspiring creative writers could identify with Richard Wright, Nella Larsen, Gwendolyn Brooks, or Chester Himes, and now the proliferating black academics served as new models for ambitious blacks who did not want careers in writing. The examples of John Hope Franklin, Montague Cobb, Horace Mann Bond, and Benjamin Quarles demonstrated the viability of academic careers for well-educated blacks.

During the postwar years thousands of African American veterans seized their GI benefits and enrolled in undergraduate and graduate programs. White southern universities were still segregated, so the top graduates of black colleges moved on to graduate work at the northern institutions reputed to be hospitable places for black graduate students. Between 1930 and 1962, Columbia University awarded 144 doctoral degrees to graduates of black colleges—more than any other American institution.[29] New York University, Ohio State, and the University of Chicago closely trailed Columbia in conferring doctorates on students from black colleges. At the time, only one black college, Howard University, offered a doctoral program.

## Integration and New Hopes

Black scholars managed to make their way into print with greater frequency during the forties and fifties. *Children of Bondage: The Personality Development of Urban Youth in the Urban South* (1940), by Allison Davis and John Dollard; *Dark Metropolis: A Study of Negro Life in a Northern City* (1945), by St. Clair Drake and Horace Cayton; and *The Negro in American Life and Thought: The Nadir, 1877–1901* (1954), by Rayford Logan, joined Horace Mann Bond's *The Education of the Negro in the American Social Order* (1934), in exploring aspects of the black condition in the United States. Black firms such as Woodson's Associated Publishers tried to buck the growing trend toward large and well-financed publishing operations by producing books that the bigger houses tended to ignore. In 1948 Woodson published Benjamin Quarles's *Frederick Douglass,* an important biography that had attracted little interest among the large publishing houses.

The book that exerted the greatest influence on the scholarly community was John Hope Franklin's *From Slavery to Freedom: The Negro Experience in America,* the first modern history of blacks in the United States. Franklin, then a professor at North Carolina College, a historically black college, wrote the book at the urging of editors at Alfred A. Knopf, who recognized the need for a scholarly account of blacks in American history. The book quickly became a staple for students and scholars of the black American experience, and it has remained in print since its publication in 1947.[30] *From Slavery to Freedom* whetted the appetite of thousands of Americans interested in black history. Its balance and comprehensiveness set a formidable standard for subsequent scholars.

The scholarship of Franklin, Logan, Bond, Drake, and Frazier could not be ignored, and academic and professional associations began to accept black scholars as members. Occasionally blacks were asked to review books and other scholarship on black life. Such contact with the mainstream academic community was reassuring to black intellectuals; they were gratified that, finally, at least some distinguished black scholars were invited to present papers at conventions. But this recognition did not lead to job offers from the major research universities. Black scholars still had to squeeze their work in between the heavy teaching loads common at the financially pressed black colleges. They had no research assistants, and only a few black scholars received major grants for academic research—invariably for studies on race. The Carnegie Corporation, in the aftermath of Gunnar Myrdal's influential *An American Dilemma,* funded the projects of several carefully selected black social scientists.

The pattern of demand for professional and semiprofessional blacks was shaped by racism. Teachers were needed to staff segregated black classrooms; social-service workers, to cope with black clients; and professionals, to provide legal, medical, and financial services to the black community. Other high-status careers remained essentially closed to blacks. Although the national economy was expanding and the labor market was becoming more diversified, discrimination limited the access of blacks to the emerging occupations in scientific and technological fields. Forever conscious of their own need for financial security, intellectually ambitious blacks elected to pursue careers as teachers. A black mathematician could not count on being hired as a statistical analyst in private industry, but he or she could always get a job teaching mathematics at a black institution. Thus blacks with advanced degrees gravitated to black colleges, and holders of undergraduate degrees settled into secure positions in largely segregated elementary and secondary schools. The dream of a society where race was not a barrier persisted, however, and intellectuals continued to press for integration.

## The Lure of Color Blindness

From 1939 to 1954 the NAACP achieved a string of favorable civil rights decisions. Slowly, the federal court system was outlawing racial exclusion in public institutions and extending to blacks equal protection under the law. The prospect that racial barriers would soon be eliminated enthralled black writers, many of whom concluded that racial integration was close at hand. Anticipating a "color-blind" society, black fiction writers began to turn away from purely ethnic or racial themes. The combative posture of older black writers such as Richard Wright and Frank Marshall Davis was roundly criticized by the new wave of novelists, poets, and critics who extolled "universal" themes. And Hugh Gloster, author of the pathbreaking *Negro Voices in American Fiction*, pleaded with black writers to move beyond the historical preoccupation with racial injustice and delve into the variegated landscape of twentieth-century black life. According to Gloster, black writers' emphasis on race had "retarded [their] attainment of a cosmic grasp of the varied experiences, humorous as well as tragic, through which individuals pass in this life."[31] The new novelists, harking back to the position taken during the 1920s by Wallace Thurman, Zora Hurston, and Rudolph Fisher, suggested themes like intragroup differences and class tensions as relatively untapped currents in black life. Works about such topics, integrationists hoped, would blunt racial enmity. From them, white readers would learn about and appreciate the basic humanness of African Americans.

An optimistic J. Saunders Redding proclaimed in 1949 that the gulf between black and white reading audiences was closing and that black writers could effectively appeal to both groups. By accepting the challenge of connecting with a white audience, black writers could at last claim the readership they deserved: "Working honestly in the material they know best, they are creating for themselves a new freedom. Though what is happening seems very like a miracle, it has been a long, long time preparing. Writing by American Negroes has never before been in such a splendid state of health, nor had so bright and shining a future before it."[32]

The small black periodicals also endorsed the assimilationist ethos. *Negro Story,* subtitled *A Magazine for All Americans,* hoped to position itself as a vehicle for writers of all nationalities and races. The editor, Alice Browning, issued special calls for whites to submit fiction and poetry for inclusion in *Negro Story.* The *Crisis* and *Opportunity,* the venerable institutional organs, along with a younger publication, *Phylon,* wholeheartedly supported the new emphasis.[33] Essays and articles in support of the explicitly universalist approach usually implied that the issue was craftsmanship and quality, not racial ideology. With the criteria so framed, the bearers of the protest tradition tended to be dismissed as untalented and unimaginative writers, rather than ideologically incorrect peers. Black literary critics associated with scholarly organizations joined the movement away from an emphasis on race.

In 1957 the College Language Association, an organization of black literature and language teachers, launched the *CLA Journal.* Remarkably, the editor, Therman O'Daniel, did not mention race or any special commitment to black culture. Unlike the *Journal of Negro History,* established in 1917, or even Atlanta University's *Phylon,* which first appeared in 1940, the *CLA Journal* chose not to define itself as an ethnic-oriented publication, even though the association's membership was overwhelmingly black. The mood of integration apparently convinced the journal's founders that an explicit emphasis on the world of black letters would be out of step with social trends. Indeed, the early issues included scholarship covering a wide range of literary topics.

Ironically, during the period of the move toward integrationist thought, very little integration was occurring in the main institutions of American intellectual life. It was still the case that few blacks held appointments at northern universities. Chicago universities were home to two black scholars: Allison Davis held a subsidized faculty appointment at the University of Chicago, and across town St. Clair Drake taught at Roosevelt University. Few publishers accepted manuscripts by black writers who rejected the popular formula of racial optimism. Frank Yerby's romantic novels about the nineteenth-century South sold well and never examined racial issues. The major white periodicals frequently had special issues devoted to "The Negro," but otherwise African American intellectuals were nearly invisible to the wider public. Instead, the integrationist ethic seemed most prominent among the black periodicals that were soliciting material from white writers. Eager to escape the label of "race publications" and to enhance their image, black journals welcomed the integration of their contributor lists.

The realities of the broader society continued to belie the idealism of the integrationist writers. Despite the hope and optimism that accompanied the civil rights victories in the courts, sober black thinkers were aware of the depth and pervasiveness of racist attitudes and became increasingly sensitive to how such attitudes sustained social and economic inequality: blacks had lower per capita incomes than whites and higher rates of unemployment; blacks suffered higher mortality rates and were less well educated. The lynching of Emmett Till in Mississippi in 1955 and the virulent resistance to school desegregation in many southern cities reminded blacks that racial injustice often led to murder and violence.

When blacks began to demand their civil rights, race resurfaced as a volatile issue in American culture. The 1954 campaign for integrated seating on buses in the South and the violent clash over school desegregation in Little Rock, Arkansas, three years later, forced Americans to grapple with the implications of color. Abstract and legalistic arguments about liberty for blacks grew dim amid the sharp images of racial conflict in Montgomery and Little Rock.

## The National Creed and Color

Guiding the early civil rights movement was a belief that every American, regardless of race, deserved equal protection under the law. Civil rights advocates maintained that the elimination of discriminatory laws would in time produce what was hopefully referred to as a color-bli.._ society. Their expectations had some basis in reality; by the early 1960s surveys showed that most white Americans agreed with the principle of nondiscrimination.[34] By planting their ideas and arguments for equality in the soil of moral suasion, intellectuals and activists gained the support of important political and cultural leaders. Furthermore, the moral emphasis enabled advocates to avoid the more ideological considerations of power and privilege that had divided the intellectual community in earlier periods. However, the new civil rights vanguard did not rely on messages from the pulpits alone. The moral appeals for equal treatment were often accompanied by demonstrations designed to produce what Martin Luther King Jr. called "creative tension" in society.[35]

In *An American Dilemma* (1944) Gunnar Myrdal had hypothesized "a tension" that Americans felt between the American *ideal* of equal treatment under the law and the *reality* of blacks being denied the full fruits of democracy. In a 1944 review of Myrdal's book, Ralph Ellison called the Swedish author's conclusions limited and possibly mischievous, for they avoided "the question of power and the question of who manipulates that power."[36] Ellison feared that an emphasis on moral "tension" could obscure the links between the power of certain interests in society and racial discrimination and subordination. The eradication of racial prejudice was a complex problem, not to be solved by simply highlighting the incompatibility of discrimination with the American creed, Ellison insisted. However, his reservations about the moral-conflict approach to race were largely ignored. Most mainstream civil rights leaders accepted the idea that moral suasion and education would bring about racial equality.

No leader represented the moral thesis more vividly than Martin Luther King Jr. In 1963 King and several supporters were arrested in Birmingham, Alabama, when they disobeyed a state court injunction prohibiting demonstrations and other forms of public protest against segregation laws. With unmatched eloquence he framed the fight against racial injustice in legal and religious terms. Writing from an Alabama jail to a group of white ministers who had challenged the moral basis of nonviolent direct action to eliminate segregation laws, King predicted,

> One day the South will know that when these disinherited children of God sat down at lunch counters, they were in reality standing up for what is best in the American dream and for the most sacred values in our Judeo-Christian heritage, thereby bringing our nation back to those great wells of democracy which were dug deep by the founding fathers in their formulation of the Constitution and the Declaration of Independence.[37]

King's cogent pleas for racial justice were firmly within the framework of American political philosophy and appealed to a wide spectrum of Americans. Frequent reference to such intellectual beacons as Thoreau, Gandhi, Tillich, and Emerson further enhanced his—and the movement's—legitimacy.

When black Americans took to the streets and demanded the rights and freedoms inherent in citizenship, the nation was caught off guard. As thinkers from Du Bois to Ellison had noted, blacks were essentially "invisible" elements in the nation's cultural and social life. While the social dominance of white culture and institutions meant that blacks had to try to understand white culture, most whites saw no reason to reflect on the black experience—until social turbulence forced them to look for explanations of the events convulsing the nation. James Baldwin became the best known of a generation of black writers who sought to explain black rage to white Americans. Well versed in the language, symbols, and sensitivities of white America, Baldwin wrote essays, poems, and novels that starkly depicted the injustice of racial discrimination and its effect on blacks. In *Notes of a Native Son* (1955), *Nobody Knows My Name* (1961), and *The Fire Next Time* (1963), he resurrected a theme from the days of the abolitionist movement: racism erodes the humanity of whites and blacks alike. "Down at the Cross," an essay in *The Fire*

*Next Time,* makes the point that racial turbulence comes from "the white man's profound desire not to be judged by those who are not white, not to be seen as he is, and at the same time a vast amount of the white anguish is rooted in the equally profound need to be seen as he is, to be released from the tyranny of his mirror."[38] The attention Baldwin received suggests that he had told some living truth. Consciously addressing a white audience, Baldwin and other black intellectuals made an eloquent case for the humanity of black people and drew up literary indictments that implicated white society in the oppression of black citizens.

Some black writers distrusted colleagues who capitalized on demands created by the civil rights movement. They understood the symbiotic relationship between black intellectuals and the civil rights movement—no one had taken much notice of black intellectuals before that turmoil. Yet they worried that rather than exploring the subtleties of black life and the meaning of black experiences, many writers—for example, Claude Brown in *Manchild in the Promised Land* (1965)—were content to simply introduce new white readers to African American life. Ishmael Reed describes the problem in terms of intended audience:

> I see some of these books that come out, and I know to whom they are directed. You can always tell when the narrator becomes an anthropologist and starts explaining black folkways in their books. . . . That's a sign. It's a tip-off because blacks know them already. Who are they writing for? I think Baldwin plays the role, a guide. He will take time out to get a footnote to explain to the white reader what's going on . . . because his audience is a white-middle class audience. There are always going to be millions of liberals who read in this country, and that's his audience. Of course, Baldwin isn't the only one who does this.[39]

The issues of "authenticity" and "representation" were also at stake. The dynamism of the black political movement made it presumptuous for any person, intellectual or not, to declare that he or she spoke for the movement. The rapidly escalating militancy of political activists left more deliberative thinkers behind. By the mid-sixties many black intellectuals came under fire from militant activists—Eldridge Cleaver, Michael Thelwell, Vincent Harding—for misrepresenting the thoughts and passions of those blacks who were taking to the streets.[40] Intellectuals were charged with minimizing the rage and anger of the black masses and creating an illusion of optimism.

In the sixties black literature often reflected the mood and frustrations of the angry and alienated. Baldwin recognized the volatility of oppressed blacks but noted some limitations. "The rage of the disesteemed is personally fruitless, but it is also absolutely inevitable; this rage, so generally discounted, so little understood even among the people whose daily bread it is, is one of the things that makes history."[41] Most black writers avoided substantive political analyses that might have provided frameworks for channeling black frustration. They moralized ("racism is wrong and it must be eliminated") but seldom discussed basic political questions relating to race and culture. Few directly addressed the political difficulties a despised minority faced in a democratic society. Fewer still proposed a framework for reconciling the class interests of different groups in the black community. The idea of relations with Africa rarely went beyond proclamations of allegiance.

Twenty years earlier Ralph Ellison had berated black intellectuals for a lack of creativity in thinking about their social conditions. Arguing for "a change in the basis of society," Ellison held that the experiences of the black masses in fashioning their lives in the face of racial oppression contained much that could be useful to political thinkers.[42] E. Franklin Frazier, in an article titled "The Failure of the Negro Intellectual" (1962), also lamented the unwillingness of black thinkers to consider the social, as well as the economic and political, meaning of integration:

> What Negro intellectuals have had to say concerning integration has been concerned with the superficial aspects of the increasing participation of Negroes in the economic and political life of American society. Practically no attention has been directed to the rather obvious fact that integration involves the interaction

of the organized social life of the Negro with the wider American community.[43]

But the moral argument held sway: racial oppression is remediable through education. Liberal social scientists, black and white, set out to educate the nation away from bigotry. Sympathetic writers, religious leaders, and eventually civil rights activists saw roles for themselves on the moral turf. Just as Myrdal had deftly avoided questions of power in society, so did the thinkers of the early sixties.

The moral thrust of nonviolent protest was in keeping with the traditions of black intellectuals in the United States. For over a century black intellectuals had steadily condemned racial bias in American life. Now, at last, their call for nondiscrimination was being heard by an important segment of white America. Young educated whites in particular, many of whom had had no association with African Americans or their culture, were drawn by the persuasive pleas of black intellectuals to join the movement against discrimination.

The engagement of black intellectuals and writers with the civil rights movement in the early sixties impressed a generation of white college students, particularly those who opposed the Vietnam War. The example of intellectuals such as Baldwin, King, and the psychologist Kenneth Clark led many young American thinkers, black and white, to believe that intellectual life should embrace social responsibility, rather than aspire to an apolitical objectivity. And that belief entailed acting on one's beliefs. Ignoring the advice of elders who cautioned against active partisanship, many of the nation's activist college students—Tom Hayden, Mario Savio, Robert Moses—headed to the civil rights battlegrounds of the South, hoping to create the moral community sketched by Thoreau and others.[44]

In the tradition of service and protest on behalf of the race, black thinkers including Derrick Bell and Marian Wright eagerly lent their interpretative and analytical talents to the civil rights movement. That black intellectuals had a special responsibility to the black community was rarely debated. Moreover, the exclusion of black thinkers from white intellectual institutions had created a feeling of solidarity with and sensitivity to other blacks who found themselves outside white society. The involvement of black intellectuals in the

struggle for change rekindled discussions about the role of intellectuals in social movements and about the connection between ideas
and action.

## Impasses and Black Consciousness

Optimistic moderates reasoned that once blacks had equal access
to social institutions and processes, they would become just another
ingredient in the American melting pot. However, despite the passage
of national and state laws outlawing discrimination in the 1960s,
change came very slowly to the South, and when it did come, middle-
class rather than poor and working-class blacks were its prime beneficiaries. Nor did poor blacks in the urban North, where state and
local antidiscrimination laws had been on the books for years, see
much improvement in their lives.

The failure of northern laws to abolish racial inequality prompted
a number of black activists and intellectuals to question whether the
struggle for social justice should be based on antidiscrimination statutes alone. John Lewis, a young leader of the Student Nonviolent
Coordinating Committee (SNCC), wrote in a speech prepared for the
1963 March on Washington, "We will not wait for the President, the
Justice Department, nor Congress, but we will take matters into our
own hands and create a source of power, outside any national structure that could and would assure us a victory."[45] The march leadership insisted that Lewis delete this and several other uncompromising
passages from his speech; the thousands who gathered at the Lincoln
Memorial heard a more moderate version.[46] But this shift in thinking
challenged the social and legal assumptions of the liberal consensus
and the nature of power in American society.

The new analysis proceeded as follows: The U.S. Constitution was
based on the notion of individual rights, yet for centuries blacks had
been denied freedom and liberty. American social institutions had
coalesced around interests and groups that excluded blacks. Trade
unions had been organized by whites and frequently maintained
exclusionary policies. Even policies that appeared to be race neutral,
like seniority, discriminated against black workers who had only
recently been allowed to join the work force. Historically, white

officials had limited housing for blacks to certain areas and refused to provide adequate services to such areas. Beyond institutional practices, the Constitution's emphasis on individual freedom and voluntary association provided great latitude for whites to act out their prejudices and enhance their privileges in various legal and extralegal ways.

The "melting pot" thesis (that the interaction and subsequent blending of ethnic and national groups into society creates a distinctly American type) had long influenced public policy on matters of race. But in *Black Power: The Politics of Liberation* (1976) the collaborators Stokely Carmichael and Charles Hamilton, a professor of political science, presented compelling arguments for the uniqueness of black problems in the United States. The legacy of black slavery and centuries of racial oppression had led to socioeconomic conditions in the black community that were qualitatively different from those of the white ethnic immigrants who came later. Racial attitudes and institutional barriers worked against the kind of assimilation that had been possible for Irish, Italian, and German immigrants in the early twentieth century. Also, in matters of culture, Harold Cruse and Amiri Baraka challenged the wisdom of black people's simply adopting the priorities, values, and aesthetics of the dominant group.[47] They insisted that cultural elements that had sustained black people throughout a history of subordination in America certainly contained much that should be preserved, and indeed cherished.

Cosmopolitan black intellectuals witnessed with pride the emergence of independent African nations during the sixties. The success of Ghana (1957), Kenya (1963), and Tanzania (1964) in winning political independence after decades of colonization and subordination effectively countered centuries-old negativism and pessimism about the potential of black Africa. Whatever the subsequent strife in their countries, articulate African leaders Kwame Nkrumah (Ghana), Patrice Lumumba (Congo), Léopold Senghor (Senegal), and Julius Nyerere (Tanzania) were highly visible symbols of black achievement. Malcolm X and other political figures with an international perspective frequently reminded black Americans of the African successes and sought to build political and economic links between American blacks and their kinfolk in Africa.

Some black intellectuals elected to ignore the sensibilities of white readers and audiences because black audiences had grown sufficiently large as a market. But often the aesthetic and cultural tastes of this growing black audience reflected those of the dominant culture. For instance, black action movies, which simply substituted black cops and robbers for white ones while glamorizing violence, attracted large black audiences. The films *Superfly, Shaft,* and *Cleopatra Jones* provided black representations of mainstream cultural preoccupations. Despite the pleadings of some nationalists—notably the poet Haki Madhubuti—the mass black audience did not elevate or refine its tastes. And although serious culturalists inveighed against the crass commercialization of black consciousness, many cultural products and expressions were reduced to commodities.

On the other hand, the determination of African American artists to reflect on and celebrate the political struggles created personal artistic anguish. Here, for instance, Gwendolyn Brooks speaks of her early perspective and the changes that the black consciousness movement wrought in her own life and work:

> I thought I was happy, and I saw myself going on like that the rest of my days. I thought it was the way to live. I wrote, these people wrote, we saw each other, we talked about writing. But it was white writing, the different bonds among whites. Today I am conscious of the fact that my people are black people; it is to them that I appeal for understanding.[48]

Several other black intellectuals came to reject or minimize the significance of their earlier work, concluding that it did not directly address the concrete problems of black people. Like Gwendolyn Brooks, the poets Amiri Baraka and Haki Madhubuti abandoned the traditional form and voice of Euro-American prose and poetry and sought to produce art that would be comprehensible to the masses, that would aid and comfort them in the search for a new cultural identity.[49]

In their desire to communicate more directly to a mass audience by producing work that was more accessible, these poets encountered what one observer has described as an inevitable impasse:

> Between the creative writer and the classes or causes he wishes
> to "represent" or "express" *there is always a gap:* the gap
> between the book and the world, between my pen at this
> moment and the miner's drill at this moment, the gap between
> a superfluous, middle-class game (literature) and those forms of
> necessary, concrete activity by which we stay alive. This gap
> brings a renewed anguish to the intellectuals generation after
> generation; and generation after generation the impulse to "go
> to the people" . . . is renewed. This impulse is both noble and
> futile.[50]

Aware of the competing impulses, but hoping to find ways to link art
to the social struggle, black creative artists joined the movement to
create a new history.

A veteran of artistic and social struggles, Ralph Ellison was skeptical about self-conscious attempts by artists to redesign themselves
and their work to fit the imperatives of activism. He accepted a "division of labor" in the fight for racial justice, with artists exploring
aesthetic provinces and social activists confronting the specifics of
social life. Ellison spoke of a more limited role for artists like himself:

> If there are people who are moved and who are moved towards
> changing their view of themselves and the world, I think this is
> all to the good. The one thing I do know is that this is no role
> for me. I am not that kind of speaker and I think I can best serve
> my people and my nation by trying to write as well as I can.[51]

But most black intellectuals answered the call for engagement, convinced that they had something to contribute to the black struggle.

# 8 «««

# STANDING
# AT THE CROSSROADS

You face reality, not the lights. The lights go off as
quickly as they come on.          —JAMES BALDWIN

THE LATE 1960S were heady times for black intellectuals. The civil
rights movement brought them visibility. Scholars and writers
who worked the rich soil of race and culture gained an audience.
Prestigious universities began to recruit African American scholars.
Major academic and professional organizations like the American
Sociological Association, the American Psychological Association,
and the Modern Language Association responded to protests by
members who insisted on a more prominent role for black scholars.
At national and regional meetings the number of panels on race and
ethnicity increased greatly, and blacks and their supporters also
insisted that more (and often different) attention be focused on racial
considerations in various disciplines. Publishers and editors of books
and magazines sought works that would explain social unrest to surprised and frustrated white audiences. Black social and political
activists boldly pressed their claims for the soul and allegiance of
black intellectuals. Never before had African American prospects for

employment in intellectual work been so favorable.

Civil rights laws enacted between 1964 and 1967 had improved the lives of many black Americans. Blacks in the South applauded the prohibition of official segregation. Public accommodations were desegregated; hundreds of public school districts grudgingly integrated their classrooms. Two years after passage of the 1965 Voting Rights Act, the percentage of blacks registered to vote in the five states covered by the legislation increased from 41 percent to 61 percent.[1] Racially conservative southern officials moderated their views so as not to alienate their new black constituencies. In 1966 Barbara Jordan went to the Texas state senate, its first black member since Reconstruction; Charles Evers, the brother of the assassinated civil rights leader Medgar Evers, was elected mayor of Fayette, Mississippi; and Julian Bond, son of the noted black intellectual Horace Mann Bond and himself a black activist, took his seat in the Georgia House of Representatives when the United States Supreme Court ruled that the Georgia legislative body could not bar him because of his outspoken opposition to the Vietnam War. As noted by one chronicler of the civil rights era, "The number of black elected officials in the South rose from fewer than one hundred in the year of the Voting Rights Act (1965) to some 500 in 1970 to 1,600 in 1975, and nearly 2,500 in 1980."[2] While such increases in black elected officials served important symbolic needs, new officeholders often became frustrated trying to improve the quality of life for their poor and working-class constituents. Black elected officials, lacking a claim on either entrenched or emerging economic interests, had no way to reorder state and local legislative priorities to benefit the black masses.

In the North civil rights legislation and political pressure opened up a range of opportunities for blacks. Some working-class and middle-income blacks were able to escape the ghetto and to integrate suburban housing. President Lyndon Johnson's "War on Poverty," backed even by several powerful southern congressmen, proceeded from on the belief that government programs, by providing education and jobs, would drastically reduce the number of poor Americans. But increasing black joblessness in some areas and violent black rebellions in northern and southern cities reminded Americans that the rising tide had not lifted all.

## Civil Rights Activism of the 1960s

Between 1963 and 1967 a fiery corps of desegregation's veterans fought fiercely to turn national attention to the black masses, whose welfare seemed beyond the scope of civil rights laws. The activists George Wiley of the Welfare Rights Organization, Stokely Carmichael of SNCC, and Floyd McKissick of the Congress of Racial Equality (CORE) cited many persistent barriers to equality—discrimination in the work force, lack of effective political control of local institutions, the displacement of workers by technology.[3] Seeking to explain the frustration and increasing militancy of some black leaders, Kenneth Clark summarized their case for white moderates:

> Successful litigation, strong legislation, free access to public accommodations, open housing laws, strong pronouncements on the part of the President, governors or mayors, and even the right to vote or to hold office were not relevant to the overriding fact that the masses of Negroes were still confined to poverty and to the dehumanizing conditions of the ghetto.[4]

Clark's message must have seemed curious, even radical, to good-hearted white Americans. Clark was not a radical. He earned a Ph.D. in psychology from Columbia in 1940 and joined the City College of New York faculty in 1942. Clark and his wife, Mamie Phipps Clark, conducted research in the forties on the effects of integrated education on black children. Their research, known as the "doll studies," suggested that racial isolation undermined black children's self-esteem. In the *Brown* desegregation case it was cited by the Supreme Court as important evidence for integration.

To the white establishment, the growing impatience of the black community seemed a sign of ingratitude. Lyndon Baines Johnson, Texas born and raised, had engineered passage in 1964 of the most comprehensive civil rights bill in history. A year later he signed the Voting Rights Act, in effect giving the vote to hundreds of thousands of rural blacks in the South. He then provided the legislative framework for the broad-based War on Poverty, which addressed employment, education, health, and housing problems of the poor. But whereas white America felt that social change was proceeding at whirlwind speed, many blacks knew these steps to be long overdue, with much remaining to be done. When establishment figures counseled patience, black activists like Malcolm X escalated the rhetoric: "How can you thank a man for giving you what's already yours? How then can you thank him for giving you only part of what's already yours? You haven't even made progress, if what's given to you, you should have had already. That's not progress."[5]

## The Nation of Islam and Malcolm X

A self-educated, charismatic, and militant spokesman for black nationalism, from 1954 through 1964, Malcolm X worked for Elijah Muhammad and the Nation of Islam. The Nation of Islam and its message posed interesting quandaries for black intellectuals during this period. For years after its birth in depression-era Detroit, the Nation of Islam (commonly called the Black Muslims) was but one of many fringe religious groups operating in black America, and attracted little attention from scholars. Through the forties and fifties, however, it recruited thousands of urban blacks disillusioned with black Christianity and open to religious ideas alien to the American experience. Elijah Muhammad taught that despite some civil rights victories, equality in the United States was impossible. The problem, he argued in unflinching terms, was not so much the laws and social system as the evil nature of the white race:

> The human beast—the serpent, the dragon, the devil, and Satan—all mean one and the same; the people known as the white or Caucasian race, sometimes called the European race. Since by nature they were created liars and murderers, they are the enemies of truth and righteousness, and the enemies of those who seek the truth.[6]

Rather than press for civil rights, Black Muslims insisted that land was the means for separate and autonomous development. As a spokesman for Elijah Muhammad, Malcolm X declared in 1961,

"Just give us a portion of this country that we can call our own. Put us in it. Then give us everything we need to start our own civilization here . . . that is, support us for 20 to 25 years, until we are able to go for ourselves."[7] Land and temporary support would be reparations for three centuries of slavery (free labor) and racial subjugation.

Despite the Muslim movement's appeal, a predominantly Christian black community was reluctant to embrace Islam. Still, some elements of the religion's programs struck a chord with the growing militancy of the 1960s. Black self-sufficiency and antiwhite rhetoric were core elements in the message of Malcolm X, whose rise in the Muslim hierarchy paralleled the growth of the civil rights movement. In 1964 Malcolm broke with the Nation of Islam, explaining that he felt constrained by the group's political conservatism and disillusioned with the moral leadership of Elijah Muhammad. At bottom, he had come to reject the idea that whites were evil by nature.

Convinced that black unity and assertive action must precede liberation, Malcolm X launched the Organization of Afro-American Unity (OAAU) in 1964. The OAAU was open to all black people committed to Malcolm's black nationalist political program. Although the notion of "black nationalism" was becoming harder for him to define and embrace, he hoped to build a broad-based vanguard group that would co-opt both the moderates in the civil rights movement and the apolitical Nation of Islam group. In January 1965, a month before his death and not far from the spot where he would be assassinated, he explained his new vision:

> I haven't changed. I just see things on a broader scale. We nationalists used to think we were militant. We were just dogmatic. It didn't bring us anything. Now I know it's smarter to say you're going to shoot a man for what he is doing to you than because he is white. If you attack him because he is white, you give him no out. He can't stop being white.[8]

In February 1965 Malcolm X was gunned down while addressing an audience at the Audubon Ballroom in Harlem. Three men with ties to the Nation of Islam were apprehended and convicted of the murder. These convictions strengthened the credibility of mainstream black leaders like Roy Wilkins, who saw little value in the

Black Muslim movement and rejected it.[9] But C. Eric Lincoln, a noted scholar of African American religion, has identified a constituency for the Nation of Islam:

> For the millions of Blacks whose lot has been measurably improved by almost three decades of America's "new" racial policies, the romance of Elijah Muhammad's Nation of Islam still represents challenge and identity; and above all, it is a visible expression of the rage and hostility that still pervades the Black undercaste. To them, it is quite clear that the denied and the disinherited are still Black, the deniers and the disinheritors are still white, and Armageddon remains inevitable.[10]

White racist violence and resistance to black demands for justice suggested that true equality lay far ahead. When confronted with this fact, many observers concluded that black self-development was a more fruitful strategy than continued reliance on white power. The shift by groups like SNCC and CORE to more nationalist assumptions drew the Nation of Islam into the dialogue about the course of the black movement. However, the religious character of Islam and its avoidance of secular political action was a stumbling block for many who were equally uncompromising foes of white racism and believers in group development.

In 1966 a public opinion poll indicated that 85 percent of all white Americans felt that "the pace of civil rights progress was too fast." As one twenty-two-year-old white woman put it, "They're asking for too much all at once. They should try the installment plan. People don't adjust that quickly."[11] A growing number of blacks, however, believed that civil and human rights were not perks to be awarded or withheld by the white majority. Militants encouraged blacks to reject gradualist definitions of advancement and accept nothing less than absolute political and social equality.

By the late sixties white America had grown more intolerant of black demands. Disruptive urban rebellions and the rhetoric of retaliation prompted many whites to retreat to their sanctuary within the dominant group. Opportunistic politicians, seeking to play on rising white fear, ran campaigns based on a return to "law and order," meaning to most whites a crackdown on black lawlessness. The national retreat from racial justice confirmed black activists' belief that America was a racist society that would never acknowledge racial equality. Leaders like Carmichael promised to continue social agitation in the name of democracy: "It is crystal clear to us—and it must become so with the white society—that there can be no social order without justice."[12]

To the rhetoric of black freedom, Malcolm X had added an element prophesying changes in the thinking of black intellectuals. His central message did not vary—the key to black social and political development resided in the black community itself; the moral endorsement of white America was superfluous. This conclusion put him at odds with civil rights traditionalists who, for tactical or philosophical reasons, appealed to whites for redress and to "make whole" a community long savaged by white supremacy. The form of this request implicitly acknowledged a subordinate moral standing for black Americans.[13] Kenneth Clark, urging more attention to power in society, warned, "The Negro must now be aware that no fundamental change in his status can come about through deference to or patronage from whites. He cannot have rights that are given as a gesture of good will (with the implication of the right to withdraw those rights)."[14]

Even so, moderate activists, focusing on short-term goals and symbols, dominated the dialogue. Roy Wilkins of the NAACP and Whitney Young of the Urban League rejected the uncompromising posture of the militants. In their view, aggressive rhetoric only frightened whites and gave them excuses for postponing reform.[15] Since the beginning of his career with the NAACP in 1931, Wilkins had been a conservative force within the organization. Assuming its leadership after Walter White's death in 1955, Wilkins had placed his faith in the political and legal institutions of American society and worked tirelessly to maintain the reputation of the NAACP as the preeminent civil rights organization.

Whitney Young, a Kentucky native who taught in the School of Social Work at Atlanta University, succeeded Lester Granger as executive director of the Urban League in 1961. An aggressive moderate, Young solicited the assistance of corporations, foundations, and government agencies in addressing problems of employment training, housing, and job placement—traditional focuses of Urban League activity.

Black thinkers less enamored of gradualism could not defer to the will and pace of the white majority. The calls from white America for patience and gradualism sprang from no intellectual or legal principle. Simple expediency, not true prudence, governed the rate of progress. How could thoughtful men and women, well versed in American philosophical traditions, accept the idea that African Americans' freedom, justice, and equality were negotiable and subject to the goodwill of the dominant group? What would moral compromise on human rights issues mean to the stature of black people?

Scholars and artists once optimistic about black equality now felt betrayed by white America. The white establishment's insistence on control over steps toward racial equality created a mood of pessimism and anger. The new cynicism prompted many black artists to concentrate on the potential within black life and culture.

## Identity as Platform

The value of maintaining ethnic identity and cohesion had echoed through the writing of black intellectuals since the nineteenth century. Edward W. Blyden, a nineteenth-century emigrationist, speculated that blackness could be a cultural and political fountainhead of social development:

> We should not content ourselves with living among other races, simply by their permission or their endurance, as Africans live in this country. We must build up Negro states; we must establish and maintain the various institutions; we must make and administer laws, erect and preserve churches, and support the worship of God; we must have governments; we must have legislation of our own; we must build ships and navigate them; we must ply the trades, instruct the schools, control the press, and thus aid in shaping the opinions and guiding the destinies of mankind. Nationality is an ordinance of Nature.[16]

Spurred by the declining fortunes of the black masses and by leaders who rejected political rapprochement based on deference to the power of whites, 1960s intellectuals raised complex questions about ethnicity and class in black America.

Much of the thinking about cultural identity was less reactive and more subtle than the rhetoric of Blyden. Ralph Ellison repudiated the idea that black culture was defined and determined by social boundaries and constraints. Despite racial oppression, blacks had themselves decided how to live their lives, he said.

> But can a people (its faith in an idealized American Creed notwithstanding) live and develop for over three hundred years simply by *reacting*? Are American Negroes simply the creation of white men, or have they at least helped to create themselves out of what they found around them? Men have made a way of life in caves and upon cliffs, why cannot Negroes have made a life upon the horns of the white man's dilemma?[17]

Starting in 1960 the Student Nonviolent Coordinating Committee worked toward a racially integrated society, but in 1966 it shifted its attention to black community empowerment. The organization, like many black intellectuals, abandoned the goal of a color-blind society within the political and cultural framework of American life. This was new only in one sense. The Nation of Islam and the Republic of New Africa had always appealed for a separate and sovereign state, but they were fringe elements in the black community.

By 1967 the rapid escalation of racial consciousness among white and black Americans had come to worry a number of black intellectuals. Bayard Rustin preferred to downplay the ethnic character of the movement and to advocate economic policies that would benefit all Americans.[18] Kenneth Clark expressed unease about the long-term consequences of race-based social policies. Harold Cruse countered that to undo centuries of racial subordination required policies that took into account the nation's history. Without directly confronting its racial legacy, how could the country redress the effects of past and present discrimination?[19]

Determined to keep the peace, most national policymakers endorsed race-specific emphases in public policy. "Affirmative action" programs sprang up in the public and the private sectors. Affirmative action called for preferential hiring in order to ensure diversity in the workplace. At a time when the national economy was expanding, the programs seemed pragmatic and nonthreatening to most whites. Few people looked beyond the moment, toward conflicts that would arise once economic growth slowed and competition for jobs increased.

Occasionally a lonely voice raised constitutional or philosophical questions. In December 1963, only four months after he had helped organize the historic March on Washington for Jobs and Freedom, Bayard Rustin denounced racial preferences, insisting that they would "create psychological and economic problems for the country."[20] But supporters of policies that went beyond formal nondiscrimination pointed to the ineffectiveness of fair employment commissions in northern states like New York and New Jersey, where the commissions had not fostered a more representative work force. Even moderates such as Whitney Young called on the government to go beyond formal nondiscrimination. The moral force of black protests and the abundant evidence of state complicity in racial oppression swayed the political culture. Compensatory affirmative action programs swept the country. This was fine for the moment, but the seeds had been sown for a bitter harvest of racial recrimination and white resistance, which would outlive Whitney Young, Bayard Rustin, Martin Luther King Jr., and other principals of the late 1960s debate.

Many whites were perplexed. If black was beautiful, did it follow that white could not be beautiful? For many Americans the shift represented a retreat from the principles of racial equality. Martin Luther King Jr. reassured whites that the black awareness phase was only temporary. He pointed out that self-acceptance and confidence had been lacking in the black population and that the assertion of group identification was necessary to allay feelings of inferiority.[21]

Other intellectuals scoffed at King's entreaties. They considered it unnecessary, even counterproductive, to explain to whites the importance of racial consciousness. After all, if the goal was black self-improvement, the good opinion and understanding of whites was a decidedly secondary consideration. The frustrated and angry, like James Baldwin, thought they saw through white liberalism: "What they want me to do is to accept their *weak will* for the *deed*. They want me, you know—they want me to sympathize with them because *they* suffer because I suffer. And they're never willing to risk themselves, their jobs, their psychiatrists, their wives or their children—or *anything*."[22]

## The Intellectuals' Search for a Role

The black consciousness, or black power, movement that convulsed black America in the mid-sixties was fundamentally political. Years earlier, during the Harlem Renaissance, learned black Americans had debated the existence and nature of a distinctive black culture in American life. One group emphasized the African sources of black culture and the other the "American" component. The black awareness movement of the 1960s, however, went beyond issues of identity and cultural content. It tried to address problems of black powerlessness. The First Modern Pan-African Congress, convened by activists in Atlanta in 1970, called on African Americans to "work to ensure that African (Black) expressive forms can be employed in the other institutional areas of our struggle, i.e., politics, economics, education, religion."[23] The new black consciousness activists aspired to remake the very fabric of American society. Such ambitious objectives raised perplexing questions for many black intellectuals.

Socialized in the traditions of Western civilization, black scholars and artists knew the value placed on objectivity and nonpartisanship. Pride of place in universities and the world of letters seemed reserved for "detached" thinkers. Yet to grow up black in America was to join a collective black consciousness. It is not so farfetched to compare this solidarity with the example of the American founders——intellectuals who took political action in a collective struggle for freedom.

In 1966 a SNCC organizer in Alabama, Willie Ricks, electrified a black rally with the chant "black power!"—and within the movement people quickly tried to capture the energy these words aroused.[24] The simplicity and starkness of the term immediately appealed to the black masses, who had long resented their powerlessness. Furthermore, the term was sufficiently general that African

Americans from many social strata could project their own meanings onto it: aspiring political leaders who defined black power in the context of their pursuit of standing and influence; artists who speculated about black power as an engine for the production and distribution of their work; would-be millionaires who viewed black power as a vehicle that would catapult them to parity with Du Ponts and Rockefellers. Ralph Ellison defended the slogan. After all, he said, "the oversimplified and very often unfortunate slogans which are advanced in the civil rights movement act as slogans always do. Why do we demand that terrible encyclopedic nuances be found in the slogans of the civil rights movement?"[25] Expansive and ultimately amorphous, the phrase allowed proponents to avoid complexities such as defining an agenda or forging concrete, goal-directed strategies.

Many activists had little use for intellectuals. They denounced scholarly detachment and individualism as regressive Western intellectual conservatism. Franz Fanon, the Martiniquan psychiatrist-revolutionary, argued that a people long oppressed needed to attract active and partisan intellectuals from among themselves. In *Wretched of the Earth* (1966) and *Black Skin, White Masks* (1967), he insisted that the proper role of black intellectuals evolved out of group oppression reinforced by dominant cultural agencies. In the beginning stages of their formal education, intellectually oriented persons from an oppressed group seek to enter the dominant group, he said; however, the contradiction between their privileged position and that of less educated people is a constant source of friction. Ever-present slights remind sensitive thinkers of their fundamental identity:

> Because he feels he is becoming estranged, that is to say because he feels that he is the living haunt of contradictions which run the risk of becoming insurmountable, the native tears himself away from the swamp that may suck him down and accepts everything, decides to take all for granted and confirms everything even though he may lose body and soul. The native finds that he is expected to answer for everything, and to all comers. He not only turns himself into the defender of his peoples' past, he is willing to be counted as one of them.[26]

But once the black intellectual immerses himself in the indigenous culture of the native, Fanon said, he is free to assume a new role: "He turns himself into an awakener of the people, hence comes a fighting literature, a revolutionary literature, and a national literature."[27]

For some black militants the social and cultural conflict in the United States seemed to call for Fanon's type of struggle, the struggle being waged in underdeveloped and economically exploited countries.[28] The American black consciousness movement, like earlier nationalist movements, stemmed from blacks' concluding that white culture was antithetical to their freedom.

Western cultural and aesthetic values were attacked by militants such as Ron Karenga, a graduate student at UCLA and later leader of the West Coast–based organization United Slaves (US), who charged the nation's schools with acculturating blacks away from their "indigenous" culture. Despite obvious differences with the classic colonial situation that Fanon confronted, Askia Muhammed Toure and other African American intellectuals stressed the parallels: "We must strive to develop a revolutionary soul—total psychic unity with the masses of our people. We must become the very embodiment of their hopes, dreams, consciences, and desires for justice. We must develop into mental and spiritual fighting machines of Black America, instruments of the people."[29] Militant leaders demanded that intellectuals fuse with the black masses and lead the way in unmasking white standards and the purposes served by the dominant norms. They declared that intellectual distance supported the status quo and that nothing less than active engagement was acceptable. As a slogan of the era had it, "You're either part of the solution or part of the problem." Activist intellectuals reserved for themselves the right to define both the problem and the solution.

## Struggling with Boundaries

Black academic intellectuals agreed with black activist intellectuals that race was a critical element in the social order and in their own lives. But their intellectual training and habits—reflection, introspection, balance, moral symmetry—shaped their perceptions of events and lessened their effectiveness in the popular movements.

Intellectual training values departures from the norms. A broader insight or imagination frequently divests the intellectual of strong, organic roots in a particular social group. Karl Mannheim respected the energy and direction of intellectuals but wondered about the social basis of their thought.[30] When intellectuals do cast their lot with a particular group, the commitment is often ambivalent and halting. As Henry Louis Gates has explained,

> I think it's hard to be committed to thirty million black people out there. It's so easy to say it. I know what you mean [by asking me] and I would usually say "Yeah." But I don't think I could say that truthfully without a lot of qualification. Thirty million people don't mean anything to any of us in the abstract. I can't even grasp the idea of that many people. All I know about are the individual folks I've been knowing.[31]

The youthful militants were contemptuous of such "intellectualizing" at a time of crisis. They insisted that black thinkers "do something." Although black intellectuals could articulate a sense of social responsibility, most felt impotent before the problems devastating poor neighborhoods.

Some argued that social change was, by its nature, slow. Even the most cogent and empirically grounded theories had to confront the vast entrenched structure of privilege and interests that supported the status quo. Martin Luther King Jr., sometimes the intellectual, at other times the activist, told an interviewer in 1965, "Our task has been a difficult one and will continue to be, for privileged groups, historically, have not volunteered to give up their privileges." Pressed for an expression of optimism about an end to racial injustice, King replied, "I confess that I do not believe this day is around the corner. The concept of supremacy is so embedded in the white society that it will take many years for color to cease to be a judgmental factor."[32]

If African Americans were in crisis, the situation was not conducive to the kind of deliberate, dispassionate analysis that might lead to long-term social transformations. The idea of a "domestic Marshall Plan," advanced by Whitney Young in 1963, and the Freedom Budget, offered by A. Philip Randolph, seemed like wishful thinking to the militants—and besides, both programs depended on the political will of the white majority.[33] Such speculations about long-range developments bored the activists, who, for the most part, preferred to "seize the time." Intellectuals who parsed out protracted analyses were bound for irrelevancy; indeed, they were part of the problem. The charge of irrelevancy, or worse, troubled Clayborne Carson and others committed to a broader view:

> Maybe we could someday reach the point where some of our work as intellectuals would not necessarily have to have an immediate social impact. That we might conceive of it as being for the benefit of society, in that society needs more knowledge, but not for the benefit of a particular group. I once considered becoming a math major, but I became more interested in politics and history. I would hate to be thought of as having abandoned the race if I had chosen to pursue math or physics.[34]

Concerning pressures on talented blacks, Richard Yarborough, a literature professor at UCLA, offered this view: "Blacks always put burdens on their leaders, and intellectuals have more responsibilities than others. Whether that's fair or not is beside the point. The black situation in this country has never been fair, so I think it's just something that must be faced."[35] Clayborne Carson valued the tradition of service but worries about the constraints it imposes:

> There is that feeling that you've got to do something that is for the benefit of the race which goes way back in black history. Du Bois in *Dusk of Dawn* talks of how you have to use your learning to benefit the race. You know, such an attitude is helpful in a lot of ways, but I hope it does not serve as a boundary on the imagination of black intellectuals.[36]

In this context, as in others, Du Bois's example is instructive. His career certainly demonstrated how much imagining was possible within and around the boundaries of race, yet even he has not escaped latter-day criticism. Henry Louis Gates wonders whether Du Bois's energies were expended on the proper subjects:

Black people like Du Bois appealed to me. He was my model. I figured I was not as smart as him, but if you had to pick a role model, it might as well be Du Bois. He did wonderful things with the *Crisis*. How can you knock that? On the other hand, I wish that he could have written his own sociology of knowledge, or pursued philosophy rather than sociology. But who's to say? He certainly thrived. . . . He wrote more than you and I together will ever write, and he wrote it wonderfully.[37]

The turmoil of racial conflict in the late sixties and early seventies increased tensions between scholarly ideals and partisan activism. The collapse of the liberal consensus on how to advance the equality of blacks angered the activists, but many intellectuals were made uncomfortable by this anger. Some—Harold Cruse, St. Clair Drake, Vincent Harding[38]—accepted the importance of group solidarity and acknowledged their moral debt to the black masses, but maintained their right to think for themselves. Not all ideas promulgated by activists in the name of blackness drew support from intellectuals, for whom freedom meant independence of mind.

# 9

## CAPTURING
## THE DEFINITION

Too great a sense of identity makes a man feel he can
do no wrong. And too little does the same.

—DJUNA BARNES

WITH THE BLACK POWER movement emerged a new form of
"blackness." Activists framed their critiques and political
agendas in the name of the black masses, who had arguably been
ignored by the traditional civil rights leadership. When the urban
revolts in Watts (1965), Newark (1967), and Detroit (1967) abruptly
captured the nation's attention, adroit activists moved quickly to link
their nationalistic agendas to the social well-being of the black community. Groups like US and the Black Panther Party represented
themselves as vanguard organizations that took their cues from the
urban masses.

The activists' announced affinity with mass aspirations lent
authority to their definition of blackness. They challenged other
blacks to conform to the definition or else be treated as outsiders.
Henry Louis Gates reminisces about his plunge into the whirlpool of
black militant symbolism at Yale during the 1960s:

The biggest transition was adapting to so many black people. That blew my mind. I remember going to the first Black Student Alliance meeting. . . . I was in a room that held about three hundred people; everybody in that room was black. And I thought I was in Africa or Harlem. I had never seen that many black people at one time. And the first order of business was how few black people were at Yale. And I couldn't believe how many black people were there.

Gates soon learned that being black at Yale went beyond ethnic identification, and the realization gave him pause.

You had people coming out of all kinds of trick bags, and I was just an innocent. I didn't know what it meant to be properly militant, to be cool, to be accepted in terms of one's own blackness. The question that always lurked beneath the surface was "How black are you?" That was the hardest thing for me, learning how to be with a group of people who were not willing to accept you merely because you were black. There was a litmus test of blackness, and you had to pass that test before you could be truly black.[1]

Like many other impressionable young thinkers, Gates would later question both the idea of a litmus test and the motives of those who insisted on it.

Increasingly, the militant activists' hostility toward black intellectuals was rooted in suspicion and fear. Militant black youths recognized that their market value had never been higher. No longer were they denied recognition and legitimacy because of an alleged lack of academic training and sophistication. Many skillfully expressed (and merchandised) their indifference to white cultural norms in their language and dress. Indeed, the adoption of African names, African-style dress, "natural" hair styles, and often profanity-laced speech signified cultural defiance. The more exotic the belief and behavior, the more "authentic" the version of blackness.

Bobby Wideman, younger brother of the author John Edgar Wideman, recalls his early days as a black militant:

I was a stone mad militant. Didn't know what I was saying half
the time and wasn't sure what I wanted but I was out there
screaming and hollering and waving my arms around and didn't
take no shit from nobody. I dug being a militant, cause I was
good. It was something I could do. Rap to people. Whip a righ-
teous message on them. People knew my name. They'd listen.[2]

Wideman and others managed to convince those who would listen
that militancy was the only path. To have opened the movement, or
even the debate, to different styles and values (ones more acceptable
to white America) would only have undermined the status of the
militants. By 1969, new ingredients were being added to the mix at
America's intellectual centers.

No less militant than Bobby Wideman, the Yale undergraduates
Armstead Robinson and Glenn E. deChabert probed the meaning of
being black in the cloistered Ivy League. Robinson, who by 1995 was
a professor of history at the University of Virginia, and head of that
institution's Carter G. Woodson Institute, argued in 1969, "To be
black here—to be aware of all the things whiteness has meant for
black people and to be asked to submit passively to being coddled
by the white power structure, being paid to come, is a fundamental
contradiction for anyone with a positive black identification."[3]

DeChabert, by contrast, did not relish trumpeting his blackness to
whites. The idea that he could educate whites about blackness
seemed at odds with his personal quest:

You realize it's hard enough to deal with yourself and other
black people and try to figure out your place in the world. . . . If
you start to deal with white people, start to be a tutor or mentor
or conscience for white people, you find after a while that you
have ceased to be a mentor for yourself. And this is the essence
of black consciousness: figuring out in your mind what you are
to yourself and what you mean to the world in terms of its
black population.[4]

After Martin Luther King's assassination in 1968, white colleges
stepped up their recruitment of black students. A majority of the
nation's universities also began to make special efforts to recruit

potential black scholars to their graduate schools. The Ford, Rockefeller, and Carnegie foundations joined federal agencies in offering
financial and other forms of assistance to aspiring black intellectuals.

Most African Americans recognized the symbolic value of black
faculty appointments, particularly those made by elite institutions.
Even while Arthur Jensen and William Shockley were espousing the
mental inferiority of blacks, black scholars were being hired at places
like Berkeley, Yale, and Columbia. Dissenters in the black community scoffed. To them, the presence of a few carefully selected black
voices on campus provided false legitimacy to the schools' self-com-
placency regarding nondiscrimination and intellectual freedom.
White authorities, militants said, would not permit autonomous and
progressive black intellectuals to flourish at white institutions.
Advanced degrees spoke not of superior academic achievement but
of their holder's ability to compromise with an oppressive educational system. Going further, individuals such as Nathan Hare challenged the validity of traditional academic criteria in selecting and
evaluating black scholars.[5] Contributions to books, journals, and
organs dominated by whites were not regarded as the best black
thinking.

Other militant but more pragmatic nationalists recognized that
able black students completing high school should seize the opportunity for a topflight education. Many such high school graduates
enrolled in elite schools, hoping to earn high-status degrees and go
on to positions of influence and leadership. It followed that black
scholars should be present on elite campuses to guide black students.

Black students arriving on campus in the early seventies found that
the standards and definitions of blackness developed by radical
urban activists had been accepted by the black student body. New
students quickly realized that they had to come to terms with the
prevailing mood of black awareness. Many privileged black middle-
class college students were sympathetic to the black awareness movement and wanted to be a part of the action. The condescending attitudes of white administrators and faculty increased their desire to
close ranks with older militants.

Yet while most black college students supported group solidarity
and empowerment, the narrow interpretation of blackness promoted
by the militant leadership bewildered many. Gates recalls his anxiety

about being out of step with the militant activists at Yale in the late
sixties:

> I thought damn! I'm just Uncle Tom up here. I don't know any-
> thing about how I should function. Are you supposed to wear
> an Afro? Wear dashikis only? Give a special handshake? Date
> white people? Listen to a certain music? Ice your white friends?
> I was worried, and very anxious to be accepted by my commu-
> nity, because I had always been accepted before and would find
> rejection bothersome.[6]

Richard Yarborough resented the merchandizing of blackness by
radicals.

> I didn't feel totally accepted by the blacks on campus, because I
> had a very different upbringing than they. I frequently felt like
> an outsider, an observer, rather than participant. I noticed
> things that other people may not have noticed—the hypocrisy
> of middle-class black students wearing denim jackets and talk-
> ing about poverty when they were driving cars. Some black stu-
> dents accused me of being "bourgeois" because of my manner,
> speech, and background when, in fact, they were often economi-
> cally from a higher social class than I was.[7]

A preoccupation with superficial manifestations of blackness led
to what Adolph Reed has described as the "commoditization" of
black nationalism. Commercial and cultural entrepreneurs rushed to
provide the latest symbol of authenticity.[8] Predictably, the "certi-
fying" products were tailored to fit the image of poor urban blacks.
During the sixties many impressionable students either denied—or
apologized for—their middle-class background and academic success. The absurdity of having to reject one's identity in order to be
considered "truly black" was not lost on some young scholars. As
one who experienced the contradictions of black consciousness,
Clayborne Carson recalls,

> Middle-class and educated people began to wonder, "What is
> my role in this movement?" Some began to really identify with

the "brother on the block," as they used to say at that time. I knew people who talked like me, and suddenly a year later they were talking like the brother on the block. It was a very conscious kind of decision to change, to rid yourself of all of that middle-class baggage. For various reasons I didn't choose to do that, and I guess that is one of the reasons I took the road which led me here [Stanford University, history department].[9]

The activists' rigid standards and narrow criteria also caused the numerical expansion of the movement to be sacrificed to the apparent cohesion of "true believers." Troy Duster, who did battle with some of the extremist factions, recalls,

In the sixties too narrow a construction of blackness was coming down on me and other people. There are now many ways of being black, whereas in 1968 or 1969 they made you feel as if there was only one way. Somebody would seize the cover of blackness, drape it over himself, and in behalf of the black nation march forward and say, "This is blackness. If you're not for me, you're against me." That has changed.[10]

Although the militants' slogans were simplistic, the stridency of their appeals and the tentativeness of their critics allowed them to monopolize debate about the direction of the Black Power movement. Most black intellectuals understood the danger posed by a small group invested with the authority to pronounce who was black and who was not. But many—particularly those who had grown up in predominantly white neighborhoods and attended mostly white schools—dared not challenge the legitimacy of those who spoke for the "masses." At one level the black community, thanks to greater opportunities, was becoming more socially diverse; in the context of college campuses, though, a vocal minority was able to mask the complexity of black existence and define racial identity by a formula that served the minority's personal interests.

The notion that academically successful African Americans had been "contaminated" by values and standards antithetical to the struggle for black power was not a new theme. Carter G. Woodson, a Harvard-educated historian, had raised it in *The Miseducation of the Negro* (1933). Woodson reasoned that blacks could succeed in white institutions only by subordinating their sense of self and cultural integrity. Fanon later made much the same point: the nationalist native who entered the schools of the colonizers emerged as a fawning assimilated intellectual.[11]

Neither Woodson nor Fanon paused to consider that their lives contradicted their arguments. Although both had been academically successful in white institutions, neither had succumbed to "assimilation." Nor had Du Bois, who grew up in a largely white town in Massachusetts.

Furthermore, militants could see that graduate work in philosophy had not alienated Angela Davis from black culture. Davis had grown up in Birmingham, Alabama, but left at age fifteen to attend the progressive Elisabeth Irwin High School in New York. She went on to Brandeis University, in Massachusetts, and, after graduating magna cum laude, pursued graduate study in Frankfurt, Germany.[12] Davis was passed off as an exception. Most militants accepted the dogma that American education only alienated blacks from their better selves.

Anti-intellectual tendencies led black radicals to reject many talented individuals—some because of the type of education they received, others in spite of it. The militants' elevation of lower-class urban black culture also devalued the rural black folk culture and the artists and scholars who had worked in that realm. Zora Neale Hurston, Sterling Brown, Charles Johnson, and even the blues were set aside as relics of a quaint, bygone era.

### For Us, or against Us

Most black intellectuals saw the shortsightedness and irrationality of much of the militants' rhetoric but avoided a public challenge. Aware that whites were growing more hostile to even "reasonable" demands by blacks, they dreaded being cast as "enemies of the people." They wanted to consider themselves a part of black unity, even if the terms imposed by militants were usually unacceptable.

The American intellectual establishment had difficulty understanding why black consciousness appealed to thoughtful African Americans. Mainstream critics and the popular media spread the erroneous message that only naive and anti-intellectual blacks were attracted to the movement. Gates recalls, almost wistfully, the mania on the Yale campus:

> I had great peer relationships with some of the strongest people here [at Yale]. We'd just sit around and talk about the "problem." We'd talk about it at breakfast, we'd talk about it at lunch, we'd talk about it at dinner, we'd talk about it at parties, and you would talk about it when you were just sitting around bullshitting! That's all we talked about . . . the ironies of being black with this kind of education in a society where—horror of horrors!—there was three and a half percent unemployment rate and a seven percent black rate, which we thought was completely unacceptable. Hell, you'd give anything to have back those figures right now.
>
> I think that was wonderful; I mean, it's a very exciting kind of thing.[13]

Other black scholars and intellectuals caught the excitement. Black activists' heated rhetoric, extreme though much of it was, captured the energy of a people awakened to, and then intoxicated by, its own potential. Predictably, the awakening produced no consensus. Black thinkers had many and varied reactions to the content of black consciousness appeals. Moreover, many had misgivings about their own role as intellectuals in the struggle for freedom.

The powerful and the powerless alike sought to draw black intellectuals into debates about goals, premises, and strategies. It mattered little whether individual intellectuals were trained in chemistry, philosophy, or European history; they could not escape organizational and institutional pressure from whites seeking advice from the "nearest Negro." By virtue of their race, not their training or interests, all black intellectuals were considered experts on race and the meaning of the black movement.

Such attention and rewards seduced many highly educated blacks. Quite a few dubious intellectual pronouncements flowed as black sociologists analyzed literary texts and black psychologists explained economic history.

## Social Determinism and Black Life

The militants' rhetorical strategy required blaming whites for the problems of black communities. Militants like Stokely Carmichael as well as social democrats like Bayard Rustin linked shortcomings in the black community to broader patterns in American life. When Martin Luther King was murdered, Rustin wrote, "Whatever deficiencies in dignity and self-respect may be laid to the Negro are the consequence of generations of segregation, discrimination, and exploitation."[14] Intragroup crime and violence, drug abuse, educational underperformance, and family instability all were attributed directly or indirectly to white oppression. Such blanket allegations were troubling to many young black intellectuals who themselves had come from poor neighborhoods. Glenn Loury grew up in a low-income neighborhood on Chicago's South Side, got married at a relatively early age, yet managed to earn a B.A. at Northwestern and a Ph.D. at the Massachusetts Institute of Technology. Loury and others like him understand the insidious effects poverty and racial discrimination have on family and communal life. They have known firsthand the ordeal of racial bigotry. Nonetheless, they survived and prospered, proof that some inner-city blacks can rise above racism and poverty. Fundamentally, they have rejected, as Ellison did years earlier, the characterization of black life and culture as a by-product of racial oppression.

These success stories were cited to counter notions of victimization. Instead of waiting for the government to step in, some blacks called for more black initiative. Thomas Sowell argued that the success of individual blacks from impoverished communities proved that the hurdles of discrimination, however significant, could be cleared.[15] The black community cannot be absolved of significant responsibility for its problems, Sowell says.

Even so, militant critiques persuaded some young black thinkers that their blackness had been diluted by their "white man's education." As anti-intellectual rhetoric increased, several vocal supporters of black empowerment launched a counteroffensive, reminding militants that individual initiative *and* broad social action were necessary. Vincent Harding, long active in militant nationalistic circles, pointed out the regressive motives and behavior among the activists.

Black intellectuals, he insisted, had to take some responsibility for weeding out or reforming those elements that, left unchecked, would devitalize the movement. They should, he wrote,

> identify the enemy within the black community, within our own people, within ourselves. . . . To identify the enemy is to identify the mesmerizing fear, the debilitating venality, the lack of moral and intellectual self-discipline, the opportunism, the pathological lying, and the self-defeating desire for public recognition and praise which dwell among us.[16]

Many black intellectuals agreed. But in the polarized sixties, it seemed clear that the United States was still a "closed" system. Sixty years earlier W. E. B. Du Bois had understood that many interests hostile to social equity touted black self-help to deflect attention from white privilege and the social inequity rooted in such privilege. No serious scholars suggested that self-help alone could overturn barriers to opportunity for blacks. During the Great Depression the federal government had quickly abandoned the policy of self-help for whites and established massive federal social assistance programs. Why was self-help alone now supposed to suffice for blacks?

All observers agreed that individual initiative, the character of the community, and societal opportunity (or the lack thereof) were crucial and interrelated elements in promoting individual and group mobility; but they disagreed about how much weight to assign each element. Thomas Sowell and other conservatives contended that recently enacted nondiscrimination policies sufficed to ensure the upward mobility of blacks. Families and individual resourcefulness had to supply whatever else was necessary.[17] Troy Duster disagrees:

> The problem with Sowell is that he's *half* right. It's his conclusions that are wrong. Sure, some people were pimping the black movement; sure, some jive students got in school because they're black; sure, some incompetent people get jobs because they're black. But access to power, to bank loans, to home ownership, had been completely closed to blacks. I think that most black intellectuals have always seen that the ideal of meritocracy has never been even close to true—that simple hard work and perse-

verance explain why whites hold power—that this has never described America. Affirmative action helped open employment doors, and college admissions doors—and it was inevitable that one can find abuses. For black intellectuals to forget or ignore this history and to denounce all affirmative action as misguided is to fall into a trap; it is in large measure to be intellectually irresponsible.[18]

Halford Fairchild, a psychologist, offers cautious support for Sowell's position:

> I think he's got a point. Welfare has in fact childrenized much of the black population. It's made many blacks feel as though they are ineffectual, incompetent, and they need to receive handouts. But I think there are some very profound institutional handicaps that make it impossible for a majority of the black poor to do what Sowell thinks they should be doing.[19]

There were new particulars to argue about—welfare, affirmative action—but the polemic essentially revived the debates between Booker T. Washington and W. E. B. Du Bois about economic and political development.

Discussions about race were further polarized by the publication in 1965, of a report by Daniel Patrick Moynihan, at the time on leave from Harvard to serve as an assistant secretary of labor in the Johnson administration. Moynihan, who taught urban politics and education, cited the increase in out-of-wedlock births and the deterioration of the family as major impediments to the social progress of the black poor, and he called for government action to provide economic opportunities for black adults. His emphasis on the pathology of families drew media attention and angered many black scholars, who resented the stigmatization of poor blacks.[20] Poor black families, it seemed to many, were being blamed for their victimization—were victims twice over.

The quixotic racial policies of the seventies offered black intellectuals of all kinds much to criticize. Occasional homilies by national leaders urging Americans to be fair produced no change. Black militancy and a stalled economy gave whites reasons to accept, or rationalize, racial exclusion or discrimination in employment, housing, and education. At the same time liberal scholars, black and white, emphasized the long-term effects of racial oppression, carefully demonstrating that poor educational achievement, inadequate housing, high unemployment rates, and criminal behavior were linked to historical discrimination. Social science researchers identified and examined patterns of black dysfunctionality. The avalanche of research prompted some blacks to ponder its moral and political implications. African Americans, especially the intellectuals, knew hundreds of individuals who bore no resemblance to the socially debilitated creatures who populated mainstream scholarship. Several historians of slavery, notably John Blassingame in *The Slave Community* (1972), Eugene Genovese in *Roll, Jordan, Roll: The World the Slaves Made* (1972), and Albert Rabateau in *Slave Religion* (1978), suggested that blacks enjoyed a greater independence in shaping their lives and forging their social institutions than had previously been thought. Such conclusions contradicted the work of E. Franklin Frazier, Moynihan, and other social scientists who saw social dysfunctions flowing from slavery and racial oppression. If black social and moral life was not devastated by slavery, skeptics asked, how could the greatest degree of freedom since Emancipation have destroyed what human bondage failed to destroy?

As anthropologists, sociologists, and other academics began to take a second look at the black family, Herbert Gutman marshaled evidence to rebut Frazier's and Moynihan's theses and show that black families had displayed remarkable stability through 1925.[21] Another writer found resilient and highly functional cultural adaptations in the male-female relationships of poor blacks.[22] But the emphasis on black strengths undermined the policy decisions of traditional advocacy groups. If black institutions were so strong and autonomous, why were so many individual blacks poor or unemployed?

In the 1960s, then, the black consciousness movement failed to bring about the social and cultural revolution that many of its leaders predicted. Ron Karenga's black nation never materialized.[23] But social and cultural movements rarely culminate in such grandiose transformations; social change is usually more subtle. The black awareness movement did greatly alter black and white attitudes toward racial imbalance in the United States. The American penchant for immediate empirical results does not recognize movements that "simply" change the way people view the social world. Mainstream critics largely succeeded in caricaturing the black consciousness movement and many of its key figures.

On balance, many thoughtful African Americans were drawn in some way to the idea of black nationalism. Henry Louis Gates describes his encounters in 1970 at Yale with the black nationalist entourage of the poet Amiri Baraka:

> I took blackness very seriously, but I thought that a whole lot of black nationalism was full of shit! I would go to Newark on weekends, and when Baraka would come in the room they would stand up and bow. I was fascinated that anybody would bow when some human being walks into a room, and where their heads would have to be in order to do that. But I was fascinated by the energy that black nationalism unleashed. I think you and I would agree that no other political movement has ever been able to do that.[24]

In other words, the posturing and theatrics that accompanied much nationalist activity should not obscure the changes the black consciousness movement wrought in the thinking of a generation of black intellectuals.

# 10 ⫷

# RUDE AWAKENINGS

A certain fragile chumminess has sprung up, notably
along the margins of blacktown and whitetown,
between the friendly and open-hearted and well-educated on both sides. But this involves a few thousands
not millions of people, is far from equality and fraternity, and is no evidence of any important social change.

—W. H. FERRY

## Enter the Brave New Scholars

FOR MANY BLACK students and faculty, a white university environment presented special problems. Students had to contend with
academic challenges while sorting out the meaning of their presence
on campus—to themselves and to whites. Said one new faculty member, "When I arrived [at UCLA] after my Ph.D. I felt like a powerful
shark, just cruising the waters. Now I feel like a wounded minnow,
just trying to survive."[1]

During the seventies activists made a morally and politically compelling case for hiring qualified black scholars. Embarrassed by the
virtual absence of black faces on faculties, many university officials
acted quickly. A moral impulse and the desire to head off, or respond
to, militant black students brought some novel developments. Rather
than being allowed, indeed encouraged, to concentrate on their academic work, many black professors were herded into nonacademic

activities.[2] Institutions that had traditionally steered younger faculty away from administrative committees and community affairs drafted young black scholars precisely for duty in these areas. As a consequence, their teaching and scholarly work suffered.

Black students made demands as well. Having clamored for black faculty, they now expected them to serve as mentors and role models. Here, at last, were the "authority figures" who would ease hostility and indifference on overwhelmingly white campuses. Black students regarded personal counseling, advocacy, political advice, and cultural invigoration as essential to the black academic's role.

Paradoxically, here student and administration interests converged. University presidents and deans wanted black faculty to maintain the peace. Contributions to research and teaching paled by comparison. Students, of course, were also less concerned about their instructor's research or intellectual development. They applauded the administration's encouragement of black faculty involvement in matters affecting black students—and the local community. Unaware of the time and energy junior faculty had to expend to meet promotion criteria, students did not see how extracurricular activities could threaten a young scholar's career. Black scholars who were thought to withhold full involvement with black student concerns were considered suspect. Campus activists argued that because their collective efforts had created the conditions that led to the employment of black faculty members, the primary obligation of those faculty was to the black student constituency. The moderate version of black faculty "obligation" meant teaching courses relevant to the past or present experiences of African American students. Some students, like the following respondent to a researcher during the Berkeley strike for a Third World college, were bluntly specific: "I was in the movement and I got my ass busted so you [instructor] could get this job. Now you are talking the white man's grade shit. Man, you benefitin' from my action. You wasn't even here when the shit came down."[3] Though sometimes dishonest and manipulative, student militancy helped break the color barrier. As the black nationalist activist Nathan Hare, who once headed the black studies program at San Francisco State, pointed out, "Our cries for more black professors and black students have padded white colleges with more blacks in two years than decades of whimpering for 'integration' ever did."[4] Not only did militant protest increase the numbers of black students, but the work of black scholars began to receive more attention. In 1982 Benjamin Quarles, whose first book, *Frederick Douglass,* was published in 1948, acknowledged a professional debt to the rambunctious young activists in the black consciousness movement:

> I think that many of the so-called black intellectuals owe whatever fleeting attention they had to the black protest movement. Some of us have seen books we have written which had desultory sales, suddenly take off—all because of the Black Power movement. I would be the last to criticize that movement, because such recognition as we have, modest as it is, would have been even less without the black thrust in the sixties.[5]

Implicit in the rhetoric of militant students was a pledge to support black faculty who conformed to their expectations at the expense of other institutional norms and expectations. But teachers who relied on student support found they had miscalculated. Even when students vociferously protested the termination of popular black professors, the judgments of promotion committees, tenure committees, and administrators prevailed. Black faculty members who were ousted for not meeting institutional standards were soon forgotten.

Ronald Taylor, a senior professor at the University of Connecticut, tells of agonizing over competing loyalties:

> I think some people can make a very clean separation and say, "Those things are characteristic of the system. There is not much I can do about that. My contribution lies in the larger world." One can do that and of course solve part of the problem, at least in terms of dealing with some of the everyday pressure, because one can convince oneself that universal questions are more important than dealing with "local" issues. And at times, I must admit, I've done that. But I haven't found it easy to forget the local scene. Many of my black colleagues find themselves in something of a bind, especially when there are issues that they care about.[6]

Black scholars usually considered themselves more sensitive than their white peers to the problems of black students and staff. Even nonactivist professors found it difficult to ignore the pleadings of individual black students. And with black faculty shouldering so much of the burden, their white colleagues were able to lessen their participation in complicated and time-consuming campus activities surrounding race.

The pull between academic and nonacademic activities reminded one Africanist scholar, Robert Cummings, of the zigzag course he had negotiated in graduate school at UCLA, when his graduate adviser constantly tried to dissuade him from engaging in nonacademic activities.

> Now, the one thing that he could never understand was why I was fooling around with these other, nonacademic issues. He says to me, "These things are nonacademic. Intellectuals don't have time for that!" My argument was, "Maybe white intellectuals don't have time for that. Blacks have to take time for such things. I have to do some other things that white students don't think they have to do. I have to fight the fight." He replied that I was spreading myself too thin, that instead of grappling with the important literature in my field, I was always getting into the black movements. He was right, but grappling with the literature in my field in a singularly absolutist manner was a luxury in that period.[7]

Youthful black intellectuals did not tend to view scholarship and activism as two distinct realms. Like the young Du Bois, they believed that they could effectively apply their insights and analyses to important social and political issues. Many graduate students, caught up in the excitement of the black consciousness movement, adopted a social utilitarian attitude. Nell Irvin Painter of Princeton University, author of *Hosea Hudson* and *Sojourner Truth: A Life, a Symbol,* attributes this utilitarianism to "the incredible amount of baggage that goes with being black." Black graduate students, she says, "want to prove so much . . . want to apply their knowledge; they want it to mean something and often want to do more than graduate students generally ought to do if they are to complete their degrees in a timely fashion and without going crazy."[8]

*Above:* William Wells Brown, considered by many to be the first black novelist and playwright, participated in abolitionist and underground slave rescue efforts.

*Above right:* Robert Purvis, a thoughtful figure who supported black rights but clashed with Douglass and others over the character of the freedom campaign.

*Right:* Frederick Douglass, born into bondage, became an outspoken foe of slavery. He was one of the more active intellectuals of the nineteenth century, supporting women's suffrage and a range of other reform issues.

*Left:* Ida B. Wells Barnett, an uncompromising and eloquent foe of lynching and racism.
*Below:* Booker T. Washington (seen with his secretary Emmett Scott) was an influential figure in American history at the turn of the century. His ideas shaped many black educational and political initiatives.

*Above:* Ernest Everett Just, a biologist whose work at Howard University in the early twentieth century transcended the constraints of his status as a black scientist.

*Above right:* Alain Locke, a Harvard Ph.D. and Howard professor, who carefully cultivated black literary talent during the Harlem Renaissance.

*Right:* Zora Neale Hurston, writer and folklorist, whose work helped draw attention to southern folk culture in black America.

*Above left:* Langston Hughes, one of the most widely read writers in African American letters. Hughes featured black folk culture in much of his creative work.

*Above:* Wallace Thurman, a provocative critic and writer during the Harlem Renaissance. Early on, Thurman expressed reservations about the artistic merit of Renaissance literary work.

*Left:* Claude McKay, an independent writer and intellectual of the 1920s and 1930s, who often bucked popular currents in black social and literary thought.

*Above:* Nella Larsen, whose novels of middle-class angst attracted much attention during the Harlem Renaissance. *Above right:* James Weldon Johnson, an author and protest leader of the NAACP during the 1920s and 1930s. *Right:* William Thompson Patterson abandoned a career as a successful lawyer in Harlem to actively pursue radical causes. His wife, Louise, was an educator with ties to several Harlem Renaissance writers.

*Above left:* Richard Wright, a formidable literary talent, author of *Native Son*. *Above right:* Countee Cullen, skilled poet associated with the Harlem Renaissance. *Below left:* Arna Bontemps, novelist, educator, and veteran of the Harlem Renaissance who served as Fisk librarian until 1965. *Below right:* St. Clair Drake, whose *Black Metropolis* (written with Horace Clayton) remains a classic in urban ethnography. Drake headed the Afro-American studies program at Stanford during the 1980s.

*Above left:* Harold Cruse, professor emeritus of African-American studies at Michigan. Cruse's seminal books *The Crisis of the Negro Intellectual* and *Retreat or Rebellion* influenced black intellectuals during the 1970s. *Above right:* Nathan Huggins, professor and chair of Afro-American studies at Harvard until his death in 1991. Huggins wrote *Harlem Renaissance,* an insightful account of the art and artists of the period. *Below left:* William J. Wilson, a University of Chicago sociologist whose 1978 book, *The Declining Significance of Race,* catalyzed debate about race and class in urban America. *Below right:* John Bracey, one of several activists who became serious scholars. The author and editor of several important accounts of black protest and black nationalism, he teaches in the black studies department at the University of Massachusetts at Amherst.

*Above:* Mack Jones is Distinguished Professor of Political Science at Clark Atlanta University. Jones, Adolph Reed, and Alex Willingham were important political thinkers in the 1970s and 1980s in Atlanta.

*Above right:* Cedric Robinson, perhaps the country's leading scholar of black radical thought, chairs the black studies department at the University of California at Santa Barbara. Robinson published *Black Marxism* in 1983.

*Right:* Toni Morrison, a Nobel Prize–winning novelist and since 1989 professor of English at Princeton.

*Above left:* Clayborne Carson, author of *In Struggle,* the prize-winning chronicle of the Student Nonviolent Coordinating Committee, is professor of history at Stanford and editor of the Martin Luther King Jr. Papers Project. *Above right:* Troy Duster, professor of sociology and director of the Institute for the Study of Social Change at University of California at Berkeley. Duster specializes in social movements, science, and social policy. *Below left:* Robert Allen, editor of *Black Scholar* and author of *Port Chicago Mutiny, Black Awakening in Capitalist America,* and, with Herb Boyd, *Brotherman. Below right:* Albert Rabateau, professor of religious studies at Princeton, wrote the highly acclaimed *Slave Religion.*

*Above left:* Armstead Robinson was director of the Carter G. Woodson Institute at the University of Virginia from 1980 until his death in 1995.

*Above:* Ronald Taylor, professor of sociology at the University of Connecticut and an authority on the social development of black youth.

*Left:* Joyce Ladner, professor of sociology at Howard and a published scholar in the area of poverty and families.

*Above:* Gerald Horne, a
highly prolific historian and
activist, is professor of history at University of North
Carolina at Chapel Hill.
*Above right:* Ishmael Reed,
one of the major innova-
tors in black contemporary
fiction.
*Right:* Nell Irvin Painter,
an American historian and
author of *Sojourner Truth*
and *The Narrative of
Hosea Hudson,* is professor
of history at Princeton.

*Above left:* Manning Marble, professor of history at Columbia and a prolific author in black political history. *Above right:* Robert Cummings, professor and chair of African studies at Howard. *Below:* C. Eric Lincoln *(right)*, a major figure in black religious history since the publication of *Black Muslims in America* in 1962, is professor of religion and culture at Duke. Alex Haley *(left)* collaborated with Malcolm X on the classic *Autobiography of Malcolm X.*

*Above left:* Kenneth Manning, biographer of the famed biologist Ernest Everett Just, is professor of history at MIT. *Above right:* Glenn Loury, a thoughtful critic of many liberal approaches to race and social policy. *Below:* Angela Davis, 1995 University Professor at the University of California at Santa Cruz, visits activists in South Africa.

*Above left:* Genna Rae McNeil, biographer of Charles H. Houston, is professor of history at the University of North Carolina at Chapel Hill.
*Above:* Henry Louis Gates Jr., W. E. B. Du Bois Professor in the Humanities and chair of Afro-American studies at Harvard.
*Left:* Thadious Davis, biographer of Nella Larsen and professor of English at Vanderbilt.

*Above:* Michael Eric Dyson, professor of communications studies at the University of North Carolina and an articulate commentator on black popular culture.

*Above right:* Patricia Williams, professor of law at Columbia and author of the provocative books *The Alchemy of Race and Rights* and *The Rooster's Egg*.

*Right:* Kathleen Cleaver, professor of law at Emory and a former radical activist.

*Above left:* Trudier Harris, a prolific literary and cultural critic, is professor of English at Emory.

*Above:* Walter Mosley, an imaginative and popular writer whose work captures the pulse and complexity of urban black communities in the 1940s and 1950s.

*Left:* Lani Guinier, professor of law at the University of Pennsylvania and a civil rights scholar.

## Guides and Guideposts

Bold rhetoric notwithstanding, black intellectuals in academic life had to fall in line. On most campuses promotion and tenure depended on "teaching excellence," "outstanding research," and "exemplary service." The informal requirements were more elusive still. Even the brightest and best-trained newly hired professors had few clues about the institutional culture and the often idiosyncratic factors that would determine their standing. Unless one secured a mentor, useful advice regarding these informal rules was hard to come by. Albert Rabateau, the author of *Slave Religion,* now at Princeton University, considers the problem to be a serious one.

> Recently I have been thinking about the problem of black intellectuals and academics not having mentors. Not just a dissertation adviser, but someone they can go to and say, "I need some advice on this and that." The mentor connection seems to work better for whites than black academics, here [at Berkeley] and at Yale.[9]

Douglas Daniels recalls his naïveté when he joined the faculty of the University of Texas:

> The first couple of years, you are not smart enough to even know what university committees exist, and that you should find out who's on them. I was not smart enough to know that. I did not realize that the ones who do not come to faculty meetings or who don't make speeches are sometimes the movers and shakers of the university . . . who sit back real quiet and make a phone call here and there, and things begin to happen for better or worse.[10]

Young black faculty and graduate students often did find senior black scholars who could articulate the unwritten rules of academic expectations. These mentors usually knew how student pressures and administration expectations came into play. Nonetheless, there frequently remained a generational or cultural gap between these senior black professors and younger, socially committed black intellectuals.

In a 1969 article Michael Thelwell wrote, "The cultural condescension and chauvinism that has dominated graduate departments, coupled with an absence of racial consciousness and cultural nationalism on the part of most traditionally trained black academics, makes them little more qualified [to serve as mentors] than their white peers."[11] Still, few young black scholars chose to ignore advice or collegiality extended by experienced colleagues. Reflecting on his graduate experience at Stanford, Richard Yarborough notes,

> One thing that black intellectuals in academia do, and I think most of them are probably very aware of it—and those that are not should be—is that as a role model they're often more influential than anything they say in class. The fact that a black professor I had in college was very successful, very intellectual, clearly competent—in fact, more competent than most of the other people in his department, by their own admission—made me recognize that there is a way to go. I mean you can read about Du Bois, Frazier, and the others, but it doesn't mean much unless you can see people whom you have contact with in those roles.[12]

Many black scholars dedicated their books to black intellectuals who influenced their careers: John Blassingame, *New Perspectives on Black Studies* (1971), to David Bishop and Myron Clemmons; Mari Evans, *Black Women Writers, 1950–1980* (1984), to George Kent; Margaret Walker Alexander, *Richard Wright, Daemonic Genius* (1988), to Richard Wright; Sterling Stuckey, *Slave Culture: Nationalist Theory and the Foundations of Black America* (1987), to Sterling Brown; and Vincent P. Franklin, *Black Self-Determination: A Cultural History of African American Resistance* (1992), to Charles Davis.

In American history, sociology, anthropology, and related fields, many white faculty members also shared the intellectual and political interests of the novice scholars. C. Vann Woodward at Yale, Herbert Blumer at Berkeley, and Thomas Pettigrew at Harvard were among the most active mentors of black graduate students and junior faculty. Some sympathetic white professors became frustrated when striving black academics hesitated to confide in them and seek advice on easing their careers along. The long history of distrust between African Americans and white authority figures—and calls for black solidarity—prevented or distorted many potentially fruitful associations.

Other scholars criticized race-specific mentoring arrangements as stereotyping. Clayborne Carson, for example, resented it when his departmental chairman routinely sent first-year black graduate students to him for advice, whether or not they were working in his specialty.[13]

## Rules of the Game

Although committed to freedom of inquiry and expression, American universities, like other institutions, generated a bureaucracy and culture that encouraged conformity. The standards for evaluating intellectual work and teaching competence were touted as objective, but no one denied that subjective factors played a role. For black scholars specializing in race and ethnic issues, those subjective factors were troublesome. When white peers criticized the quality of their work, were their objections well founded or were they the product of racial bias or of political conservativism? Were an institution's measures of academic merit intellectually defensible, or were they expressions of white or Euro-American privilege, status, and power?

Some black professors, such as Richard Yarborough, accepted these subjective factors as the price of remaining within academia:

I think that as soon as you take a job in any kind of mainstream university, you've got to compromise. The institution's got a tremendous amount of inertia and, beyond that, an institution has mechanisms which are going to work to defend it against threat, against change. When I accepted this job, I knew I would be judged by the standards and values of some people who might consider black literature to be an invalid field to start with. But I also had to ask myself, "If I'm not going to follow those rules and play the game, then why am I here?"[14]

Such talk, of course, was nonsense to the militant activists, who responded that black intellectuals were supposed to lead the assault on biased academic standards. But Clayborne Carson defends, at least in part, the value of intellectual standards:

> There are a number of people I knew in graduate school who were extremely hostile to the whole notion of doing intellectual work and saw their role primarily as political, rather than as a person doing intellectual work that may have an impact on politics, which is a different thing. Intellectual work has to be serious enough to stand the test of time. When you look at the work that came out in the turbulent period, how many of those articles would stand up?[15]

## Stigma

In the 1970s the hiring of blacks for numerous high-status faculty positions triggered a counteraction. From white quarters came cries of double standards and reverse discrimination. But some black intellectuals also criticized affirmative action programs for African Americans in higher education. Thomas Sowell argued that such programs were unnecessary because the civil rights legislation passed in the sixties would in time lead to fair representation in academia. Moreover, he said, they implicitly endorsed lower expectations for African Americans and tainted the accomplishments of the most talented blacks: "If a black kid graduates first in his class at Harvard, he is still going to be thought of as someone who got his degree because of affirmative action."[16] And black professors would be constantly challenged to prove that they were indeed competent and not merely beneficiaries of an unjust system. Sowell also warned that white competitors for high-status positions would resent individuals or groups that seemed to benefit from affirmative action and that this hostility would outweigh any temporary benefits to black competitors.

Aligned against Sowell, supporters of affirmative action questioned his assumption that university officials would see the error of their ways and now conform to the letter and spirit of the antidiscrimination laws. John Hope Franklin contended, "Quotas existed long before affirmative action, but the figure for blacks was zero."[17]

Critics of affirmative action who worried that preferential policies would lower the self-esteem of blacks and women had never spoken about the other side of the coin. For generations white southern males rarely had to compete with blacks or women. Actual laws and sexist customs had seen to that. Yet the outpouring of literature by white southern writers and scholars contained no titles like "Reflections of a Racial Privilege Product."

Most black scholars were unaffected by the imputations of inferiority. Supportive families and other social networks had, over time, provided them a sense of their self-worth. It mattered little that some whites resented their success and attributed it to affirmative action. Nell Irvin Painter expressed consternation, not self-doubt, when an unemployed white male doctorate holder implied that she owed her appointment at the University of Pennsylvania in 1979 to her race and her gender:

> I never questioned the justice of my position. I should have a job, a good one. I had worked as a graduate student and had written a decent dissertation. I knew foreign languages, had travelled widely and had taught and published. I thought I had been hired because I was a promising young historian. Unlike the man beside me, I didn't think my teaching at a first-rate university required an extraordinary explanation.[18]

While some black scholars ignored racial stigmatizing and others responded assertively, still others, like Norris Johnson, an anthropologist at the University of North Carolina, brooded: "Sometimes I get nauseated just coming onto the campus. I feel I am suspect. Sometimes you can see the contempt on students' faces. They just watch you, to see if you can speak coherently."[19]

Having confronted and countered racial stigmatization, some successful black scholars grew in status at elite institutions. Fearful that the presence of black colleagues with less than exceptional qualifications would reflect negatively on their own status, they enforced existing standards with a vengeance. Troy Duster laments this "gatekeeping" mentality:

When it comes to assessing other blacks, there is a certain type of "eye of the needle" black professor in the academy who always shows that he or she has only the highest of standards. All of us have met and argued with this type, perhaps because there is a little bit of that in all of us [black professors] as we argue with ourselves. Is there room for the mediocre black graduate student? Is there room for the average or mediocre black professor? For this type, to which I refer, the answer, in practice, is unequivocally *no!* To put it another way, when evaluating the files of prospective black candidates, one becomes Branch Rickey looking for Jackie Robinson.[20]

Whites could afford to be simply satisfactory scholars, but African Americans had to be brilliant.

Complicating the outlook for black scholars was the historical notion that talented blacks had a special responsibility to be paragons of the race. J. Saunders Redding, who grew up in an achievement-oriented family in Wilmington, Delaware, in the 1920s, recalled his father's admonitions when he was about to leave home to attend an integrated university:

Son, remember you're a Negro. You'll have to do twice as much better than your classmates. Before you act, think how what you do may reflect on other Negroes. Those white people will be judging the race by you. Don't let the race down, son. . . . Out East you may feel it less because there're fewer Negroes, or for the same reason, you may feel it more. Some say one thing, some the other. But no matter where you go in this country, you'll never get away from being made to know that you are a Negro. . . . A Negro's just as good as anybody else, but he's always got to prove it.[21]

Redding added, "Thus burdened, I went off to college."

## Standards and Realities

Some black students who headed for prestigious universities in the seventies arrived academically unprepared and at a distinct disadvantage. How were sympathetic black professors to treat them? Ronald Taylor wrestled with this question at the University of Connecticut:

> I have vacillated in my thinking about my responsibility toward black students once they are enrolled in this university. The problem has given me some difficulty. I've resolved it in this way: I decided that I cannot take fully into account where these students come from. Because by doing that I am then caused to treat them in a way that cannot be helpful to them in the final analysis.[22]

The problem, he noted, was institutional and had both moral and political dimensions:

> On one hand, I am aware of the conditions that affect a great many black students and, on the other hand, I have to take a somewhat different attitude when it comes to classroom performance. But that is related to the circumstances under which black students are recruited, which is another source of consternation to me, especially at this school. My feeling is that the university tends to act dishonestly when it recruits students that it is just not prepared to train or educate adequately . . . that it accepts no such recruitment for white students. It seems dishonest and immoral to do that, to recruit black students with some different basis. That has been again another source of inconsistent and schizophrenic behavior on my part. I have not always known what position to take.[23]

## Black Studies and Intellectual Problems

Through the mid-1960s the study of black America hardly ever appeared in a university curriculum. Individual scholars could be found at several schools: Kenneth Stampp, Leon Litwack, Lawrence Levine, and Winthrop Jordan at Berkeley, C. Vann Woodward at Yale, and Thomas Pettigrew at Harvard. But there were no research units or degree-granting departments. Large universities employed dozens of specialists in European studies but rarely hired anyone who specialized in African American or African history.

Early on, black students called for courses on the black experience. Black studies advocates proclaimed that the invisibility of blacks in the curricula was not inadvertent but part of a design to minimize the contributions of blacks to American society. Black studies, they asserted, would help redress that imbalance.

Many universities accepted the legitimacy of this call but reported difficulty in finding credentialed and able instructors. This insistence on academic credentials was perceived by student activists as a ploy. To them, white authorities' concerns about academic standards seemed irrelevant; in fact, they were symptoms of the very problem that needed redress. Nathan Hare, the black sociologist hired to head the black studies department at San Francisco State, agreed with the students: "[The universities] would rather have a white moderate professor with a Ph.D. teaching a history sequence starkly barren of blackness than a black man without a degree who has spent long hours in research on the subject."[24]

The demand for more courses soon turned into a call for independent black studies departments. Activists like Michael Thelwell demanded "autonomous" departments, claiming that autonomy was necessary to put the unit beyond the control of hostile white administrators and faculty. Fearful of co-optation, Thelwell insisted that "the program had to be free of domination, control, and influence, overt or covert, from and by whites."[25] Unencumbered by traditional academic requirements, these units could design curricula that would better serve black students and, by extension, all black Americans. Supporters doubted that the educational objectives of black studies could be achieved in previously existing departments. Bold symbolic actions and dramatic departures from the status quo carried the day.

Students also lobbied for black professors in the new departments. A plausible case was made for the experiential value of blacks researching and teaching black culture. Some advocates, however, drifted into the epistemologically dubious posture of insisting that no whites could understand—and hence research or teach—material on blacks. Few went this far—they knew that such scholars as Kenneth Stampp, Louis Harlan, Robert Hemenway, and Eugene Genovese had offered important insights into the world of black Americans. But opponents of black studies, recognizing how the students' argument discredited the movement, pounced on this contention in their critiques of black studies.

Robert Merton attacked what he called the "extreme insider" position, "the principle that particular groups in each moment of history have monopolistic access to particular kinds of knowledge."[26] Scholars rushed to agree with Merton. Less quoted was Merton's acknowledgment that "there is a *tendency for, not a full determination of,* socially patterned differences in the perspectives, preferences and behavior of people variously located in the social structure" (emphasis in original).[27] That is, experience in black culture often produced a heightened and nuanced sensitivity that outsiders lacked.

Paralleling the claims about the advantages of "insiders" was the contention that "outsiders" had certain advantages in analyzing social phenomena. The belief that outsiders, presumably unaffected by the interests and sentiments of a culture, could recognize things often unnoticed by indigenous observers, was a fixture in American social thought. The two most famous examples are *Democracy in America* (1835), by Alexis de Tocqueville, and Gunnar Myrdal's *An American Dilemma* (1944). Indeed, this "outsider knows best" theme had influenced the Carnegie Corporation to select Myrdal, a Swedish sociologist, to study American race relations. Some critics complained that Myrdal's analyses suffered from his unfamiliarity with American culture. To his credit, Myrdal had recognized the value of insider perspectives and had hired E. Franklin Frazier, Ralph Bunche, and Abram Harris to research and write several sections of the book.[28] But many black thinkers conceded no interpretative advantage to outsiders.

Another controversial demand arose: blacks insisted that university programs assign a prominent role to community involvement and service. To traditionalists, black and white, community action strayed from the proper mission of a university. Why should the university impose on students' time and energy in this new way? John Blassingame, a historian who was a key actor in the development of black studies at Yale University in the 1970s, bluntly asked,

Are contemporary students that different from those of my own generation? Do they really have that much time after studying?

In many cases investigation has shown that at the same time that students demand more community action programs, they rarely participate in those that the colleges have already established.[29]

Militants and their sympathizers responded that the university was not value free or detached from social and political interests. Universities and faculty members had, through research and development, contributed to the U.S. involvement in the Vietnam War, and had directly and indirectly buttressed the interests of powerful corporations. Community programs, utilizing students, would offer a minor and symbolic counterbalance to academia's connections with establishment interests.

Hundreds of colleges responded to the call for black studies programs. By 1991 over 250 of America's 2,100 four-year institutions had established some type of black studies program.[30]

Fashioned hastily and under pressure, these programs sometimes hired academically marginal people to direct or teach in them. John Blassingame complained, "It is clear that Urban League officials and local black preachers are not, in very many cases, prepared to teach the college-level courses in black studies that they have been assigned." He charged that "in many cases predominantly white schools have deliberately organized ill-conceived programs because they are intended solely for Negro students. In short, a number of institutions are not seriously committed to Afro-American Studies."[31] Frequently black students themselves, seeing the value of intellectual rigor in the new undertakings, functioned as checks against the academic capitulations of university officials. A black student at Yale in 1969 made a persuasive case:

> Traditionally any white person who did a minimum amount of research could pass as an authority on black America, and so could any black man for that matter. You didn't have to do any real research; you didn't really have to examine what you were saying. What we're calling for now is for people to do some really intensive reflection about what black America is, and what our role in America has been, what we've done, and so forth. That's rigor, and that means a lot of people who have passed for authorities will be severely questioned.[32]

Indeed, few deans responsibly shepherded the growth of black studies; most cynically allowed inexperienced black studies advocates just enough latitude to ensure that the programs would collapse under the weight of impossible expectations.

The existing tension between energetic black students and seasoned black intellectuals also hindered the development of academically solid programs. While the impetus for black studies came from students, such departments were endorsed by such black scholars as St. Clair Drake, Harold Cruse, and Vincent Harding. These intellectuals envisioned programs seriously committed to sound scholarship. In many instances the advice of such supporters of black studies was ignored both by students, who cared little for their ideas, and by administrators, who were not about to provide financial support for major projects. Because the senior black intellectuals posed no threat to institutional calm, their arguments to students and to officials for rigorous academic grounding and adequate financial support were usually ignored. These scholars had little choice but to retreat and apprehensively await the outcome of campus upheavals. White intellectual sympathizers were also marginalized by black students who believed that the involvement of whites would detract from the symbolism of black studies.

Under fire from student activists, universities responded to political threats rather than to the intellectual challenge posed by the idea of black studies. By focusing the dialogue on students' politically symbolic demands, administrators effectively subverted discussion of the more fundamental challenges that black studies posed to the organization of knowledge in the academy

Shorn of rhetoric, black studies represented an integrative approach to knowledge about black people in American life. Traditionalists argued that existing departmental structures could accommodate the academic thrust of black studies. But questions like "How was African American culture influenced by slavery?" did not conform to existing disciplinary boundaries. Was discourse on this topic to be guided by the discipline of history, anthropology, psychology, or folklore? What of the economic and linguistic dimensions? Such an obviously interdisciplinary topic could best be investigated by a team of rigorous scholars and teachers who shared an academic interest in black life and recognized the value of collegial interaction and coordination. The permeability of disciplinary boundaries in modern scholarship within the social sciences, humanities, and natural sciences had already been widely accepted. The next step was to establish interdisciplinary departments—black studies, American studies, women's studies, environmental studies.

Many issues were oversimplified or ignored by the activist students who insisted on "complete autonomy," an all-black faculty, and a politically uniform orientation. Critics carefully publicized, then attacked, extremists in the black studies movement and thus avoided the more seminal implications of the black studies idea. Yet it seems fair to ask whether universities would have paid attention to more moderate arguments. For years pioneers like Benjamin Quarles, John Hope Franklin, J. Saunders Redding, Rayford Logan, and St. Clair Drake had articulated the need for more and better scholarship on black Americans. But it was the clamor of nineteen- and twenty-year-old black students that brought results. The black nationalist poet, playwright, and activist Amiri Baraka, who taught in several black studies departments in the sixties and seventies, contrasted the achievements of the two groups:

> The inclusion of Black Studies on these campuses came only as a result of student struggles, and if some of the rhetoric which accompanied these struggles was overblown, even metaphysical and idealistic, the revolutionary core of those struggles was correct. Black Studies would not yet be on these campuses, nor will it remain, if it had to depend solely on the efforts of Redding-type intellectuals and their pleas for "moral uplift" among the bourgeoisie. Black Studies came only as a result of struggle and confrontation.[33]

Eventually many of the seventies programs buckled under the weight of addressing so many concerns all at once. In addition to teaching students of all races about black life, programs undertook responsibility for increasing the self-esteem of black students, solving the social problems of the local black community, liberating oppressed blacks throughout the diaspora, serving as a political base for black interests on campus, and fulfilling as many other "objectives" as well-meaning students cared to add. Institutions like Yale,

Ohio State University, Harvard, and the University of California at Berkeley, however, weathered the excesses of the early seventies and achieved a degree of stability and success in advancing scholarship, some traditional, some innovative, concerning African Americans.

## Competition Within

During the 1970s higher education contracted, and competition for the fewer and fewer slots in colleges, professional schools, and university faculties intensified. Affirmative action and other preference policies were challenged as unconstitutional. Whereas black faculty in the early seventies had to decide how they would function on campuses, they now had again to worry about access. Appropriating the rhetoric of the early civil rights movement, critics called for a color-blind society in which individuals, not groups, would be evaluated on the basis of prevailing ideas about merit.

In a lawsuit filed in 1974 against the University of California at Davis Medical School, Allan Bakke charged that the institution's admissions policies were unconstitutional, that absent the special admissions program established for racial minorities, he would have been admitted to Davis's medical school. In October 1977 the case was argued before the United States Supreme Court. Seven Jewish organizations and several other associations representing white ethnics filed amici briefs on Bakke's behalf. In June 1978 the Supreme Court ruled that the UC Davis policy was unconstitutional.[34] But the majority opinion stated that admissions policies in which race was only one of several factors were constitutional.

The *Bakke* case placed Jews in an anomalous position. In the twenties and thirties a high proportion of Jews had populated leftist organizations and movements that called for expanded rights for blacks. During the sixties organized Jewish groups unhesitatingly denounced the exclusion of blacks from voter rolls, discrimination in public accommodations, and segregated housing and schools in the South. Many of the northern college students who had traveled South to assist with black voter registration and direct action protest activities were Jewish. Groups like the American Jewish Congress and the American Jewish Committee, recognizing the relevance of antidiscriminatory policies for Jewish Americans, had aided the struggle throughout the South. Thus, when Jewish organizations sided with Bakke, many black intellectuals felt betrayed.

Organizations representing Italians and Poles had also supported Bakke, but black intellectuals and mainstream culture focused on the black-Jewish tension. The spectacle of these two minority groups at odds on civil rights attracted popular commentary and media attention. At the bottom of this opposition lay different histories.

## Different Realities, Different Paths

Unlike blacks, Jews were never formally discriminated against in the nation's elementary and secondary public schools.[35] Jewish families pushed education for their children, believing that academic success would make their lives much easier. First-generation factory workers were determined that their offspring would not have to endure grinding manual labor.[36] Along with youths from other white ethnic groups, talented Jews became acculturated and moved up like other hardworking white immigrants during the early twentieth century. Colleges and universities, particularly in eastern cities, where most Jews lived, became the next beachhead for aspiring intellectuals. Growing numbers of Jewish students made their way to elite institutions and, despite frequent social snubs, performed well. Nervous about how a preponderance of Jews would negatively affect the upper-class Anglo-American character of their institutions, several prominent private universities limited Jewish enrollment. The percentage of Jews in the student body at Columbia dropped from 40 percent in 1916 to 21 percent in 1918. Harvard and Yale also sharply reduced admissions of Jewish students. However, the quotas imposed by some elite institutions in the Northeast did not spark a national trend. Most universities did not restrict enrollment of Jews. At the same time, though, social discrimination often ran rampant in the student body.[37]

During the first half of the century informal quotas on Jewish professors quietly held, although gradually the need for scholars and experts overrode nativist pressures. Intellectually oriented Jews went in any direction they wished. Decades earlier, Jews had been hired primarily to teach Hebrew or Judaic studies, but their movement into more secular academic fields in the 1920s was unimpeded. Of course, bigotry occasionally surfaced. Lionel Trilling, the first Jew hired by Columbia University's English department, was encouraged by his chairman in 1936 to move on because Trilling was "a Freudian, a Marxist, and a Jew." But soon after World War II, according to Lewis Feuer, "the barriers against Jews in the university world were dismantled almost completely."[38]

Most Jewish intellectuals eagerly advocated traditional meritocratic principles. Stephen Steinberg has explained, "The meritocracy benefitted Jews because they had the economic and educational prerequisites to compete for scarce places at all levels of higher education."[39] In contrast, a pattern of formal and race-based discrimination against blacks at all levels had made arguments about merit irrelevant.

Having gained access to prestigious institutions, Jews in the sixties were worried (with justification) that group preferences would reduce their opportunities. But blacks, traditionally excluded, reasoned that any preference that included them was a positive and necessary first step. After all, considerations of merit had not kept Alain Locke, Ernest Just, and John Hope Franklin from the faculties of major American universities—racial discrimination had. Whereas educated Jews were advancing in the academic world because of their merit, blacks were barred because of their color.

In the post–World War II period, the disparity between Jews and blacks in academic life, medicine, and law continued to increase. Arthur Goren calculated that "by 1970 over 10 percent of American professors were Jewish and in the most prestigious universities that proportion reached 30 percent."[40] Blacks, a much larger population group, held less than 2 percent of the university faculty appointments, and many of those appointments were at the historically black colleges. During the civil rights movement, with its emphasis on outlawing racially exclusionary and discriminatory policies, the group interests of Jewish Americans were well served by the visible and vocal leadership of African Americans. Indeed, black activism allowed Jews to assume a supportive but less confrontational role on matters of human rights. According to Bernard Rosenberg and Irving Howe, such a dynamic had long prevailed:

The American Negroes have served as a kind of buffer for American Jews. So long as deep-seated natural resentments and hatreds were taken out primarily on blacks, they were less likely to be taken out on Jews. If Jews have been the great obsession of Christianity, blacks have been the great obsession of America. And as long as this situation obtained, both organized and spontaneous haters in America concentrated on blacks, and only secondarily on Jews.[41]

## Who Gets Heard?

The competition for high-status training and work in the stagnant economy of the 1970s was not the only source of conflict between black and Jewish intellectuals. Blacks often lamented that what Jews said about blacks seemed to carry more authority than comparable work by black scholars. A scholar of black literature opined,

Jewish intellectuals, at least in the academic setting, have for a variety of reasons accepted the role of ethnic spokespersons. Many Jewish intellectuals have made their careers speaking for and interpreting the works of other ethnic groups. And they have been allowed to take that position. Not only by the ethnic groups who up until recently haven't had much to say in the matter, but by mainstream society. WASPs have said, "You are an ethnic group. We will allow you to explain what this black novel means." White Americans will accept the closest thing to themselves, rather than go the step further.[42]

More than hostility toward Jewish scholars, black intellectuals felt resentment toward a wholesale willingness in the United States to accept the authority of others on the black experience. Here was racism. Why was no one asking blacks to offer their special insights into Jewish life?

Black intellectuals doubted that the outsider status of both blacks and Jews gave Jewish intellectuals a special empathy for the black reality. For most blacks, the "whiteness" of Jews defined them more than their Jewishness. Troy Duster reflected on his experience as a college student at Northwestern, where he encountered for the first time the concept of white "ethnicity":

> I had grown up totally immersed in blackness, but when I went to college, for the first time in my life I was around people from all over the world, with all kinds of accents. I found myself making distinctions that I never thought were possible. For example, I got more gentile and Jewish taxonomy in one month than I had gotten in my first seventeen years.
>
> I'd meet Jews, and they'd say, "You know, I'm Jewish." I'd say, "What?" "I'm Jewish, my name is Steinberg, I'm just like you, I'm discriminated against." It struck me how quickly the Jews would come up to me and tell me who I was and who they were, why we had something in common and why we should be friends. I was put off by that and a bit resentful that somebody should presume that they shared this common grievance, and as far as I was concerned they were white.[43]

## Telling the Story

Black scholars, particularly those in the social sciences, wanted to use their training and professional standing to revise the black historical record. Highly sensitive to the bias that had shaped scholarly material about blacks, they saw themselves as "corrective" agents on a mission to set the entire record straight, not just to work on projects of personal interest. Nell Painter suggests why a majority of historians who are black elect to write about race, unlike Jewish historians, who are freer to roam the globe:

> We've had very little choice, given what other historians have written about black people and the racial politics of blackness in the country. There's not an intellectual tradition of Jew-baiting in the way that there has been pernicious scientific racism stigmatizing blacks. Their not having that intellectual burden freed them to do a wider range of things, and that breadth gives them more prestige in the profession.[44]

Black scholars studying race in society frequently found their ideas in conflict with the received wisdom of established authorities, many of them Jewish. Stanley Elkins's *Slavery: A Problem in American Institutional and Intellectual Life* (1959) drew sharp rejoinders from many black scholars for its suggestion that a "sambo" personality was normative among slaves. Nathan Glazer, another Jewish scholar and coauthor of *Beyond the Melting Pot* (1963), had disparaged the idea of a viable black culture. Robert Fogel, coauthor of *Time on the Cross* (1974), tried to demonstrate that slavery was not as harsh and repressive as most historical accounts portrayed it. Insurgent intellectuals challenging established and older peers was nothing new. The overlay of ethnic as well as ideological and generational differences was.

Occasionally an intemperate voice objected to any presence of white or Jewish scholars in black studies. Such claims for racial exclusivity achieved notoriety, but they were rare. In his penetrating book on "objectivity" in the American historical profession, Peter Novick has suggested a difference in the aspects of black history addressed by Jewish and gentile scholars.

> While there are some exceptions to the rule, those who have written the most influential studies of white attitudes and behavior toward blacks were almost all gentiles—David Brion Davis, George Fredrickson, Winthrop Jordan, Morgan Kousser, James McPherson; those who wrote of blacks as subjects, were overwhelmingly Jewish—Ira Berlin, Herbert Gutman, Lawrence Levine, Leon Litwack, George Rawick.[45]

In Novick's opinion the Jewish scholars, though white, prided themselves on "thinking black."

It rankled with some black scholars that while whites were listened to in the milieu of African American studies, blacks were ignored outside of it. Robert Cummings, an Africanist political historian, describes his resentment at being pigeonholed:

> If I start talking about the Arab-Israeli conflict, nobody wants to hear me. I have spent six of the last ten years on the ground researching, studying the problem. Now, intellectually I want to

pursue this issue. But when I stand up, they want me to tell them why Jesse Jackson said so-and-so. I don't know why Jesse Jackson said anything. Because of the racial reality in the minds of whites, I'm not allowed to talk about the Middle East. When they need to quote someone, they quote someone who went there on a two-week trip. He can talk about the hard, substantive matters, but black folks can't. All they think I know is what Jesse Jackson or Andy Young thinks.[46]

Nell Painter concludes that the black studies movement had an unanticipated effect on Jewish intellectuals:

They had played the role of being the intellectuals regarding blacks, having reached the point where they did not feel the need to spend all of their time studying Jewish history. Ironically, one of the things that happened is that the movement of blacks to take over black intellectual concerns has served as a model for Jews to go back and reexamine their own group. There has been a revival of ethnic consciousness among Jews as a result of the black awareness movement of the sixties.[47]

# 11 ⋘

# IMAGINING
# FOR THE PEOPLE

For blacks, describing needs has been a dismal failure
as political activity. It has succeeded only as a literary
achievement.               —PATRICIA WILLIAMS

As a cry for racial justice rang across the United States during the
sixties and early seventies, black artists found themselves in a
strong black mainstream. Black artists had languished for years on
the fringes of American cultural life; now the public was interested
in what they were thinking and doing. Eldridge Cleaver's *Soul on Ice*
(1967) and Alex Haley's *The Autobiography of Malcolm X* (1964)
sold well and prompted vigorous debates in scholarly circles. Charles
Gordone's drama *No Place to Be Somebody,* a sharply etched portrait of American lives confounded by racism, won the Pulitzer Prize
for drama in 1969.

Black activists courted creative artists, reasoning that their work
could and should complement the political goals of the black consciousness movement. The overtures were tentative, however; activists were wary of the artists' ideological unpredictability. Larry Neal,
who spent much of his short life trying to reconcile the roles of artist
and activist, proposed a relationship: "Black Art is the aesthetic and

spiritual sister of the Black Power concept. As such it envisions an art that speaks directly to the needs and aspirations of Black America."[1] Other activists, less egalitarian in framing the relationship, preferred a parent-child analogy, with the parent (politics) defining what the progeny (art) should be. The black nationalist Ron Karenga held that aesthetic concerns had to be subordinated to explicitly political objectives: "All art must reflect and support the Black Power Revolution, and any art that does not discuss and contribute to the revolution is invalid."[2] And proscriptive slogans like Neal's or Karenga's avoided defining their own terms. For example, what *were* "the needs of the black people"? Who decided what constituted the "Black Power Revolution," and who determined what kind of art contributed to it?

This political emphasis elicited both support and criticism from the black creative community. The poet Haki Madhubuti, who changed his name from Don Lee in 1970, established Third World Press and published *We Walk the Way of the New World* (1970), *Dynamite Voices* (1971), and several other collections by black nationalist writers.

No writer symbolized the shift to militant cultural nationalism more than Amiri Baraka. Born in 1934, Baraka grew up as LeRoi Jones in Newark, New Jersey, and in the early fifties attended Howard University, which he described in his autobiography as "the pimple of pretended progress by the 'colored few.'" After a stint in the air force, Jones settled in New York and became a fixture in beat generation poetry circles. Jones received an Obie award for the best off-Broadway play in 1964. *Dutchman,* a scaring account of a subway encounter between a black middle-class man and a white woman, established Jones as one of America's most talented young dramatists. His *Blues People* (1963) was one of the first serious attempts to examine jazz in the context of American culture. By 1973 Jones had changed his name to Imamu Amiri Baraka (translated as "poet / priest," "warrior," "blessing") and in such books as *Home: Social Essays* (1966) and *Black Music* (1968) signaled his break from what he termed decadent white Western values. He urged black artists actively to promote cultural and political liberation. Baraka was contemptuous of writers like James Baldwin who explored individual feelings and downplayed political content in their work.

To the younger generation the tension between aesthetics and politics seemed new, even revolutionary, though decades earlier Langston Hughes, Claude McKay, George Schuyler, Wallace Thurman, and Zora Hurston had wrestled with many of the same questions. Richard Wright, in an essay boldly titled "Blueprint for Negro Writing," had argued in 1937 that the distinctive character of black writing evolved from the writer's acceptance of social responsibility: the duty of the black writer is to "create values by which his race is to struggle to live and die."[3] During the black consciousness period, Wright's relatively moderate ideal was transposed into a more militant key, as in the following lines by Amiri Baraka:

*We want "poems that kill."*
*Assassin poems. Poems that shoot guns.*
*Poems that wrestle cops into alleys*
*and take their weapons leaving them dead*
*with tongues pulled out and sent to Ireland.*[4]

Black literary intellectuals, many recently installed in universities, proposed theoretical and aesthetic justifications for politically saturated black art. Hoyt Fuller, Addison Gayle, and Stephen Henderson placed the new work in the context of broader developments in the culture and the legacy of African American folk traditions. As editor of the magazine *Negro Digest* (renamed *Black World* in 1970), Fuller published fiction, poetry, and critical essays reflecting and justifying a symbiotic relationship between aesthetic values and politics. Gayle edited *The Black Aesthetic* (1971), an anthology of essays that endorsed strengthening the link between art and politics. Most of the contributors called on black artists to demolish, or at least expose, the bias inherent in Western cultural standards. White American aesthetic canons had to be neutralized before a politics beneficial to black people could be created.

Although militant nationalist intellectuals, reinforced by political activists, commandeered national platforms to lecture about the uniqueness of a black cultural vision, other black intellectuals scoffed at the "black aesthetic" rhetoric, at least its more extreme forms. Ralph Ellison saw black aesthetics as reductive: the richness and complexity of African American life could not be exhausted by simple and sterile slogans. Black life in the United States had produced many distinctive cultural products, but rather than emphasize their separateness, Ellison stressed their pervasive influence on American culture. In rejecting the more nationalistic expressions of African American culture, Ellison asserted that the interconnectedness of blacks and whites in mass society made impossible the development of an autonomous "American Negro culture":

> It must, however, be pointed out that due to the close links which Negro Americans have with the rest of the nation these cultural expressions are constantly influencing the larger body of American culture and are in turn influenced by them. Nor should the existence of a specifically "Negro" idiom in any way be confused with the vague, racist terms "white culture" or "black culture"; rather it is a matter of diversity within unity.[5]

Ellison's notions of cultural pluralism and symbiosis annoyed the separatist nationalists and, at least on one occasion, puzzled some white intellectuals. When Ellison rejected the assimilationist thinking of some panelists at a 1965 conference of the American Academy of Arts and Sciences, he argued that blacks would and should fight to retain features of their subculture. Another panelist pressed him, claiming that Ellison's plea for the Americanization of all groups contradicted his strong commitment to the black subculture. Ellison retorted, "I defend the subculture, because I have to work out of it, because it is precious to me, because I believe it is a vital contributing part of the total culture."[6]

Albert Murray agreed with Ellison. In *The Omni-Americans* (1970) he argued that American blacks were the quintessential shapers of American culture. Like Ellison, he charged sociologists and politicians with corrupting the originality and vitality of black ethnic culture, reducing the richness to a few problematic political points. In truth, Murray said, "ethnic differences are the very essence of cultural diversity and national creativity."[7] Moreover, the diversity of the black population in the United States rendered moot the ethnic cultural cohesion and solidarity premised by black nationalist rhetoric. And though references to blues and jazz appeared often in the writings of black cultural nationalists, Murray accused them of being blind to the very essence of the blues and jazz tradition.

> So far, incredible as it may be, no Negro leader has made political use of the so-called survival techniques and idiomatic equipment for living that the blues tradition had partly evolved in response to slavery and oppression. Even more incredible is the fact that most Negro leaders, spokesmen and social technicians seem singularly unaware of the possibility of doing so.[8]

Murray was referring to the improvisational mind-set so fundamental to jazz. Rather than marching lockstep with ideologies and dogma, he implied that African Americans should keep their options open and respond creatively to changing conditions.

The disputes between the black nationalists and such figures as Ellison and Murray were fundamentally political and perhaps generational. Intellectually, the positions were not as far apart as some assumed. Ellison and Murray both wrote essays skewering various staples of the American cultural menu. Certainly Ellison's opinions about the limitations of writers like Faulkner in addressing race squared with the polemics of the activists. Ellison's intellectual thrust and parry, however, was eclipsed by the more strident formulations of nationalist activists and intellectuals.

Black culture had developed over centuries of what Nathan Huggins, the historian and former head of Afro-American studies at Harvard, called Afro-Americanization, and contact with American values and institutions had irreparably modified cultural forms that may at one point have been distinctively African.[9] By selecting elements from their ethnic province and filtering them through the dominant culture, African Americans had in many instances created something new.

The more assertive promoters of "the black aesthetic" did not believe that it was particularly important to define the construct. Larry Neal insisted, "There is no need to establish a black aesthetic. Rather it is important to understand that one already exists. The question is: where does it exist? And what do we do with it?"[10] Langston Hughes and Richard Wright had argued earlier that models for black literature should be based on blues and folklore. However, as Jennifer Jordan noted, the artistic wellspring of folk culture was distant from the experience of the urban black middle class.[11]

Old debates were being revisited. In 1926 George Schuyler had ridiculed as "hokum" the claim of Langston Hughes and other black creative artists that the art of black Americans was distinctive. Schuyler scoffed, "As for the literature, painting, and sculpture of Aframericans—such as there is—it is identical in kind with the literature, painting, and sculpture of white Americans: that is, it shows more or less evidence of European influence." The allegedly shared circumstances of African Americans had not led to a distinctive aesthetic or perspective, Schuyler continued, and social class and economic background determined cultural predilections more than race did: "In the homes of the black and white Americans of the same cultural and economic level one finds similar furniture, literature, and conversation. How, then, can the black American be expected to produce art and literature dissimilar to that of the white American?"[12] Schuyler ignored the fact that many artists, convinced of the superiority of European standards, consciously imitated white art. During the 1920s important black intellectuals were not inclined to discount the opinions of the white critical establishment. Frequently, the promoters of black creative artists leaned on the opinion of white critics, because only their imprimatur meant anything in the high councils of culture. During the Harlem Renaissance, Charles Johnson and W. E. B. Du Bois strategically included white judges on panels for their black literary competitions, in hopes that white approval would add luster to black achievements. As long as black thinkers and creative artists felt it necessary to view their work through the lens of prevailing culture, creative possibilities remained limited.

No real victors had emerged from the controversy about black art in the 1920s. Individual black writers and other creative artists continued to draw on their experiences to produce a range of work that mirrored their diversity. In 1968 Saunders Redding, responding to a journal's inquiry about the existence of a black aesthetic, rejected the concept. Redding argued that "aesthetics has no racial, national or geographical boundaries. Beauty and truth, the principal components of aesthetics, are universal."[13] Redding's position on absolute standards of truth and beauty sidesteps the ways in which both standards are socially constructed. Robert Hayden, the winner of the Grand Prize for Poetry at the 1965 First World Festival of Negro Arts, in Senegal, also rejected the idea of a black aesthetic and testily asked, "Isn't the so called 'black aesthetic' simply protest and racist propaganda in a new guise?"[14]

## The Search for Standards

The mainstream cultural establishment followed with keen interest the debate about the nature of the black aesthetic. If black artists were reflecting sensibilities significantly different from white sensibilities, then white establishment critics would lose currency.

In 1968 Richard Gilman, a reviewer for the *New Republic*, announced his unsuitability as a white critic to pass judgment on such works as *Soul on Ice* or *The Autobiography of Malcolm X*. The more political black authors, he wrote, "take their blackness not as a starting point for literature or thought and not as a marshaling ground for a position in the parade of national images and forms, but as absolute theme and necessity."[15] Given these intentions, which made the traditional imperatives of literary criticism irrelevant in his eyes, Gilman appealed to white intellectuals to agree to the following proposition:

> It would be better for all of us if we recognized that in the present phase of interracial existence in America moral and intellectual "truths" have not the same reality for Negroes and whites, and that even to write is, for many Negroes, a particular act within the fact of their Negritude, and not the independent, universal "luxury" work we at least partly and ideally conceive it to be.[16]

Gilman's manifesto provoked a barrage of criticism from white intellectuals. How dare he impugn their authority to speak about certain kinds of black writing! Their standards and criteria were surely universal and applicable to all creative work. Gilman pondered these reactions and later wrote,

In all the letters I received from white readers there was evident an anxiety, which mostly expressed itself as anger, over the threat I had posed, or revealed, to tradition, to the ways in which judgments have always been made and so to the very principle of judgment, or criticism, as that which allows us to distinguish for the militant purposes of our culture among the multifarious phenomena that minds and imagination are constantly throwing up.[17]

Opponents of Gilman's thesis rallied. Ethnic particularism in artistic standards opened the door of relativism, they claimed, and invited anarchic demands for all sorts of special pleadings.

Calling black literature "our mutual estate," Theodore Gross contended that black literature was merely an offspring of white Western culture and therefore was fully within the comprehension of white intellectuals:

Every important Negro writer, including Malcolm X and Eldridge Cleaver, has been intellectually shaped by a white western tradition. So long as he builds his experiences upon a white western intellectual tradition, the Negro author speaks to whites intellectually; and he speaks to Negroes intellectually and empirically.[18]

Ralph Ellison had earlier rejected the axiom that whites could not understand black cultural forms, but he qualified his rejection: "I think there are certain things that are accrued over so many years and which are so subtle that no outsider can take them on. But if there is anything viable about expression and cultural or artistic form, it is available to all the people who will pay their dues."[19] Many members of the white critical establishment resisted any suggestion that they had to "pay their dues." Critics with national reputations were not novices in need of schooling in their craft. Their training, credentials, power, and status confirmed in their own minds that their standards and judgments were universal, not parochial. Ishmael Reed agreed—with savage irony: "After all, in this country Art is what White people do."[20]

Gilman's contentions paralleled arguments made by Harold Cruse in *The Crisis of the Negro Intellectual* (1967). Cruse took black intellectuals to task for having failed to articulate artistic standards and criteria that were based on African American experience. Work produced to satisfy white critical norms, he warned, would never fulfill the promise of a vibrant and original ethnic art.[21]

Most black artists saw the point as moot. Alice Walker, for example, wrote of her joy and exhilaration in devouring the work of Dostoevsky, Tolstoy, and Turgenev and acknowledged that white southern writers like Flannery O'Connor and William Faulkner had helped her, a daughter of the South, find and develop her literary voice.[22] In John Wideman's complementary view, the standards of the American establishment were troublesome only when they were not applied fairly to black writers.[23] The question of who decided what was "fair" was not answered.

Such writers as Walker, Albert Murray, and Ernest Gaines took it for granted that their work was shaped by their experiences as blacks. They insisted on the legitimacy of values and aesthetics that emanated from the black group. In their minds the cultural distinctiveness of their work did not represent an impenetrable barrier to readers who were not African American. But most doubted that the white critical establishment was sufficiently free of cultural prejudice to approach black art on its own terms. In Robert Merton's terms, these black artists claimed "insider" status within black culture, asserting that their work embodied nuances and perspectives that were often not understood by outsider (white) critics.[24]

Black creative artists and intellectuals also observed how entrenched cultural forces, and society itself, prevented the emergence of distinctly ethnic criteria. Those persons, white or black, who rose to positions of authority in the literary establishment had been trained at mainstream institutions to apply the critical methods of the dominant culture. Works outside the dominant norms ran the risk of being misunderstood, or worse, ignored. Nathan Huggins described the labyrinth of self-doubt from which some black artists could not escape:

> The black artist had to convince himself that he had something to say worth saying, and that he had the skill to say it well; then

he had to defy the white eyes which were often his eyes as well. Such doubt, however, takes a heavy toll from the traveler. For what is art and beauty, after all, except what other men have applauded? And the world will only salute you, one thinks, when those who make judgments and pronouncements discover you. The more profound one's doubt, the more his work is likely to be recognizable echoes or reflections of past greats.[25]

Adrienne Kennedy, the award-winning playwright, came to understand the importance of strong support from cultural and intellectual insiders. Reflecting on her early attempts to have her work published and taken seriously, she acknowledges the significance of a high-profile "sponsor."

I had written *Funny House of a Negro* and sent it to Ralph Ellison and a lot of other people. They said, "Well you're talented, but" ... whatever. I decided to take a course at New York City's Circle in the Square. Edward Albee was teaching the course. I was the only black person in the class and one of only two women. Paddy Chayefsky and Rod Serling were the rage then, and all the guys would try to write like them. My play was done at the end, and the class read it and said it wasn't any good. Albee was gay and very sophisticated. He understood what it was to be an outsider and didn't look at my play with the prejudice that others did. When he said my poetry was as good as Dylan Thomas's, the class got very angry. Well, Albee had a very caustic tongue, and he would not let them dismiss my play. He insisted that the play be done at Actors Studio that week. When your play was presented at the studio, you just sat there, while New York playwrights, actors, and directors criticized it. They started in on the play, saying it was terrible. But Albee, who had taken a seat in the front row said some of the lines in *Funny House* were as good as T. S. Eliot's *Wasteland*. He attacked them for not understanding my metaphors and imagery. He made them feel like idiots. When he insulted someone, it took them weeks to recover. They revered him, but they were more afraid of him. On the spot, he almost forced Molly Kazan to make me a member of the Playwrights Union. There is no way I could have gotten into that exclusive little literary world without his support and callous temperament. It's too strange not to be true, isn't it? [Laughing][26]

The need for a valid and relevant standard of criticism had similarly troubled Romare Bearden in the 1930s. Disappointed at the lack of originality in the work of black visual artists, Bearden attributed the problem not to an absence of talent but to the absence of informed criticism that would encourage black artists and their audiences: "We need some standard of criticism then, not only to stimulate the artist, but also to raise the cultural level of the people."[27]

In 1971 Darwin Turner, who the following year become a professor of literature at the University of Iowa, renewed the call for more blacks who could provide serious criticism of black cultural works. The ascendancy of trained black critics, whose assumptions and artistic frameworks would differ from those of "outsiders," would free black artists from having to defend their right to make artistic judgments and choices.[28] Turner acknowledged the existence of obstacles to the training and establishing of authoritative critics who were black, but noted that the civil rights movement had opened the doors of elite training centers and that if the blacks entering universities could master the European-based standards, yet retain their African American sensibilities, the problem of relevant criticism would be solved.

The rhetoric of black nationalists had convinced many Americans that black thinkers brought special insights to the assessment of African American cultural products; and yet, refining and formalizing the insights presented a challenge. A body of perceptive black literary critics emerged from the cultural ferment of the seventies well trained in traditional Western criticism. Inspired by the debates about the character and distinctiveness of black aesthetics, they turned their attention to black cultural material as well. Arnold Rampersad, Barbara Christian, Stanley Crouch, Robert O'Mealy, Gerald Early, Trudier Harris, and Henry Louis Gates, among others, expanded the debate about blacks and American culture.[29]

Such critics often advanced new literary interpretations and theories, but no critical unanimity evolved among them. Debates as vigorous as those with the white critical establishment took place within black circles. Ishmael Reed squared off against Baraka; Larry Neal challenged Henry Gates's view of the black arts movement; and some younger writers predictably attacked the older ones, which by this time included Baldwin, Wright, and Langston Hughes.

Once the mode and value of intragroup intellectual scrutiny was established, other issues surfaced. The intellectual ferment surrounding cultural issues expanded beyond the agenda of the nationalist vanguard. Black women intellectuals and writers, in particular, had much to say about a male-dominated black aesthetics movement. Audre Lorde, for example, spoke of what she thought were characteristic differences between how black male and female writers expressed their emotions: "Black male writers tend to cry out in rage as a means of convincing their readers that they too feel, whereas Black women writers tend to dramatize the pain, the love. They don't seem to feel the need to intellectualize this capacity to feel; they focus on describing the pain itself. And love often is pain."[30]

Ignoring the charge of some militants that airing intragroup differences was counterproductive, black women intellectuals pressed the issues and problems that defined and sometimes constricted their reality, including the sexism of black men. Over the next ten years, the hegemony of the early group of militant nationalist writers over the nature and direction of black creative culture was challenged by women, gays, formalists, and multiculturalists, and as well by iconoclasts like Stanley Crouch, the self-proclaimed "hangman" for black literary and political poseurs.[31] Crouch admitted his own complicity in some of the bizarre currents in the sixties ethnic nationalism movement. But in 1990 he declared himself "hostile to its ideas." In the introduction to *Notes of a Hanging Judge*, he wrote,

Where there was not outright foolishness, there was mongering of the maudlin and a base opportunism. Those qualities tainted a good deal of the writing that came out of that period and supported more than a few of the conceptions that many are only now coming to recognize as the self-destructive double standards they always were. What I frankly consider cowardice or intellectual dishonesty among Afro-American intellectuals and commentators allowed for the sustained power of more than a few silly ideas.[32]


## The Avant-garde

A number of black artists ignored the activists who pressed them to address the relations between imaginative work, the character of the black experience, and the activists' political agenda. Rather than mount a frontal attack on political and social oppression, Ishmael Reed and Clarence Major, for example, elected to besiege Western aesthetic ideals. Reed, in particular, saw possibilities in the path of artistic innovation: "You let the social realists go after the flatfoots out there on the beat and we'll go after the Pope and see which action causes a revolution. We are mystical detectives about to make an arrest."[33] The avant-gardists scoffed at traditional notions of form and frequently inverted familiar cultural symbols. Reed challenged those who dismissed the role of literary innovation. "No-one says the novel has to be one thing. It can be anything it wants to be, a vaudeville show, the six o'clock news, the mumblings of wild men saddled by demons."[34] Reed's assault on dominant values, however, baffled many social activists, who sought more familiar weapons of cultural advocacy.

The experimentalists were largely dismissed as aesthetes whose values and ideas had no bearing on social experience. But Larry Neal saw the connection between the creation of radical forms and the social predicament of African Americans: "On one level there is the tendency of the modern artist to seek innovative forms. But in the context of political insurgency, the quest for new forms becomes an aspect of the larger quest for freedom and identity."[35] Charles Wright, Carlene Hatcher Polite, and John Wideman also experimented with writing that challenged conventional ideas about form and narrative.[36] But although rooted firmly in African American culture, their work was ignored in the highly polarized climate of the late sixties.

An experience of Adrienne Kennedy's illustrates the complex broth of avant-gardism, racial sensitivity, and critical acclaim. Growing up in a close-knit African American community in Cleveland, where she did very well in school, Kennedy thought that the path to a conventional black middle-class existence was straightforward: "college, career, comfort." But when she graduated from high school and enrolled at Ohio State University in the early fifties, she collided with racial prejudice and privilege in a way that dramatically affected her imaginative world:

> The white kids in my dorm were really nasty people. They would give parties in the corridor, and they wouldn't invite blacks. For the first time in my life I started to feel lost. It hurt, but what saved the day was that there were still these poor black kids at Ohio State. Their fraternities and sororities saved the day. I became very embittered toward the white world. . . . It's something I have to this day. Maybe it was there all along, but it really flowered at Ohio State. It was like "I'm going to show these people!" By the time I graduated, I was very, very angry. I somehow felt it wasn't enough to wear pretty clothes, join AKA [a black sorority], and go back to Cleveland.

Several years later, Kennedy married and moved to New York City with her husband, a graduate student at Columbia. There she found what she called her vindication:

> In the fifties I took classes at Columbia and managed to write a novel. The professor in one of my classes was the editor of the *Writer,* which was an important magazine in the New York literary world. Anyway, he read my novel and told the class it was a work of genius. I guess this was my first revenge because the class was all white. This was a turning point. People in the class would come up and try and talk to me. If I can be totally frank, they were all white and they looked up to me. I got a lot of gratification out of that. I felt vindicated in a sullen kind of way. The experience was an outlet for my anger. The people in the class were all upper-middle-class whites, and this famous professor had given me a special place in the class. For the first time since elementary school, white people wanted to hear what I had to say. For some reason, I felt I had to have that—their attention when I'm in a winning position.[37]

Like innovators of any hue, the black avant-gardists, because of their complex art and vision, found only a very limited audience. They never enjoyed the popularity of social-realist authors like Lorraine Hansberry, Ed Bullins, or Claude Brown. Instead, they were attacked as dilettantes by those who demanded an art comprehensible and uplifting to the masses—a demand reminiscent of the call for "proletarian literature" by Communists in the thirties. However, the independence and self-confidence of the avant-garde writers enabled them to weather the indifference of the era. By the 1980s a less prescriptive view of art had led many African Americans to new assessments of Reed, Major, and other innovators.

## Jazz's Different Course

Despite the ascent of black writers and critics during the 1960s and 1970s, they did not match the success of black musicians. Not only had black musicians created highly innovative music, but it was invariably they—not professional critics—who defined the day's musical standards. When the music that was to be named bebop was launched in New York by Charlie Parker, Thelonious Monk, Dizzy Gillespie, and Max Roach (all African Americans), mainstream critics were nearly unanimous in disparaging it. But the musicians who came to the clubs along Fifty-second Street in New York recognized the artistry of these musical revolutionaries. Acclaim for bebop swept the country. Mainstream critics had little to do with it. Rather, musicians, insiders who understood the nuances and tradition on which bebop was based, called the tune. Within five years jazz had undergone a virtual revolution.

Of course not everyone was convinced. Louis Armstrong, himself a jazz innovator of an earlier period, ridiculed the music, contending that Charlie Parker was playing the wrong chords.[38] Just as fellow artists are the first to spot innovation, they are also the most strident critics of new work that displeases them: "Wherever there appears an art that is truly new and original, the men who denounce it first and loudest are artists. Obviously because they are the most engaged. No critic, no outraged bourgeois, can match an artist's passion in repudiation."[39] While the critics' outrage may not have matched Armstrong's, many relentlessly attempted to control the criteria that governed innovation. Amiri Baraka (LeRoi Jones) pointed out the divide that separated the innovators from those who tried to interpret and analyze bebop:

> The irony here is that because the majority of jazz critics are white middle-brows, most jazz criticism tends to enforce white middle-brow standards of excellence as criteria for performance of a music that in its most profound manifestations is completely antithetical to such standards; in fact, quite often is in direct reaction against them.[40]

Nor was Jones charitable to the notion that the middle-brow critics could learn to appreciate new music. "Critics are supposed to be people in a position to tell what is of value and what is not, and, hopefully, at the time it first appears. If they are consistently mistaken, what is their value?"[41]

If the mainstream critics had prevailed, bebop would not have strayed from the beaten path. But the support of an indigenous cultural-critical community encouraged creative black jazz musicians to trust their artistic vision. Larry Neal, who revered and respected both black letters and music, ventured to explain why the musicians felt freer to develop their own styles and voices:

> The historical problem of black literature is that it has, in a sense, been perpetually hamstrung by its need to address itself to the question of racism in America. Unlike black music, it has rarely been allowed to exist on its own terms but rather has been utilized as a means of public relations in the struggle for human rights.[42]

In asserting that music is less discursive than literature, Neal was at least half right; but many black writers argued that it was not their preoccupation with race as much as white critics' perceptions that all black writing was at heart about—and only about—black experience that hamstrung them. The problem was not the author's intentions but the critics' jaundiced perceptions. Toni Morrison was convinced that this parochial arrogance precluded a sensitive evaluation of black writing:

Critics generally don't associate black people with ideas. They see marginal people; they see just another story about black folks. There's a notion out in the land that there are human beings that one writes about, and then there are black people or Indians or some other marginal group. If you write about the world from that point of view, somehow it's considered lesser.[43]

## Blackness and the Cultural Marketplace

Black creative artists who emphasized ethnic distinctiveness wondered whether society would accept products of the black imagination. Ralph Ellison was less possessive about black cultural material than most, but he conceded that American society, in appropriating African American idioms, frequently diluted those forms for a mass audience. Wynton Marsalis, an acclaimed young musician and student of American musical culture, lamented the dilution of black musical traditions by commercial interests. He hoped the work of such masters as Louis Armstrong and Duke Ellington would be accepted on their own terms: "I want the public to understand the real significance and beauty of the music, not by watering it down, but by getting to such a place in my art that it will be obvious to all who listen that I'm coming from a great tradition."[44]

Even when black artists garnered critical and popular acceptance, few benefited in ways commensurate with their actual contributions. Ellison, himself an amateur jazz musician, recalled how original art was appropriated in the postwar period.

It was a time of big bands, and the greatest prestige and economic returns were falling outside the Negro community—often to leaders whose popularity grew from the compositions and arrangements of Negroes—to white instrumentalists whose only originality lay in the enterprise with which they rushed to market with some Negro musician's hard-won style.[45]

Too often, successful black creative artists were appreciated only as "natural talents," as though their years of preparation and training had played no part in their originality and genius. Wynton Marsalis used the example of Louis Armstrong to illustrate the patronizing approach of many mainstream critics.

> They think because Louis Armstrong sat back all folksy, that in his mind he didn't *know*. How many times have you heard, "Louis Armstrong was an intuitive genius"? That implies he didn't know he was great, he could just naturally do that. It implies that he was just lucky. But if you're lucky, you can't be consistent. Pops was not an intuitive genius! He knew what he was doing.[46]

Black intellectuals noted that African American artists had contributed generously to the national culture, but that society at large had often not given due credit to the contributors. The mainstream establishment held the power to decide which black cultural elements would be assimilated and disseminated and which would be ignored or attributed to others. By not controlling black cultural products, black intellectuals were leaving the choices to those who would relegate blacks to a subordinate or "entertainment" role.

### New Stages

The passion for genuine cultural democracy that enlivened artistic debates in the sixties and seventies invigorated the next generation of African American intellectuals. Still, history had demonstrated that such democracy could not be achieved without some measure of material support from the black community. Nathan Huggins drew important lessons about black art and white patronage from the Harlem Renaissance; Harold Cruse exposed contradictions between the nationalist objectives of Baraka's Harlem Black Arts Theater and the state support that it relied on in the 1960s.

Early in the nineties the filmmaker Shelton "Spike" Lee, a product of Brooklyn and a graduate of Morehouse College and New York University's Tisch School of the Arts, rekindled the debate about who should interpret black cultural products. After making several relatively low-budget, critically acclaimed films, including *She's Gotta*

*Have It* (1986) and *Do the Right Thing* (1989), Lee proposed to make an epic film on the black nationalist leader Malcolm X. After contentious negotiations, Warner Brothers studio committed $18,000,000 to the making of the film. Lee eventually raised an additional $12,000,000. The total of $30,000,000 was the most ever spent on a black-directed film. When the battle about the amount necessary to film *Malcolm X* was resolved, Lee confronted controversy over the film's content and message. Amiri Baraka publicly chastised the filmmaker for his past films and accused him of planning to make a film that would "make middle-class Negroes" sleep easier.[47] Black intellectuals rallied to Lee's defense, with political and personal attacks on Baraka. Playthell Benjamin, the journalist and essayist, wrote, "Spike Lee, and all artists, must fervently resist any effort to reduce them to nothing more than vehicles for political propaganda."[48] Yet Lee had argued forcefully that a black director had to do the film on Malcolm X, warning that a white director would dilute the message and meaning of his life. Some could argue that this stance was just another variation on the politics-and-art conundrum. Lee himself, however, viewed Baraka's attack as professional jealousy. In an interview with Henry Louis Gates, he dismissed Baraka in these terms:

> I think he looks around today and he's seeing young black people doing stuff, enjoying access to the media, access to the people. I mean, how many people can you reach as a poet or playwright? How many people ever saw *Dutchman?* Ten thousand at the most? How many people saw the movie? I think that gets to him, the fact that we have access to so many people, and we're making money at it.[49]

While Baraka's objections to Lee's film were explicitly political, intellectuals drew together in defense of Lee's artistic freedom. However, August Wilson's insistence on a black director for the filming of one of his works was not so easily dismissed. Wilson, whose plays earned a Tony Award and two Pulitzer Prizes, declared in 1991 that the film version of his play *Fences* (1985) must have a black director. Lloyd Richards of the Yale Drama School had directed the New

York stage version. Now Wilson wanted a director who "shared the cultural responsibilities of the characters." He acknowledged that certain cultural ingredients are shared by all Americans, but held that there are "specific ideas and attitudes that are not shared on the same cultural ground." He explained that he declined a white director "not on the basis of race but on the basis of culture." Staking out a position close to Ellison's and Cruse's, Wilson asserted, "Therein lies the crux of the matter as it relates to Paramount and the film *Fences*—whether we as blacks are going to have control over our own culture and its products."[50]

The importance of African American backing was widely recognized. However, by the mid-eighties, cultural entrepreneurs were chastened by the fact that the much awaited support from the growing black middle class had not yet materialized, and few black institutions were able (or willing) to finance journals and publishing ventures. Even Atlanta University's *Phylon* and Howard University's *Journal of Negro History* appeared irregularly during the 1980s. However, Howard University Press began an ambitious publications program, releasing such titles as *From the Dark Tower* (1981), by Arthur Davis, and *The Wayward and the Seeking: A Collection of Writings by Jean Toomer* (1980), edited by Darwin Turner.

The magazine *Black World* (until 1970, *Negro Digest*), backed by the Johnson Publishing Company, the largest black-owned publishing house in the United States, had featured serious literary work and criticism. But in 1976 the nationalist-oriented monthly folded. The publishers claimed that sales and advertising revenues for *Black World* did not make it solvent. By contrast, the company's other ventures, *Jet* and *Ebony*, geared more toward a mass audience, sailed nicely into the nineties.[51] Lerone Bennett wrote highly informative essays on black history for *Ebony*.

Economic realities prompted black intellectuals to be more flexible in regard to external support. The rigid ideologies and separatist rhetoric of the earlier nationalists were neither feasible nor effective in the politically conservative climate of the eighties. Moreover, black intellectuals were more confident of their ability to build and shape cultural agencies within the context of mainstream institutions.

The feisty and resilient *Black Scholar,* founded in 1970 by Nathan Hare and Robert Chrisman has published scholarly and literary pieces by the likes of Robert Staples, Hortense Spillers, Joyce Ladner, and Harry Edwards. Frequently it has devoted an issue to a theme or controversy in African American life—the January 1976 issue explored "Black Popular Culture" and that of January 1981 high-lighted "Police Violence." In 1992 *Black Scholar* compiled a set of essays about the Clarence Thomas–Anita Hill conflict under the title *Court of Appeal.*

Charles Rowell, an English professor, established the art and literature journal *Callaloo* in Baton Rouge in 1976. In 1985 Rowell moved to the University of Virginia and quickly obtained financial support for *Callaloo* from his new institution. Johns Hopkins University Press began publishing the journal in 1990. *Callaloo* describes itself as "devoted to creative works by and critical studies of black writers in the Americas and Africa. Studies of life and culture in the black world and visual art are also published in *Callaloo.*"

In 1990 Henry Louis Gates and Wole Soyinka played a key role in reviving *Transition,* a journal first published in Uganda in 1961. Oxford University Press supported the venture. Slightly more expansive in its scope, the new *Transition* promises its readers that "though keeping an emphasis on African and African American concerns, the new *Transition* has taken on the world. No idea, thought, person, belief or subject is considered out of bounds."[52]

Also in 1990 Randall Kennedy, a Harvard law professor, launched *Reconstruction.* With substantial funding from the Rockefeller Foundation, the quarterly provides a forum for "commentary on African American politics, society and culture." *Reconstruction* has devoted space to such controversial issues as transracial adoption, race and faculty hiring, the significance of Clarence Thomas's appointment to the Supreme Court, and the 1992 rebellions in Los Angeles.

Since the early seventies the cultural nationalists had been relentless in insisting that black artists address the concrete concerns of the broader black community. Ron Karenga, architect of Kwanza, the now widely celebrated African American holiday, wrote of aesthetics in 1971, "Or in terms of painting, we do not need pictures of oranges in a bowl or trees standing innocently in the midst of a wasteland. If we must paint oranges and trees, let our guerrillas be eating those oranges for strength and using those trees for cover."[53] The idea of artists going about their creative business with no ties to the black masses was attacked as traitorous. Ishmael Reed, who rejected a foot soldier's role in the "black revolution," still wrote and spoke frequently about political issues, and Alice Walker also challenged the racism and sexism in American life.

By the late eighties the nature of the political issues had changed considerably. Influenced by postmodern critiques, several talented black artists and literary critics joined white structuralists in the turn to linguistic and textual analyses. Black postmodern critics of language and form argued that their work was vital because it challenged and deconstructed symbols and canons of the dominant culture. Some, like Henry Louis Gates, entered the national debate about the appropriateness of American canons of literature and of literary criticism. Gates argued convincingly that the texts that constitute the American literary canon are narrow reflections of the country's literary landscape. And women, black, and other nonwhite intellectuals presented impressive reasons for more representation in the curriculum of schools and colleges.[54] Traditionalists including Stanley Crouch, Dinesh D'Souza, and William Bennett objected and characterized the arguments of the multiculturalists as political rather than intellectual. Both sides in the curricular wars recognized that the issue was not purely intellectual; power, jobs, and resources in institutions were involved. But regardless of which side prevailed, the power, jobs, and resources at stake would go primarily to middle-class intellectuals, black and white. Hazel Carby, a literary scholar at Yale, had misgivings about the controversy: "I feel it is appropriate and important to question the disparity between the vigor of the debates about the inclusion of black subjects on a syllabus and the almost total silence about, and utter disregard for, the material conditions of most black people." Carby expressed concern that if multiculturalists succeeded in introducing more black texts into the curriculum of mainstream institutions, these texts would "become fictional substitutes for . . . any sustained social and political relationships with black people in a society that has retained many of its historical practices of apartheid in housing and schooling."[55]

## Literature and the New Individualism

In the late 1980s outstanding African American creative writers and literary critics produced work that stressed the autonomy of imagination. Charles Johnson's *Oxherder's Tale* and Toni Morrison's *Beloved* are two examples. Although black people populated their fiction, drama, and poetry, these writers avoided racial politics and dismissed the notion of "representativeness." Black critics, mindful of past battles, dodged any suggestion of a "common" aesthetic or concern and accepted the artistic variety of the younger writers. Nor was there talk of a black literary "essence." Rejecting as reductionist the conflict and group-based formulations of earlier critics, sophisticated thinkers like Hortense Spillers, Henry Louis Gates, and Jay Edwards mined language and form for elements of individual and cultural style. Somewhat paradoxically, the cosmopolitan perspective and diversity of some younger writers prompted Trey Ellis, author of the experimental novel *Platitudes* (1988), to resurrect the much maligned term *black aesthetic* to capture the essence of their work.

A 1989 essay by Trey Ellis in *Callaloo* sought to define a "New Black Aesthetic."[56] He acknowledged an artistic and political debt to black figures of the sixties, but observed that many young black artists had moved on. According to Ellis, the New Black Aesthetic was less defensive about blackness, leaving black artists free to explore all cultural orbits. Influenced by postmodernism, the black aesthetic purported to transcend any boundaries to the black imagination and to critique representations of black cultural material that evinced arrogance or ignorance.

Younger artists, Ellis stressed, had to reach beyond an ethnic experience and appropriate material from other subcultures. For many in his generation, this approach qualified as new, or at least "neo," though Ishmael Reed had launched the multicultural review *Yardbird Reader* in 1976: "*Yardbird reflects cultural exchange!* A fact of everyday ordinary existence in the complex civilization in which we live. We feel that there are enough Black Worlds, Yellow Worlds, Red Worlds, Brown Worlds, and White Worlds for people who crave that."[57] Ellis described the blending of different cultural perspectives as a type of "cultural mullatoism": "Just as a genetic mulatto is a black person of mixed parents who can often get along fine with his white grandparents, a cultural mulatto, educated by a multi-racial mix of cultures, can also navigate easily in the white world."[58]

Ellis offered a compelling portrait of young cosmopolitan black artists, informed by the collective black past but not shackled by ethnic exclusivism. But the artists whom Ellis identified as purveyors of the New Black Aesthetic—Wynton Marsalis, Lisa Jones, Spike Lee, Reginald Hudlin, Terry McMillan, and Eddie Murphy—displayed no common theme or set of artistic values. Citing age as the sole commonality, one critic derided Ellis's effort as "a false totalizing of a generation of intellectuals."[59]

The art and intellectual work of blacks in the late eighties and early nineties reflected the cosmopolitanism that Ellis had in mind. The harsh urban settings of black writing in the sixties appeared less frequently. Desperate and angry voices, such as those projected by Cleaver, Ron Milner, and Haki Madhubuti gave way to introspective accounts like Jake Lamar's *Bourgeois Blues* (1991) and Lorene Cary's *Black Ice* (1994). No less legitimate than the earlier community-focused work, the new black writing put individuals at the center.

There were, of course, exceptions. Toni Morrison's novels brilliantly illustrated how African American communal and family traditions shaped individual lives. As sophisticated as writers who extolled what was fashionably called their multiculturalism, Morrison kept a sense of African American community at the forefront of her work. In her novels *Beloved* (1987) and *Jazz* (1992), she shared her ideas about how the black cultural traditions and the racial environment in the United States propelled the characters in her books. This concern with social context earned her the critical wrath of Stanley Crouch, who complained that "Morrison rarely gives the impression that her people exist for any other reason except to give a message." Reviewing *Beloved,* Crouch wrote, "As in all protest pulp fiction, everything is locked in its own time, and is ever the result of external social forces. We learn little about the souls of human beings, we are only told what will happen if they are treated very badly. . . . *Beloved* means to prove that Afro-Americans are the result of a cruel determinism."[60] Crouch would rather read less about historical context and more about individual souls. Susan Willis offered a broader, more positive assessment in her discussion of Morrison's intentions in the novel *Tar Baby* (1981):

> The novels may focus on individual characters like Milkman and Jadine, but the salvation of individuals is not the point. Rather, these individuals, struggling to reclaim or redefine themselves, are portrayed as epiphenomenal to community and culture; and it is the strength and continuity of the black cultural heritage as a whole which is at stake and being tested.[61]

# 12 ⋘

# WHAT SHALL I RENDER?

If anything I do, in the way of writing novels or whatever I write, isn't about the village or the community or
about you, then it isn't about anything. I am not interested in indulging myself in some private exercise of the
imagination . . . which is to say yes, the work must be
political.                                    —TONI MORRISON

B Y THE 1980S many black intellectuals had established themselves
on university campuses across the country and navigated their
way into professional conventions, foundations, and other inner
sanctums of the intellectual world. The newcomers were frequently
disappointed to find that their white peers, for all their sophisticated
training, were not the broad-minded, pluralistic intellectuals Karl
Mannheim had described:

> Although they are too differentiated to be regarded as a single
> class, there is, however, one unifying sociological bond between
> all groups of intellectuals, namely, education, which binds them
> together in a striking way. Participation in a common educa-
> tional heritage progressively tends to suppress differences of
> birth, status, profession, and wealth, and to unite the individual
> educated people on the basis of the education they have
> received.[1]

The literature professor Richard Yarborough questions the efficacy of intellectual training in expanding or altering a person's social vision:

> I find that intellectuals have the same biases and racism and prejudices as nonintellectuals; they just justify it in different ways. You can find an intellectual to support every kind of political action there is. Intellectualism is an outlook on life; it is a mode of thinking. As a black professor, I had in graduate school defined it for me: "An intellectual is one whose life is governed by thinking rather than other modes of behavior." You may think much of the time that you are awake, and you are very self-aware about that. That has nothing to do with values, tastes, behavior, politics, or anything else. There were intellectuals in Hitler's Germany who justified what he was doing . . . so I have very little faith in intellectualism per se; it doesn't mean anything.[2]

Interviewed on the campus of Wesleyan University, Clarence Walker, an American historian, cautiously accepts the possibility of a limited communality among intellectuals, based on their disposition and mode of thinking, but adds a caveat:

> I accept the notion that there may be a community of scholars, but then they are driven by social and cultural biases. The only way that wouldn't be so is if we'd all been cloned from the same individual. The fact of a nation with a multi-ethnic body of thinkers seems to ensure competition among interests. In a nation now approaching a great deal of internal crisis because of unresolved economic and political problems, those people whose ideas are going to receive the greatest dissemination are those people closest to power—simply because they, in some ways, will be defending their asses against the people who want to get to where they are. The classic case of this, of course, is our historical allies, the Jews. Their position, being one of the preeminent groups in American academe, is now, it seems to me, one of defending the center against the onslaught of the Left and the Right.[3]

For black thinkers critical of the status quo, gauging the political leanings of whites around them had practical value. They needed to know the possible sources of support or opposition when the inevitable debates over racial inequality sharpened. Some had concluded from the visible support that many American intellectuals gave the 1960s civil rights movement that a consensus existed among serious thinkers in favor of racial justice for blacks. Blacks soon learned differently—that many intellectuals operate comfortably within the prevailing social system and that others have no strong political views one way or another. Troy Duster analyzes the dual function of intellectuals in society:

> Intellectuals are both bulwarks of the established order and the instigators of social change. The order needs people to justify inequalities, and intellectuals can be pretty good at that. And another breed of intellectuals comes along and does the analysis of the nature of social organization and says it's all socially constructed; therefore it all can be reconstructed, and that's threatening. I think intellectuals perform both functions with a vengeance.[4]

Historically, black intellectuals have been asked to engage themselves on behalf of the black community, yet such appeals can create ambivalence. In *On Being a Negro in America* (1951), J. Saunders Redding bemoaned the weight of expectations placed on him by both blacks and whites. Unlike other thinkers, he said, black intellectuals are expected to know about race, to think about race, and to hold themselves up as models for other blacks and as shining exemplars to whites. Bidding farewell to all that, Redding wrote,

> I hope this piece will stand as the epilogue to whatever contribution I have made to the "literature of race." I want to get on to other things. I do not know whether I can make this clear, but the obligations imposed by race on the average educated or talented Negro (if this sounds immodest, it must) are vast and become at last onerous. I am tired of giving up my creative initiative to these demands. I think I am not alone.[5]

Like Frederick Douglass and others before him, Redding saw blackness as just one of many factors shaping his social world. He felt entitled to explore a wider range of ideas and interests. But to refuse the "special" and "onerous" duties that fall to the black intellectual is seen as severing oneself from a tradition with deep historical roots and to put one's identity at risk.

In the first quarter of the twentieth century, some intellectuals resisted the "spokesperson" role, preferring to concentrate on nonracial material—in Ernest Just's case, on theoretical biology. But the Justs were the exceptions. More typical was the career of Alain Locke. Trained at Harvard in the philosophy of values and ethics, Locke was attracted to the writers and artists of the Harlem Renaissance. As a scholar, literary critic, and agent for aspiring black artists, Locke understood and endorsed the symbiotic relationship between the activities of the talented few and the general welfare of the group. "Negro writers must become truer sons of the people, more loyal providers of spiritual bread and less aesthetic wastrels and truants of the streets."[6]

## Power, Influence, and Black Intellectuals

By the 1980s black intellectuals formed a visible, but still marginal, element in American life. The persistence and changing character of white supremacy posed unique problems. Though black intellectuals were pushed or pulled into the foreground of many political and cultural events during the decade, most were wary about assuming explicitly political roles. Scholars like John Hope Franklin valued the traditional independence and nonpartisanship of the intellectual's role. Writing about the dilemmas of African American scholars, Franklin conceded that "the task of remaining calm and objective is indeed a formidable one. . . . This is especially true if the area of his interests touches on the great questions in which he is personally involved as a Negro."[7]

A few voices, however, questioned the wisdom of remaining "above politics": Why should the brightest and best educated hold themselves aloof from the adjudication of social and cultural power?

Many thinkers labored to draw a distinction between influencing power (which is perhaps possible in Franklin's model) and actually assuming power. Like Dostoevsky's protagonist in *Notes from Underground,* some wondered whether intellectuals suffered from "acute consciousness." When faced with a "nasty problem," the intellectual, unlike the man of action,

> succeeds in creating around it so many other nastinesses in the form of doubts and questions, and adds to the one question so many unsettled questions, that there inevitably works up around it a sort of fatal brew, a stinking mess, made up of its doubts, emotions and of the contempt spat upon it by the direction of men of action who stand solemnly about it as judges and arbiters, laughing at it till their healthy sides ache.[8]

In the 1980s Henry Louis Gates expressed the distinction between *doer* and *thinker* in less acerbic terms:

> I saw Khomeini come back from Paris. His return from exile was a very moving thing to behold. I thought he was wrongheaded and extreme. Still, it was very inspiring to see someone who's been in exile come back and take over. . . . You know he killed the giant through the force of an idea. I certainly don't mind being a part of something like that, but I want my role. . . . I'd rather watch it on a hill than be down there cheering the chief, because there are very few moments of which I could ever be an unambiguous part. . . . I think about it too much.[9]

Along with earlier idealists, Gates and many other scholars were interested in political matters, but in contrast to, say, Du Bois and Ralph Bunche, they wanted no part of the anxiety-ridden political process. As W. Russell Ellis, a sociologist, who was a vice-chancellor at Berkeley, observes,

> Some decisions made by people who wield power need more ideas in them—ideas that reflect an understanding of the world that can be used by those who craft policy and those who then turn the policy into rules and regulations. But intellectuals, and

I include myself, shy away from the bottom line. That's why I won't run for office. I get lost in the idea, and then ten people arrive at my door for the adjudication of their multiple struggles for scarce resources.

Intellectuals, he believes, should recognize their proper place:

Intellectuals, to the extent they're any good, are like albatrosses in the Baudelaire poem. You know, they're beautiful in the air but cannot walk worth a damn!* They are not to be trusted with power, because I think typically their route to their status has not been a dues-paying one. Most have not seen what people really have to go through.[10]

Duster seconds these points, in elaborating on the shortcomings of intellectuals when faced with practical and contentious matters.

What people in power have to do is to act; they have to make decisions about how you allocate resources. Now, one can be reflective about it, but the act is an act. And people get categorized and shot, or beaten up, or praised, based on the act, not on their reflection about the act. So when intellectuals take power, what makes them important is their capacity to act and what they do, not their reflections about it. Outside of power, intellectuals are interesting because of the character and the quality of their reflections about power and the social order. Their conceptualizations can provide new ways of thinking about things. You function as a clarifier of ideas and issues. When you assume power, the function changes. The case of Julius Nyerere of Tanzania is a good case in point. If you ask, would I want people in positions of power who are reflective and intellectually inclined, I'd say yes. But I would want something else too—administrative savvy. Intellectuals, at least in this country, have a history of not ever having to deal with the allocation of resources. They often don't understand that you have to make enemies. Once you are in a position of authority, you

* "The Poet shares the fate of this prince of the clouds, who rejoices in the tempest and mocks the archer down below: exiled on earth, an object of scorn, his giant wings impede him as he walks" (from Baudelaire's "The Albatross" [1859]).

are going to make enemies. That's why I don't trust intellectuals. I would not go to a university to pick some intellectual who spends most of his or her time in front of a classroom. They couldn't understand; they would be upset if someone wrote a nasty article in the *New York Times* about them. I would get someone who is reflective about the condition, but understands the need for distance. Not someone who would go sulking off into a corner if someone wrote a nasty editorial about them. I think a lot of my colleagues would dissolve into a mass of nothingness if they had to confront conflicting interests.[11]

## Diversity

Although racial subordination has always affected all African Americans, individual reactions and responses to racial barriers have been far from uniform. Slaves differed in assessing their lives and the world they lived in. Freedom meant different things to them, and they did not agree on the best way to gain it. All black thinkers agreed that slavery and racial discrimination had to be abolished, but the small group of educated blacks who gathered at annual conventions in the nineteenth century debated issues like black violence against slaveholders and the suitability of racially separate institutions. While Frederick Douglass urged blacks to fight for human rights in the United States, John Russwurm concluded that the situation in America was hopeless for blacks, that blacks should emigrate and build a viable nation on the African continent.[12] Within the small group of educated blacks, none was reluctant to attack the ideas (and often the motives) of those who held different views about the most effective means of achieving and exercising liberty and freedom.

After Emancipation, blacks clashed over the next phase of social development. In the first quarter of the twentieth century, the Garvey movement and the NAACP offered different agendas to the black community.[13] One cultural anthropologist has argued that most of the intellectual discourse was between self-described vanguards like Washington and Du Bois who were jockeying to lead the less educated masses. "Mutualist" approaches (like the Garvey movement) evolved out of contact and cooperation with all strata in the black community and occasionally competed with the vanguardist approaches.[14]

The 1920s brought more vigorous debate among black intellectuals. Indeed, it has been suggested that much of the vitality of the Harlem Renaissance flowed from the clash of ideas.[15] Creative artists chose sides and replayed and recast ancient arguments about the role of art and artists in society, the nature of criticism, and the place of folk traditions in modern and industrialized societies. Writers and scholars argued about goals, tactics, and values. Overall, the specter of a hostile white establishment tended to forge a confederacy of black opinion about racial issues. No matter how vigorously Alain Locke and Claude McKay debated the relation of art to politics, both knew that there were millionaires, senators, newspaper publishers, labor leaders, and presidents who wanted blacks to remain only partly free.[16]

In the fifties and sixties the civil rights movement stirred up black intellectuals. Few disputed the fundamental goals of nondiscrimination and greater opportunities for blacks, but differences about emphases and tactics quickly surfaced. In part these differences reflected the increasingly varied social experiences among black intellectuals. Once the antidiscrimination laws were passed in the mid-sixties, no single issue remained to mobilize the black intellectual community as a whole. Because liberals had been their strongest allies in the battle against discrimination, most black thinkers remained loyal to the liberal sector of the political spectrum, despite their frustration with the timidity and unreliability of the liberal camp. But several thoughtful and combative blacks rejected liberal ideology and championed social and economic conservatism as the best hope for black freedom, justice, and equality in the post–civil rights period. No person was more involved in stimulating intragroup dialogue about American social policy during the seventies than Thomas Sowell.

## Sowell: A Different Drummer

Thomas Sowell was born in Gastonia, North Carolina, and grew up in the Harlem of the 1950s. Although an excellent student in high school, he dropped out in the tenth grade to help his family. After attending night school, he served a tour in the Marine Corps. Sowell enrolled at Howard University but soon transferred to Harvard, where he graduated magna cum laude in 1958. He later earned a doctorate in economics from the University of Chicago. One of Sowell's professors at the University of Chicago, the Nobel Prize–winning economist Milton Friedman, wrote of the job options considered by the young black Ph.D.:

> He talked to several of us about which to accept, expressing a strong preference for one of the least attractive offers—at Howard University in Washington—on the purely emotional grounds that it would enable him to make the greatest contribution to members of his race. I tried to dissuade him—as did others of my colleagues.[17]

Sowell went to Howard but left after one year, frustrated with what he considered to be loose academic standards in the university.

In the 1970s and early 1980s, Sowell published a number of books and articles challenging the liberal black intellectual establishment.[18] In often polemical prose, he marshaled statistics and advanced interpretations against the affirmative action movement and policy initiatives based on preferential treatment in remediation for past racial injustice. He argued that the struggle for social equality and group progress would be better waged by the free market than by government intervention. Affirmative action and minimum-wage legislation had slowed black economic progress. The differential success rates of various ethnic groups could be explained in terms of characteristics, whether functional or dysfunctional, in the economic life of modern societies.

Quick to join the national dialogue about race, Sowell at first hesitated to speak about social policy and black Americans. In the preface to *Ethnic America,* he explained that he had intended to write a book on Marxism but was implored by colleagues to write a monograph about racial policy instead.[19] Doubtless, his colleagues and supporters understood that a book critical of liberal social policies by a black who moved from Harlem through the University of Chicago would carry impressive symbolic meaning.

Black intellectuals disagreeing with Sowell's ideas could not easily recycle their criticisms of white critics, liberal or conservative. They could not, for example, charge that Sowell did not understand the black experience. Indeed, Sowell would cite his family's poverty and his childhood in Harlem as a source of insight not available to those blacks who came from more privileged settings.[20] Sowell's assault on the ideas and the motives of black intellectuals guaranteed that his scholarship would fall under the scrutiny of liberals. Christopher Lasch, Ronald Takaki, and Troy Duster were among the many who took issue with various of Sowell's formulations and interpretations,[21] but most *black* intellectuals focused on Sowell's motives or on the presumed consequences of his positions. In rebuttal Sowell steadfastly maintained that his policy proposals might well help the black community, and that surely many of the social programs that originated in the liberal assumptions of the 1960s had hurt African Americans.

Riding the wave of popular conservativism that put Ronald Reagan in the White House in 1980, Sowell, Glenn Loury, and other black conservatives applauded legislation that eliminated state-imposed racial barriers, but they decried group-based social policies and remedies, citing the worsening condition of poor and undereducated blacks as evidence of flawed liberal social policies. The conservative regime liked what it heard. In the 1980s Sowell was often mentioned as a prospect for an appointment in the Reagan administration.

In 1978 William J. Wilson, a professor of sociology at the University of Chicago, aroused controversy in black intellectual circles by publishing a book provocatively titled *The Declining Significance of Race*.[22] Wilson's central thesis was that race was becoming less important as a factor in the mobility and life chances of black Americans. This rather modest assertion drew heated criticism from many scholars who feared that Wilson's thesis would be used to justify further retreats from affirmative action and race-based social policies; many questioned his accuracy and ignored his historical analyses. At least one nationally respected sociologist, G. Franklin Edwards, a student of E. Franklin Frazier's in the forties, expressed surprise at the tempest over Wilson's book: "One of the main things critics have said is that he's arming white folks with arguments they can use against movements in the black community. But I don't think Wilson's book does that, for the simple reason that he hasn't said anything that whites haven't already discussed. It's actually nothing new."[23] Nevertheless, a number of conferences were held that explored Wilson's data and analyses. The popular media seized the opportunity to feature debate and discord in African American circles. Charles Willie, a Harvard professor, challenged Wilson's thesis, drawing on empirical evidence and questioning his interpretation of trends,[24] but many black critics never moved beyond ad hominem attacks. Some liberals were incensed that a black intellectual would advance explanations other than racism to account for the growth of the black underclass. Wilson stood by his analysis and aggressively defended his ideas in the pages of national publications. His courage earned him the respect of Gates, who posited a broader obligation for an intellectual:

> For Wilson to publish that thesis he had to be willing to say, "This is how I looked at the evidence. I've thought about it, and this is the way I think it is. I know everybody's going to beat on my head, but I have to be willing to hang tough." To me, you're in the wrong profession if you don't have that kind of courage. You're not running for the president of the Black Nation; you're running for a kind of immortality, and it's contingent upon a kind of honesty.[25]

## Freedom of Choice

Throughout the nineteenth and twentieth centuries, the issue for many black intellectuals has not been whether they had special responsibilities to their race but how best to fulfill them. Few could precisely define their constituency, and there was no consensus about which activities would most benefit it. Self-proclaimed representatives of the community often sought to help black intellectuals determine their responsibilities. Troy Duster described how he negotiates requests made of him "on behalf" of black interests.

If someone knocks on your door and in the name of blackness demands something, and you don't want to deliver, you can conveniently say, "I don't know who elected you to represent the community." But if the person asking you does represent a broad constituency, it's harder to say no. I think blacks should make more claims upon their intellectuals. Jews are right! They get Jews in positions of power, and they come knocking at the door. "We're part of this group called Jews, and we ask you on behalf of the Jewish people to do this." If you're Jewish and Saul Steinberg comes up and says it, you can say, "Go to hell!" But if B'nai B'rith asks you, it's different. So if the NAACP or someone with a wide black constituency comes to me and says, "In the name of Blackness, would you do this?" I would have a very hard time, given my self-conception, saying no. Now, I may have a disagreement, but that's a different issue. That's different from saying, "I don't have any dues to pay you." Blacks should act more like Jews. They treat Jewish intellectuals as *their* intellectuals.[26]

The idea that black people could and should make claims on the resources of intellectuals was controversial. With justification, thinkers under siege pleaded that the demands of first-rate scholarship or truly creative writing were challenging enough. During the sixties the strident rhetoric of some activists had forced many powerful thinkers to the sidelines. Rayford Logan, who had spent his long career studying blacks in the social order, turned against the new wave of militancy. Logan was particularly outraged at the widespread acceptance of the word *black* in place of *Negro*. His biographer explains that Logan "claimed that black was exclusionary, for he and so many other mulattoes were not dark."[27] Logan resigned his fifty-five-year membership in the Alpha Phi Alpha fraternity when, in the late sixties, it began referring to itself as a black fraternity.

In 1966 Langston Hughes publicly attacked black writers like Amiri Baraka whose uncompromising politics and language were not, in his view, in the African American tradition—writers who "talk about whites badly right in the middle of the whites' own parlors, lecture halls and libraries."[28] Other older thinkers objected to the political positions advocated, and some rejected the assumption that they were obligated to help. As the Atlanta University political scientist Mack Jones recalled in the early eighties, the pressures confused and alienated some black scholars:

> In spite of the militant posturing, the whole generation of black academics trained in the sixties and seventies have no understanding of the black predicament that transcends the conventional interpretation of it. Therefore, their imagination about what is to be done does not in any way go beyond that. And so what I think is clear and detrimental is that increasingly we will have a black community which has no intellectual servants. I think it's pathetic and horrible.[29]

In *The Crisis of the Negro Intellectual*, Harold Cruse argues that twentieth-century black intellectuals have failed to fashion a way of thinking and acting that fuses the ethnic sentiments of the black community and the individualism of American social life. While Cruse is primarily concerned with the content of black social thought about race relations, his thesis is relevant to an analysis of the role of black intellectuals as a group. Black intellectuals who do not project an autonomous ethnic vision in their work are sidestepping an important responsibility, he says. The void they leave means that black aesthetic perspectives cannot be represented in the battle that WASPs and other ethnic groups are waging for American cultural influence. Cruse criticizes twentieth-century black intellectuals who, he claims, are content to let other ethnic group intellectuals, particularly Jewish intellectuals, frame the examination of black life.[30]

Given the widespread discrimination and racial oppression that have characterized black social experience during most of the twentieth century, many black intellectuals have felt compelled to focus their attention on issues affecting the black community. Consequently, their intellectual institutions and products are designed to challenge racial subordination and address problems like segregated and unequal schooling, employment discrimination, and fair housing. Black colleges, literary journals, professional organizations, and much of the creative literature are steeped in the tradition of protest and racial affirmation. Since the raison d'être of traditional black intellectual institutions was the fight against state-endorsed discrimination, the passage of civil rights legislation and the waning of overt discrimination in the sixties posed a peculiar challenge: was there still a role for race-based institutions and, if so, what was it?

As more and better opportunities for black intellectuals opened a wider range of fields and occupations, black academics were freer to desert the historically black colleges—with their low salaries and punishing teaching loads—for predominantly white colleges. Many did just that. During the seventies J. Saunders Redding, Darwin Turner, Samuel DuBois Cook, and Blyden Jackson all resigned from posts in predominantly black institutions and accepted appointments in major American universities that provided them greater status, more visibility for their work, and research support that black colleges could not match.[31] Soon there was talk of a "black brain drain." Critics lamented that professors once devoted to black students and colleges would now be providing their talents and skills to students at predominantly white universities. A survey by Henry Allen during the 1981–82 academic year found otherwise, however:

> Was there a "brain drain" of Black faculty from Black to White colleges and universities in the early 1980s? The evidence assembled here leads one to doubt it. The job offers mobile Black collegiate faculty in the present study received from White colleges during 1981–82 were relatively few in number, and salary data do not reveal any great mobility advantage for Black collegiate faculty.[32]

The "brain drain" hypothesis may have been advanced by black college heads, anxious to retain talented scholars. Yet, even as the racial boundaries that so frustrated earlier titans like Du Bois, Frazier, Hurston, and Just seemed quite penetrable to accomplished intellectuals in the eighties, racial inequality persisted and the circumstances of less educated blacks grew bleaker. The Columbia University law professor Patricia Williams has pondered the passage of civil rights legislation and the predicament of the black minority in American society: "My dispute is perhaps not with formal equal opportunity. So-called formal equal opportunity has done a lot but misses the heart of the problem: it puts the vampire back in the coffin, but it was no silver stake. The rules may be color-blind, but people are not."[33]

Study after study confirmed the prominent role of racial discrimination in employment, housing, health care, and education.[34] Structural changes in the labor market were depriving large numbers of the black urban poor of any meaningful prospects for social mobility, and this despairing and often unruly group loomed ominously in the psyche of middle-class Americans. Fixated on dysfunctional behaviors of the black poor, many Americans charged that black communities were suffering from a breakdown of individual responsibility.[35]

Historically, black spokesmen across the ideological spectrum—from Richard Wright to Malcolm X and Martin Luther King—had always acknowledged the importance of individual responsibility in social life, but they invariably felt compelled to point out social injustices that were beyond the scope of individual remedy. By the 1980s, however, the problem of inequality had been recast. No longer did social scientists (and ultimately the public) acknowledge discrimination and economic injustice as primary factors in the worsening straits of poor and working-class blacks. Instead, they concluded that the culture of the black poor was the main factor contributing to high unemployment, low educational achievement, high rates of out-of-wedlock births, and rising crime rates. Conservatives, and a growing number of liberals, were content to exhort individual African Americans to somehow transcend social and economic inequalities that beset the race. The call went out for a community of heroes.

In an oblique way the successes of black intellectuals, particularly those from economically disadvantaged backgrounds, confirmed the conservative premise that the most serious social barriers to black progress had been dismantled. The talent demonstrated by people such as Adolph Reed, Glenn Loury, bell hooks, Patricia Williams, and Stanley Crouch suggested that social conditions, no matter how dire, could not hold back those individuals who took responsibility for themselves, rather than blaming society for their life circumstances. The analyses of the impact of racial discrimination focused on "diversity" or "difference," more benign frameworks for debate and discussion.

Today Cornel West, a professor of Afro-American studies at Harvard, writes of searching for a moral "common ground" to bridge the fissures of class, race, individual responsibility, and gender. In a mode reminiscent of Martin Luther King's political posture toward the end of his life, West seeks to advance ideas that go beyond what he considers the confines of race-based thinking. Never minimizing the importance of historical specificity in thinking about race, West, like King, Frazier, and certainly Du Bois, links racial oppression to economic decline and moral decay in American society. One of the tasks of black intellectuals, West contends, is to demonstrate the less apparent linkages between race and opportunity.

In one of the few examinations of the role of black intellectuals, West acknowledges humanist, Marxist, and poststructuralist intellectual traditions, but sees them as limiting for black thinkers. Considering himself a legatee of black intellectual engagement with American society, West advances the notion of an "organic catalytic black intellectual," a thinker who would have a symbiotic relationship with the broader black community, unlike the clusters of self-conscious thinkers who inhabit elite academic centers. West is blunt: "This model privileges collective intellectual work that contributes to communal resistance and struggle."[36]

West's vision of intellectuals nurturing a symbiosis with a particularistic community runs counter to prevailing ideas about the intellectual's role. Most American intellectuals today hold views similar to those articulated in the 1960s by Edward Shils and Milton Gordon—that intellectuals should (and do) abandon sentimental links to ethnic or other social groups.[37] Shils wrote approvingly of how intellectual training weans individuals away from primal affiliations and group sentiment and teaches them abstract and ostensibly universal intellectual values and methods.

Earlier in the century the premise that intellectuals should forgo group allegiances and affiliations was challenged by the Italian political theorist Antonio Gramsci.[38] He maintained that social groups should generate their own distinct intellectuals. Unimpressed with the abstract quality of much that passed for intellectualism in modern Europe during the early twentieth century, Gramsci saw "groundedness" in some group as necessary to ensure the relevance of intellectual work. Reflecting on the direction and fate of European working-class movements in the first part of the twentieth century, he concluded that organic relationships develop (and should develop) when intellectuals are experientially connected to a social process or condition. Under such circumstances the contours and outcomes of the intellectual's work tend to be closely linked to the defining process or condition. West echoes Gramsci's idea about the importance of black thinkers' articulating issues and ideas relevant to their ethnic community.

Although his liberalism prevents him from prescribing what other individuals should be interested in, or what kind of work they should do, West resuscitates and extends the traditional black intellectual role that embraced the idea of service. He suggests that black intellectuals have a moral obligation to look beyond the conventions and priorities of privileged intellectual centers and beyond the offering of personal quandaries that fascinate the broader public. His idea of an organic catalytic black intellectual stands as a critique of much of the impressive academic work by black scholars, especially those who have drifted into esoteric explorations of literature. Convinced that "race matters," West calls for black intellectuals who will work to extend freedom to blacks and other subordinated groups.[39]

But, as we have seen, a growing number of black intellectuals resist the idea that race is a defining element in their social and psychological world. While few deny the past and present facts of racial discrimination, they feel that they, individually, are less affected by racial boundaries, that race does not weigh as heavily in their experience as it may have in that of their predecessors. Citing the waning of overt racial discrimination in the intellectual community, they feel justified in subordinating racial to other considerations in their intellectual framework. The movement away from particularistic interests is in fact a move toward the dominant ethos in American intellectual life—a "free floating" or "unattached" posture. Not coincidentally, such an abandonment of ethnic attachments would be welcomed by white colleagues who embrace the universalistic ideal.

During the mid-nineties black intellectuals gained a new visibility. Magazines like the *Atlantic* and *The New Yorker* published articles suggesting a seminal role for the "new black intellectuals" in American culture.[40] The *Atlantic* piece highlighted the "public" character of the new black intellectual activity, especially that of Henry Louis Gates Jr. and Cornel West. Predictably the acclaim heaped on Gates, West, and several other academics drew critical fire. In a free-swinging essay in the *Village Voice*, Adolph Reed sharply criticizes the political views of both Gates and West and, more significantly, the role as spokespersons for blacks that white society conferred on them.[41] Rather than projecting independent visions, West and Gates, according to Reed, interpret the ways of black folk to a nervous white America. Reed finds the role reminiscent of the position of Booker T. Washington, who "became the singular, trusted informant to communicate to whites what the Negro thought, felt, wanted, needed."[42] As in his 1986 critique of the Jesse Jackson presidential campaign, Reed calls for leaders or spokespersons with more of an institutional base in the black community.[43]

Reed also minimizes the intellectual contributions of West and Gates, asking, "Can the reader familiar with their work recall without hesitation a specific critique, a concrete formulation—an extended argument that is neither airily abstract nor cozily compatible with what passes as common sense? I'd bet not."[44] Michael Eric Dyson and Gloria Watkins (bell hooks), two of the more prolific writers on the "cultural studies" front, come in for blistering criticism: "Dyson and Watkins / hooks are little more than hustlers, blending bombast, clichés, psycho babble, and lame guilt tripping in service to the 'pay me' principle."[45] Skeptical about the trends in cultural studies, Reed writes, "The public intellectual's style has baleful effects on the scholarly examination of black American life. In rejecting all considerations of standards and evidence as expressions of naive positivism, the cultural politicians get to make up the story as they go along."[46]

By the nineties a counteraction of intellectuals—including Randall Kennedy, Thomas Sowell, Henry Louis Gates, Clarence Walker, and Adolph Reed—had convinced many in the black community that black thinkers did not have to look to some "common" agenda in thinking about black life. Independent and individualistic blacks refused to be constrained or even guided by the popular sense of what was valid about race and society. Their resistance was effective. The African American community became more accepting of ideological diversity, perhaps recognizing that such diversity simply mirrored the growing political and economic heterogeneity of the black community itself.

Black scholars such as Gates and Stephen Carter hit hard at occasional acts or statements suggesting an intolerance of differences within the black community. Given the record of far more coercive attitudes and actions emanating from black activists during the sixties and seventies, their protests seemed hyperbolic. The irony did not escape Martin Kilson of Harvard's government department and Derrick Bell, who was terminated from his position as professor of law at Harvard because he refused to teach unless an African American woman was appointed to the faculty. Both pointed out that moderate and conservative black critics of the traditional civil rights agenda enjoyed great standing and popularity in mainstream American life.[47]

The reorientation of the black dialogue from a group-centered emphasis on inequality and conflict to an emphasis on individual behavior and morality enhanced the standing of black literary figures who focused on their personal expressiveness and downplayed social and historical elements. Successful black intellectuals were said to prove the power of human agency to overcome societal boundaries and attitudes. Whether they liked it or not, they were cast as representatives of their race and, as such, were granted an authority far beyond the context of their own individual experiences.

Even the debates about national policies like affirmative action were dominated by the often eloquent (but singular) testimony of individuals. Furthermore, accounts like that of Stephen Carter, the holder of an endowed chair at Yale Law School, agonizing over the paradoxes of affirmative action in his professional life, lent credence to the idea that race-related policies erode the self-esteem of black intellectuals.[48]

Carter argues that black intellectuals can earn the respect of whites by excelling on the playing fields of academic and intellectual life. His own prominence supports the argument that whites can and do acknowledge good black scholarship. But as Glenn Loury and others have suggested, Carter, for all his achievements, seems somewhat insecure about his standing. Commenting on Carter's *Reflections of an Affirmative Action Baby* (1991), Loury notes how Carter downplays race as a suitable subject for serious intellectual work:

He makes sure that the reader is aware that this writing on racial topics is just a part-time pursuit, that his real academic work focuses on constitutional law and intellectual property issues. . . . And though he holds a named chair at an Ivy League law

school, a fact which should leave little doubt that he is an intellectual heavyweight, he still finds it necessary explicitly to state
that this book is merely a digression from his more serious
work.[49]

The national fascination with intellectuals who explore race within a
personal framework deflected attention from the historical and social
forces that defined the terrain from which these individuals
emerged—or failed to emerge.

The growing economic and social diversity within the black community complicated the once simple allegiance of black intellectuals
to "the group." The moral authority of black demands, grounded in
history and widely accepted in the seventies, was now placed in a
less noble perspective by persons like Shelby Steele, who insisted that
emphasis on their victim status undermined the moral autonomy of
African Americans: "Since the social victim has been oppressed by
society, he comes to feel that his individual life will be improved
more by changes in society than by his own initiative. Without realizing it, he makes society rather than himself the agent of social
change."[50] Steele argued that with the civil rights laws on the books,
blacks should eschew "collective" challenges that provoked further
undue emphasis on race. Racialization and its frequent consequence,
polarization, only worsened the prospects of blacks. Instead, Steele
appealed for renewed attention to individual effort and responsibility
in the black community. To replace the collective challenges that
dominated the sixties, he proposed individual "bargaining" with
white authorities for rewards and benefits. Individual negotiations
over advantage and recognition would reduce the likelihood that
conflict and contests would be viewed in the guilt-victim praxis.

Steele's influential idea of individual self-reliance clashed with the
sense of things perceived by Mouse, a notorious character in the popular novels of the black author Walter Mosley. In *Devil in a Blue
Dress* (1990), Mouse admonishes his friend, and the novel's protagonist, Easy Rawlins: "But Easy, you gotta have somebody at yo' back,
man. That's just a lie them white man give 'bout makin' it on they
own. They always got they backs covered."[51]

From the campuses of elite universities, reviewers generally
endorsed the call for individual-centered action. But while negotia-

tion may have been a reasonable option for black intellectuals who had marketable cultural capital and were well positioned to bargain as individuals, it was not clear how individual negotiations could do much to remedy the consequences of deindustrialization and segregation that were dislocating working-class blacks. Nor did the substandard public educational systems in urban centers seem amenable to the "bargaining" of poor individual blacks, especially since middle-class parents with far more "bargaining" clout were frequently opting to send their children to private schools.

Yet many intellectuals, only tenuously linked to the problems of the black masses, favored a strategy that separated and elevated them from the thorny issues of class and race. Many intellectuals and scholars who were beneficiaries of the racial protests and often clumsy political activities in the sixties drifted toward depoliticized and amorphous appeals for "goodwill" and "increased understanding." In the sixties such pleadings had been criticized by such intellectuals as Martin Luther King Jr. and Bayard Rustin.[52] In the changed context of the late eighties, such rhetoric seemed "responsible," and its purveyors received considerable attention.

# EPILOGUE ⫷

# OR CRUST AND SUGAR OVER

Privatized terms so dominate the public discourse that it is difficult to see or appreciate social evil, communal wrong, states of affairs that implicate us whether we will it or not. —PATRICIA WILLIAMS

T HE LIVES AND WORKS of black intellectuals have always been strongly linked to the position of African Americans in the United States. From the thoughtful, barely literate slaves of colonial America to recent Pulitzer Prize winners, all African Americans have had to come to terms with the racial burden in society. The other interests they shared with American thinkers have always competed with a need to make peace with the racial issue. Slavery, emancipation, segregation, and the civil rights movement all posed unique problems to black scholars and artists. Unlike whites, they could not choose to ignore the question of what it meant to be black in America.

Until the mid-twentieth century the barriers that defined or limited intellectual horizons for African Americans were institutionalized. Few opportunities for intellectual training were open to able blacks. The inferior education in primary and secondary schools took a toll on many blacks who had the potential to develop into intellectuals;

universities limited the number of blacks, particularly at the post-graduate level; and the literary world was also inhospitable. Those blacks who persevered and managed to obtain superior training were nonetheless excluded from employment in mainstream intellectual centers. W. E. B. Du Bois, after returning from graduate work at the prestigious University of Berlin, took a position teaching Latin at Wilberforce University, a small black normal school in Ohio, not because he had aspired to such work but because at that time it was the best job available to a black with a Ph.D. from Harvard.

Even as intellectuals were being penalized by mainstream institutions for being black, they were being asked by the black community itself whether they were "black enough," whether they were applying their talent and training to black political and social agendas. The sentiments of racial solidarity within the black masses held that highly educated blacks should identify with and champion the interests of the broader black community. That many brilliant African Americans had no interest in immersing themselves in the work and roles assigned them by that community made little difference. Operating behind the walls of a segregated society, they had little choice. Consequently, "service to the race" became part of the black intellectuals' function in American life.

Since the 1960s the standing and roles of black intellectuals have changed dramatically. As the formal institutional barriers fell, black intellectuals able to negotiate the system enjoyed unprecedented opportunities. Universities, now the primary centers of intellectual life, recruited students and offered faculty appointments to African American scholars. The admission of blacks to graduate schools and the appointment of black scholars to faculties provided access to resources unavailable to earlier generations. African Americans took advantage of the hard-won access, and the outpouring of scholarship after 1970 was impressive. The ministry, once an important career for black intellectuals, declined in importance. The eminence of theologians such as Howard Thurman, Gardner Taylor, and later Calvin Butts could not stem the tide of blacks aspiring to secular intellectual careers.

Greater access to training and employment was accompanied by a change in how black intellectuals related to the broader black community. In part this was a simple matter of numbers. As the pool of trained intellectuals grew, the pressure on individual intellectuals to function as race advocates decreased. For example, the presence of ten black faculty members, rather than three, on a campus meant that the work of providing counseling and advice to black students and addressing community racial issues could be spread around.

More important, the lowering of institutional barriers raised for black intellectuals new questions about their role. In the 1980s many of them began to view the historical tradition of engagement with racial injustice as less necessary. Distancing themselves from ideas and policies that framed the problems of black America in group terms, more black intellectuals became aligned with modes of liberalism and conservatism that located social change or mobility in the individual. A decade earlier the writer Al Young had presaged the shift in emphasis: "I've always believed the individual human heart to be more revolutionary than any political party or platform."[1]

As the belief that race was not a significant impediment to the progress of African Americans became popular among black intellectuals, historical and empirical studies on race yielded ground to ruminations about the tensions in individual lives. Jerry Watts of Wesleyan University has candidly expressed his anxiety about the attention paid to the personal lives of black intellectuals:

> Finally whatever anxiety I experience as a result of my marginalization from the broader black community, I cannot become too self-consumed at my plight. After all, my writings will not feed the numerous black homeless. . . . While I have some contributions to make to the betterment of black life, I can easily understand the low priority that many blacks give to my situation as an anxiety-ridden bourgeois black academic intellectual.[2]

Scholarly monographs suffered by comparison with melodrama.

Douglas Massey and Nancy Denton's *American Apartheid* (1993), a penetrating empirical work on racial segregation in urban America and its impact on millions of Americans, especially black Americans, was forced to compete with the authority of the singular voice of Shelby Steele describing his ascent from a black working-class neighborhood, and his discomfort when people ignored his individuality and lumped him with other blacks.[3] Elijah Anderson's textured analyses of social organization in urban black neighborhoods, *Streetwise* (1990), generated little interest among a public seeking something simpler—one person's story.

Empirical studies documenting continuing racial discrimination in employment and housing competed for space in the public's attention span with writings by Stanley Crouch, who single-mindedly searched for, and found, many behavioral and moral shortcomings in the African American community. Lani Guinier, Patricia Williams, and Derrick Bell, intellectuals who endorsed individual responsibility but insisted that race was a significant impediment to the opportunities of African Americans, were outflanked by blacks like Clarence Thomas, who touted what they had achieved in spite of the barriers. It was increasingly difficult to find an audience for the proposition that race mattered.*

Ultimately, of course, the choices of intellectuals about what they do and how they do it are based on the moral sensibilities of individuals. Conservatives insist that the long and difficult struggle of African Americans to secure the rights of citizenship was fundamentally about blacks' being able to have the same options as other citizens. The American creed of individualism provides sturdy support for this position. With the lowering of formal racial barriers, black intellectuals feel free to reject any identification with the black community at large, free to sidestep the troublesome questions posed by ongoing racial inequality. Under the elegant banner of individual freedom, the new individualists ask whether it's fair to expect black intellectuals to act differently from white intellectuals and to assume a larger burden than they.

Both camps—intellectuals who advocate an organic relationship with the black community, and those who aspire to transcend ethnic considerations—are part of the unfolding saga of race and social thought in the United States. And members of both camps today are products of the same historical forces; they are intellectuals who have benefited from the victories of those who challenged racial barriers

---

* A significant number of black women have opted for careers as legal scholars, examining links between law and society. Patricia King, at Georgetown, Kimberley Crenshaw, at UCLA, Kathleen Cleaver, at Emory, Angela Harris, at Berkeley, and Mildred Robinson, at the University of Virginia, are in this group.

in earlier periods. Now, the individualists say, they are ready to move on, to take advantage of expanded opportunities. In doing so, they are well received by the political and cultural authorities who deny the lasting significance of race in American society. By emphasizing their own individual successes and accepting the thesis that being black is no longer a limiting factor, the individualists affirm the essential openness of the social order.

In contrast, intellectuals such as Cornel West, Adolph Reed, Manning Marable, Derrick Bell, and Lani Guinier remind us that individual successes are not the measure of social justice, that the accomplishments of the newest Talented Tenth should not blind that Tenth to the group reality that still limits the choices of African Americans.

# SELECTED
# BIOGRAPHIES «

ROBERT ALLEN, a historian and editor of *Black Scholar,* is a native of Atlanta. He received a B.S. in mathematics from Morehouse College in 1964 and an M.A. in sociology from the New School for Social Research, in New York. Allen spent more than a decade as an active journalist and in the seventies began his teaching career in the black studies department at San Jose State University. He has since taught at Mills College and the University of California at Berkeley. He wrote *Black Awakening in Capitalist America* (1969) and *Reluctant Reformers* (1974) and, most recently, edited (with Herb Boyd) *Brotherman: An Anthology of Writing by Black Men* (1994).

MOLEFI KETE ASANTE, a prolific advocate of Afrocentric philosophy, was born Arthur Smith, in Valdosta, Georgia, in 1942. Asante's early years were split between Georgia and Tennessee. He received a Ph.D. in communications from UCLA in 1968 and held appointments at that university and the State University of New York at Buffalo before joining the Temple University Afro-American Studies Department. At Temple he developed the nation's first doctoral program in Afro-American studies. The author of *The Afrocentric Ideal,* (1987) and *Afrocentricity and Knowledge* (1990), he edited the *Journal of Black Studies* during the eighties.

JAMES BALDWIN, a prolific writer, activist, and social critic, was born in Harlem in 1924. Unmarried at the time of his birth, James's mother married later, but Baldwin never got on with his stepfather. Always a sensitive boy, he underwent an intense religious conversion at age fourteen—the basis for his 1953 book *Go Tell It on the Moun-*

*tain*—and subsequently attended the predominantly white DeWitt Clinton High School in the Bronx, where he received his diploma in 1942. After growing weary of New York life, he left the United States for Paris in 1948 and lived there until 1956, when he returned to the States. Two of Baldwin's books, *Notes of a Native Son* (1955) and *Nobody Knows My Name* (1961) eloquently drew attention to the problem of race in American society. The publication in 1963 of *The Fire Next Time,* essays that reflected black frustration with the pace of racial justice, coincided with the outbreak of urban disturbances in the summers of 1963 and 1964. Baldwin was gradually drawn into an activist role in the civil rights movement, and his writing, in works like *Blues for Mister Charlie* (1964) and *Tell Me How Long the Train's Been Gone* (1968), captured the militancy of the period. He weathered criticism from militant blacks for his brand of personalistic humanism, and whites had difficulty accepting their complicity in the social and psychological problems of blacks. In his later years he alternated between the relative calm of Europe and the turbulence that surrounded him in the United States. He died in Paris in 1987.

BENJAMIN BANNEKER, a self-taught mathematician, astronomer, and inventor, was born in 1731 in Baltimore County, Maryland, and died there in 1806. His mother, the great influence in his life, was an indentured Englishwoman who completed her servitude and purchased a tobacco farm, for which she bought two slaves; one she later freed, and the other she married. Though taught to read and write by his grandmother, Banneker received no formal education, yet he was able to prepare almanacs. In 1790 he helped design and implement a survey of the District of Columbia. He wrote to Thomas Jefferson, at the time secretary of state, challenging the prevailing beliefs about the inferior mental capacity of blacks. Jefferson acknowledged Banneker's letter but never conceded blacks' intellectual equality.

AMIRI BARAKA (formerly LeRoi Jones) was a leading beat poet and a central figure during the sixties rebirth of African American arts and letters. Jones was born in Newark, New Jersey, in 1934 and attended Rutgers University extension before enrolling at Howard in 1951.

After flunking out of Howard in 1954 and spending three years in the air force, Jones settled in New York's Greenwich Village and became a mover in the "beat" scene. Books like *Blues People* (1963) signaled his shift to a more nationalistic theme. He abandoned the beat scene and plunged into the art / politics vortex that was swirling in the black community. A play, *Dutchman,* received an Obie Award for the best off-Broadway production of 1964. By 1966 Baraka was a fixture in the black aesthetic movement, rejecting art that, in the words of the critic William Harris, "permits the artist to ignore the world while he busies himself with the disinterested creation of beauty." Harlem was the locale for Baraka's Black Arts Theatre institution. In 1965 he returned to Newark and established a cultural / political center, Spirit House, and became involved in the campaign of Kenneth Gibson, a black mayoral candidate in Newark. Since 1964 Baraka has aligned himself with Islam, Pan-Africanism, and Marxist-Leninism. Despite his ideological twists and turns, his creative talents have remained unmistakable. He currently works as a professor of Africana studies at the State University of New York at Stony Brook.

J. MAX BARBER, a journalist and an outspoken critic of racial discrimination, championed African American suffrage and the use of the ballot as a means of achieving socioeconomic parity. Barber was born in Blackstock, South Carolina, in 1878; his parents were ex-slaves, and he worked to put himself through school. He completed a teacher's course of study at Benedict College in Columbia, South Carolina, and in 1903 earned a B.A. from Virginia Union University. He helped establish *Voice of the Negro,* a successful black literary and political journal that encountered hard times when it dared challenge the powerful and vindictive Booker T. Washington. In 1909 a financially struggling Barber attended dental school. He graduated in 1912 and opened a dental practice in Philadelphia. There he was extremely active with the NAACP and worked as a dentist until his death in 1949.

ROMARE BEARDEN, perhaps the preeminent black visual artist, was born in Charlotte, North Carolina, in 1912. An only child, he moved to New York with his parents when he was three years old. There, his father worked as a sanitation inspector for the Department of Health. His mother was politically active and served as the New York correspondent for the black weekly *Chicago Defender.* Intending to go into medicine, Bearden received a B.S. from New York University in 1935. After changing his focus to art, he studied at the Art Students League from 1936 to 1937 with the German artist George Grosz and at the Sorbonne, in Paris, from 1950 to 1952. Bearden frequently wrote about the status of African American artists. During the sixties he became interested in collage and recast that medium with a distinctly African American flavor, making use of historical and cultural material. His work has been featured on the covers of *Time, Fortune,* and *The New Yorker* magazines, and his paintings have been exhibited around the world.

LERONE BENNETT, a widely published historian and journalist, was born in Clarksdale, Mississippi, in 1928 and educated in the public schools of Jackson. He attended Morehouse College and was editor of the school newspaper. After graduating, he worked as a reported for the *Atlanta Daily World,* a local black newspaper. In 1960 he became the first senior editor at *Ebony,* a popular monthly. His books include *Before the Mayflower* (1964), *Confrontation: Black and White* (1965), and *What Manner of Man: A Biography of Martin Luther King* (1968).

MARY MCLEOD BETHUNE may well have been the most influential black woman in the history of American education. Born in 1875 near Mayesville, South Carolina, Bethune was the fifteenth of seventeen children, whose parents' enslavement had ended with the Civil War. In South Carolina she received the equivalent of a high school education, graduating in 1894, and spent one year at a missionary preparatory school before assuming a teaching position at Haines Institute in Augusta, Georgia, in 1896. A year later she founded a school for poor children in Augusta, an act she repeated numerous times elsewhere throughout her life, culminating with Bethune-Cookman College in 1923. She was active in the black women's club movement and worked with the National Association of Colored Women (NACW). She became president of the NACW in 1924 and of the National Council of Negro Women in 1935. In 1936 President Franklin Roosevelt named her director of the Negro division of the National Youth Administration. Bethune led an informal black cabinet and provided a sounding board for White House initiatives affecting blacks. After 1932 she was a loyal friend and supporter of First Lady Eleanor Roosevelt. Awarded the NAACP's Spingarn Medal in 1935, Bethune died in Daytona Beach in 1955.


EDWARD W. BLYDEN, a colonizationist who spent most of his life studying, living, and working in Liberia, was born in St. Thomas in the Caribbean in 1832, to free parents of Ibo descent. In 1850, white missionaries, recognizing his budding literary talent, brought him to the United States to further his education. Denied entry into theological school here, on the basis of race, he traveled, with aid from the New York Colonization Society, to Liberia. There he received his only formal education, graduating from Alexander High School. In 1856 he published his first pamphlet, *A Voice from Bleeding Africa,* and in 1858 he was ordained and became principal of his alma mater. Blyden assumed the editorship of the *Liberia Herald* newspaper and held many high public offices in Liberia before moving to Sierra Leone in 1885. Between 1850 and 1896 Blyden traveled often to the United States, where, with his friend Alexander Crummell, he advocated black emigration to Africa. Many African Americans resented his anti mulatto biases. Blyden died in Freetown, Sierra Leone, in 1912.


HORACE MANN BOND, a scholar and educational leader, was born in Nashville in 1904. Bond's minister father and teacher mother decided to educate him at home. In 1923 he received a B.A. from Lincoln University, in Pennsylvania, and three years later an M.A. from the University of Chicago. Bond was one of the pioneering scholars in the education of blacks in the South. His dissertation, "Social and Economic Influences on the Public Education of Negroes in Alabama, 1865–1930," won a prize for the best doctoral thesis in the social sciences at the University of Chicago, which awarded him a Ph.D. in 1936. His thesis was published in 1941 as *Negro Education in Alabama: A Study in Cotton and Steel,* which enjoyed critical acclaim. After holding faculty appointments at Fisk and Dillard universities, he accepted the presidency of Fort Valley State College in 1939. There he launched several innovative programs to link collegiate studies to the social and economic conditions of rural blacks in Georgia. He returned to Lincoln University as president in 1945 and remained there until 1957, when he became dean of the School of Education at Atlanta University. Bond died in 1972.

EDWARD BOUCHET, the first black to receive a Ph.D., was born in New Haven, Connecticut, in 1852. His father, servant to a white man with whom he had migrated north, was a deacon and became a prominent member of New Haven's black community. Bouchet graduated as valedictorian from Hopkins Grammar School in 1870 and entered Yale, where he was elected to Phi Beta Kappa. On receiving his Ph.D., he taught at the Institute for Colored Youth in Philadelphia for twenty-six years before resigning to protest the discontinuance of the school's college preparatory program. He held a number of teaching positions between 1902 and 1916, when illness forced him to retire. He died in New Haven in 1918.

JOHN BRACEY, a prominent historian and editor, was born in 1941. As an undergraduate at Howard, Bracey participated in a militant student movement that included Stokely Carmichael and Michael Thelwell. Veering from the career trajectory of some other militant students, Bracey moved on to graduate work in history at Northwestern. He joined the faculty of Northern Illinois University and, with August Meier and Elliot Rudwick, edited several seminal collections in African American history. Bracey is a professor of black studies at the University of Massachusetts at Amherst.

DAVID BRADLEY, a writer, was born in 1950 and grew up in Bedford, Pennsylvania. He graduated from the University of Pennsylvania in

1972, and received an M.A. from the University of London in 1974. He has written two novels, *South Street* (1975) and *The Cheneysville Incident* (1981). The latter won the 1982 PEN / Faulkner Award as the best work of fiction by an American writer. His essays and reviews have appeared in various periodicals, including the *New York Times Magazine, Esquire,* and *Dissent.* He has been a professor of English at Temple University since 1976.

GWENDOLYN BROOKS, born in Topeka, Kansas, in 1917, was raised in Chicago and became poet laureate of Illinois in 1968. Brooks, who began writing poetry at age seven, attended predominantly white high schools. At sixteen she met the poet Langston Hughes, who read her work and encouraged her to continue writing; she remembers the encounter as an important turning point in her life. After graduating from high school, she attended Woodrow Wilson Junior College and graduated in 1936. The highly acclaimed poet went on to garner numerous awards and honors, including Guggenheim Fellowships for the years 1946 and 1947 and a Pulitzer Prize for poetry for *Annie Allen* (1950), making her the first African American ever to receive a Pulitzer in any category. Her other books include *A Street in Bronzeville* (1945), the novella *Maud Martha* (1953), and *Blacks* (1987), as well as a number of books for children. She was greatly influenced by the black power movement of the late sixties, and in 1969 decided to publish her books exclusively with black presses.

CLAUDE BROWN was born in 1937 in New York City, to parents who had migrated from the South. From a very young age, he was involved in small-time crime on the streets, and was in and out of institutions—including a psychiatric hospital and a reform school— until age sixteen, when he entered Washington Irving High School in Manhattan. Brown graduated in 1957 and held many jobs to support his studies, enrolling at Howard, where he earned a B.A. in 1965. That year his novel *Manchild in the Promised Land* was published to mixed reviews, particularly among black critics wary of its negative portrayal of black life. Nonetheless, Brown received widespread acclaim—James Baldwin was one of his strongest supporters. He attended Stanford University's law school and later ran unsuccessfully for the Harlem congressional seat once held by Adam Clayton Powell.


STERLING BROWN, the "Dean of American Negro Poets," was also an important and influential educator and literary critic. He was born in Washington, D.C., in 1901, to an educated black family. His father taught religion at Howard and knew both Frederick Douglass and Booker T. Washington. Brown received a B.A. Phi Beta Kappa from Williams College in 1921 and an M.A. from Harvard in 1923. *Southern Road,* his first book of poetry, appeared in 1932, and his poems have since been included in numerous journals and anthologies. From 1936 to 1939 he served as editor on Negro Affairs for the Federal Writers' Project. He received a Guggenheim Fellowship in 1937, the year he wrote *The Negro in American Fiction.* The classic *Negro Caravan* was edited by Brown and Arthur Davis. Credited with being among the first to identify the foundations of the black aesthetic tradition, Brown was an early champion of black folk culture, particularly the blues. As a professor of English at Howard, he influenced figures like Amiri Baraka and Michael Harper. Brown died in Washington, D.C., in 1988.


WILLIAM WELLS BROWN wrote *Clotel* (1853), long believed to be the first novel by an African American. He was born in 1814 near Lexington, Kentucky; his father was a white slaveholder and his mother a slave. He escaped to Cleveland in 1833 and soon became active in the Underground Railroad. The ambitious Brown taught himself to read and write and was a member of the organizing committee of the first Negro convention, in 1843. He was an energetic antislavery activist and eventually became an effective full-time lecturer for the Anti-Slavery Society. He moved to Boston in 1847 and wrote his *Narrative* that same year. Despite his activism, Brown wrote a dozen books before his death in Chelsea, Massachusetts, in 1884.


RALPH BUNCHE, a political scientist and statesman, was born in Detroit in 1904. Both of his parents died when Bunche was eleven.

He attended UCLA on an athletic scholarship and graduated with honors in 1927. Bunche received an M.A. from Harvard in 1928 and immediately began teaching at Howard. In 1934 he completed a Ph.D. at Harvard. He held various public offices, worked with the U.S. Department of State and the United Nations, and won the Nobel Peace Prize in 1950 for negotiating a temporary peace between Palestinian and Israeli factions. In 1963 he was awarded the Presidential Medal of Freedom. He died in 1971.

STOKELY CARMICHAEL, a civil rights activist during the sixties, came to prominence as chair of the Student Nonviolent Coordinating Committee (SNCC) in 1966. Carmichael, a native of Trinidad, attended the prestigious Bronx High School of Science and subsequently graduated from Howard. He was admired for his courage and organizing ability among poor blacks in the rural South. As chair of SNCC, he reflected the black movement's frustration and shift toward more nationalistic and militant positions. With Charles Hamilton, he wrote *Black Power: The Politics of Liberation in America* (1967), a highly influential treatise on the political position of blacks during the late sixties. Carmichael began a self-imposed exile in Conakry, Guinea, embraced Pan-Africanism, and changed his name to Kwame Toure.

GEORGE WASHINGTON CARVER, an influential educator and applied scientist, was born in Diamond, Missouri, in 1865. His enslaved father was killed in an accident shortly after Carver's birth, and while he was still a baby, his mother, also a slave, was kidnapped in retaliation for her owners' alleged antislavery sentiments, never to be seen again. The white family that owned his mother raised Carver, and at age ten he was allowed to leave home to pursue an education. Carver finished high school in Kansas and entered Simpson College in 1890, first studying art but later turning to science. In 1891 he entered Iowa State College, where he completed his undergraduate degree. When he earned an M.S. there in 1896, Booker T. Washington persuaded him to head Tuskegee's new agricultural department and experiment station. Despite meager resources he successfully tested the growth of peanuts, sweet potatoes, and other crops and taught black and white farmers soil conservation techniques. The relationship between Washington and Carver was so strained that Carver threatened to resign almost annually. Carver received the NAACP's Spingarn Medal in 1923. He died in 1943 in Tuskegee.


HORACE CAYTON was born to middle-class parents in Seattle in 1903. He earned his B.A. from the University of Washington in 1931 and taught at Fisk in 1935–36. His time at Fisk was difficult, and he was happy to return to Chicago and enroll at the University of Chicago. In 1945 he coauthored, with St. Clair Drake, *Black Metropolis,* which won an Anisfield-Wolf Award for the year's best book on race relations and which is still considered one of the finest studies of black urban life. Cayton died while working on his friend Richard Wright's biography in Paris in 1970.


CHARLES WADDELL CHESNUTT was one of the earliest literary craftsmen working in the black tradition. Born in 1858 in Ohio, Chesnutt moved to North Carolina after the war. A lynching that he observed at the age of nine left an indelible impression. Rising rapidly in North Carolina black education circles, he became a school principal at twenty-one. Frustrated by the southern color bar, Chesnutt returned to Cleveland and worked as a legal stenographer before passing the Ohio bar with one of the highest scores ever. Confronting northern racism in the legal profession, he concluded he could do better in his stenography business. In 1887 he began publishing short fiction pieces in magazines like the *Atlantic Monthly;* in 1889 *The Conjure Woman,* a collection of his short stories, was published. His later novels, including *The House behind the Cedars,* dealt primarily with racial themes. He gave up the hope that great literature would make a difference in the treatment of black people. He died in 1932.


KENNETH CLARK, born in 1914 in the Panama Canal Zone, immigrated with his family to Harlem. Clark attended George Washington College Preparatory High School at his mother's insistence, in spite of advice from a junior high counselor that he seek a vocational education. In 1931 Clark enrolled at Howard, receiving a B.S. in 1935 and an M.A. in 1936. At Howard he studied with Sterling Brown, Ralph Bunche, and Alain Locke, but he was most profoundly influenced by the psychiatrist Francis Cecil Sumner. Clark earned a Ph.D. in psychology from Columbia in 1940 and was a Julius Rosenwald fellow that same year. In 1942 he began a thirty-three-year teaching career at the City College of New York and in 1960 became the first African American to achieve tenure in any New York City university. He participated in the effort to desegregate public schools during the fifties. His research on the impact of racial isolation on black children was cited by the Supreme Court in the 1954 *Brown* v. *Board of Education* case, which outlawed racial segregation in public schools. The Harlem Youth Opportunities (HARYOU) program, which he founded in 1964, was one of the first and more ambitious programs designed to tackle urban poverty. He served as president of the American Psychological Association in 1970–71.

ELDRIDGE CLEAVER, born in 1935 in Wabbaseka, Arkansas, migrated with his poor parents to Los Angeles. Cleaver had a tense relationship with his father and eventually turned to a life of crime. Between 1947 and 1966 he spent much of his time in correctional institutions. He earned his high school diploma while in prison and was deeply affected by the teachings of Malcolm X. When paroled in 1966, he settled in the San Francisco Bay Area and soon joined the Black Panther Party, eventually becoming its minister of information. His autobiographical *Soul on Ice* (1968) thrust him to the forefront of the Black Power movement and was acclaimed by literary critics. After a confrontation with Oakland police officers, Cleaver left the country to avoid returning to prison for parole violations. After stays in Cuba and Algeria, he returned to the United States and underwent several political and religious transformations. At one point he was a follower of the Korean evangelist Sun Myung Moon and ran for political office in Berkeley, California.

MONTAGUE COBB, a distinguished scientist, was born in Washington, D.C., in 1904. He received a B.A. from Amherst in 1925 and an

M.D. from Howard in 1929, as well as a Ph.D. from Western Reserve University in 1932. He joined the Howard medical faculty in 1928. From 1947 to 1969 he was the director of Howard's medical school and from 1969 to 1973 its Distinguished Professor of Anatomy. He was also the leading historian of African Americans in medicine, held numerous professional memberships, served on the board of directors of the NAACP, and received a host of awards and honorary degrees before his death in 1990.

ANNA JULIA HAYWOOD COOPER, a civil and women's rights pioneer, was one of the earliest black women activists in the realm of higher education. She was born in Raleigh, North Carolina, in 1858, to an enslaved father and a free mother, and showed great academic promise at an early age. She entered Oberlin in 1881, where she earned a B.A. in 1884 and an M.A. in 1887. She delivered her paper "The Negro Problem in America" at the Pan-African Conference in London in 1900 and was subsequently named to the Pan-African Executive Committee. She did graduate work at the Sorbonne, in Paris, during 1911–12 and at Columbia in 1913–16. She received a Ph.D. from the Sorbonne in 1925. Cooper taught, or served as principal, at Dunbar High School (formerly M Street High), long the only academic high school for blacks in Washington, D.C., for thirty-nine years. She died in 1964.

SAMUEL CORNISH, an abolitionist minister, is best known for having founded a number of black newspapers. He was born in Sussex County, Delaware, in 1795 and was ordained a Presbyterian minister in 1822. He ministered to free blacks near New York City and was associated with various churches in the New York and New Jersey areas between 1830 and 1840. With John Russwurm he founded the first African American newspaper, *Freedom's Journal,* and his later editorial work on the *Colored American* led him to join the American Anti-Slavery Society. He founded its New York chapter and coauthored a pamphlet entitled *The Colonialization Scheme Considered* (1840), which challenged the idea of repatriation to Africa and advocated "hard work" and "moral uplift" as means of achieving socio-economic parity. Cornish died in Brooklyn in 1858.

STANLEY CROUCH, recipient of a MacArthur grant, was born in 1946 and grew up in southern California. After graduating from high school in 1963, he attended several Los Angeles community colleges. During this period he came in contact with the artistic wing of the black protest movement and began writing poetry. His work on the southern California jazz and poetry scene led to an appointment as poet-in-residence at Pitzer College on the Claremont College complex. He moved to New York City in 1975 and began writing jazz criticism and promoting artists. In 1980 he became a regular columnist at the *Village Voice* and used that platform to attack a range of left or liberal black cultural figures. His first collection of essays, *Notes of a Hanging Judge* (1991), was followed by *The All-American Skin Game* (1995). Crouch serves as artistic consultant to the Jazz at Lincoln Center Program, in New York.

ALEXANDER CRUMMELL, a pioneer of black nationalism and one of the preeminent African American scholars of the nineteenth century, has been called an intellectual and political forerunner of W. E. B. Du Bois and Marcus Garvey. Crummell was born in New York City in 1819, to a formerly enslaved father, who was born in Africa, and a free mother. He attended the African Free School, Canal Street High School, and Noyes Academy in Canaan, New Hampshire (where he watched whites drag the school into a swamp). He graduated from the abolitionist-run Oneida Institute in 1839. He was ordained a minister in 1844, after four years of private study, having been barred from a formal theological education on the basis of race. He was active in the Negro convention movement and worked closely with Frederick Douglass. Traveling abroad to escape American racism, he finally received his B.A. from England's University of Cambridge in 1853. In 1857 he went to Liberia and for the next fifteen years pursued a variety of professions. He returned to the States in 1873 and worked vigorously to end racial oppression. He taught at Howard from 1895 through 1897, when he helped organize the American Negro Academy. His numerous books include *The Relations and Duties of Free Colored Men in America to Africa* (1861) and *The Attitude of the American Mind toward the Negro Intellect* (1898). He died in Brooklyn in 1898.

HAROLD CRUSE, professor emeritus at the University of Michigan, was born in Petersburg, Virginia, in 1916. After spending time in the military, Cruse began a career as an activist and social critic in New York. His thinking about the roles of black intellectuals in the United States was spelled out in *Crisis of the Negro Intellectual* (1967), one of the most controversial and influential books written during the Black Power period. He joined the Afro-American studies program at Michigan in 1969. His most recent book is *Plural but Equal* (1987).

COUNTEE CULLEN, a skilled poet associated with the Harlem Renaissance, was born in New York City in 1903 and raised by his maternal grandmother. A white Methodist Episcopal couple (the Cullens) unofficially adopted the bright and vibrant lad. Cullen distinguished himself academically at the predominantly white DeWitt Clinton High School and went on to receive a B.A. from New York University in 1925 and an M.A. from Howard in 1926. His advocacy of Alain Locke's New Negro philosophy is reflected in his poetry, and his desire to be known as a *poet* rather than as a *black* poet is one subject of his well-known "Yet Do I Marvel." Cullen won numerous prizes for his poetry throughout his academic and professional careers, including a 1928 Guggenheim Fellowship. His poetry has been widely published in collections and periodicals. Harlemites were shocked when he married Yolanda Du Bois, daughter of the venerable scholar. The marriage lasted less than a month. Cullen died in New York City in 1946.

ANGELA DAVIS was born in Birmingham, Alabama, in 1944 to middle-class parents. She left at fifteen to attend Elisabeth Irvin High School in New York. In 1965 she graduated from Brandeis University magna cum laude. While an undergraduate she studied philosophy at the Sorbonne and at Goethe University in Frankfurt, Germany. She received a Ph.D. from the University of California at San Diego and began teaching at UCLA. Active in antiprison protests and a member of the Communist Party U.S.A., Davis was dropped from the teaching position at UCLA. Shortly afterward she was charged with involvement in a kidnapping that led to the death of a judge and three prisoners. Brought to trial after ten months in jail, she was acquitted. Afterward, she continued to personify the scholar-activist role so prevalent in African American history. Davis is the author of five books, including *Angela Davis: An Autobiography* (1974) and *Women, Race and Class* (1982). Currently she is professor of the history of consciousness at the University of California at Santa Cruz and in 1995 was named to the presidential chair, one of the university's highest awards.

FRANK MARSHALL DAVIS, a poet, was an outspoken critic of racial and social injustice. Born in Arkansas City, Kansas, in 1905, Davis moved to Wichita after his high school graduation in 1923. The following year he enrolled in the Kansas State Agricultural College School of Journalism, but left after two and a half years for the excitement of Chicago. In 1930 he went to Atlanta to help develop and write for *Atlanta World* (later *Atlanta Daily World*), which would become an important black newspaper. Heavily influenced by jazz, as evidenced in his volume *Black Man's Verse* (1935), he never abandoned the protest tradition. In 1948, while in Hawaii on vacation, he decided to make the islands his permanent home. Davis died in 1987.

MARTIN DELANEY, the first African American to attend Harvard Medical School, was born in Charleston, West Virginia, in 1812, to an enslaved father and a free mother. He worked for Frederick Douglass's *North Star* and in 1848 decided to study medicine. He attended Harvard in 1850–51, but Oliver Wendell Holmes Sr., dean of Harvard's medical school, succumbed to white student protests and expelled Delaney. Since doctors were not required to finish medical school at that time, Delaney could nevertheless practice as a physician for the remainder of his life. Taking great pride in his blackness, he became very political and favored emigration to South America or Africa. In 1852 he published *The Condition, Elevation, Emigration and Destiny of the Colored People of the United States,* one of the early and coherent explications of black nationalism. After the Civil War, he participated for a while in the Reconstruction politics of South Carolina. Delaney died in Wilberforce, Ohio, in 1885.

FREDERICK DOUGLASS, the best-known nineteenth-century abolitionist and an early advocate of women's rights, was born into slavery in Talbot County, Maryland, around 1817. His father probably was his master, and his mother was a slave. Douglass taught himself to read and write and passed his knowledge on to other slaves. After years of physical, mental, and emotional confrontations with slaveholders and their agents, he successfully escaped on his third attempt. In 1845 his *Narrative of the Life of Frederick Douglass* was published, and in 1846 he left the United States for a year, fearing recapture. The energetic Douglass founded the *North Star* newspaper upon his return. During the Civil War he was an adviser to Abraham Lincoln and recruited blacks to fight to destroy slavery. During Reconstruction he became one of the most influential black leaders in the country, holding a number of positions in national politics between 1871 and 1891. He spoke out often for suffrage and other rights for women. He died in Washington, D.C., in 1895.

ST. CLAIR DRAKE, an anthropologist and educator, was born in Suffolk, Virginia, in 1911. After graduating from Hampton, Drake worked for the Society of Friends at a number of schools and movements in the South. A Hampton mentor, Allison Davis, involved him in an anthropological study later published as *Deep South*. Excited about the potential of social science research to effect change, Drake enrolled at the University of Chicago. Working with the eminent sociologist W. Lloyd Warner and a fellow student, Horace Cayton, Drake immersed himself in black Chicago and in 1945 published the classic *Black Metropolis*. Drake was one of the first black faculty members at Roosevelt University, where he taught for twenty-three years, leaving in 1973 to chair the African American studies program at Stanford. He knew a number of African and Pan-Africanist leaders, including Kwame Nkrumah and George Padmore. His *Black Diaspora* appeared in 1972. A legendary smoker, Drake died in 1990.


W. E. B. Du Bois, arguably the most important and productive black intellectual of the nineteenth and twentieth centuries, was born in 1868 in Great Barrington, Massachusetts. Raised in a single-parent home, Du Bois entered Fisk University just after his mother died, earning a B.A. (1888) and an M.A. (1891). He received a Ph.D. from Harvard in 1895, after doing graduate work in Berlin from 1892 to 1894. His 1899 book *The Philadelphia Negro* was a pathbreaking study of urban blacks in America, and *The Souls of Black Folks* (1903) remains a seminal text on race relations and the "color line." Du Bois underwent many political shifts during his long career. He was a founding member of the Niagara movement (1905), an organization of black intellectuals that broke ground for the founding of the NAACP five years later. At its inception, he was the only black officer of the NAACP, serving as its director of publicity and research for twenty years. In that capacity he founded the *Crisis,* the NAACP's official organ. Though often at odds with many of the young Harlem Renaissance writers—and with a number of his more mature colleagues—Du Bois envigorated that cultural movement. He came to be known as the father of Pan-Africanism, and later would be a target of governmental anti-Communist paranoia and probing. In 1958 he received the Soviet Union's Lenin International Peace Prize, and in the early sixties he formally joined the Communist Party. In 1961 Prime Minister Kwame Nkrumah invited him to come to Ghana. Du Bois renounced his U.S. citizenship in 1963, just before dying as a Ghanaian citizen on the day of the famous March on Washington.


Paul Laurence Dunbar, the most popular black poet at the turn of the century, was born in 1872 in Dayton, Ohio, to former slaves. His father, who fought in the Civil War, escaped to Canada via the

Underground Railroad, and his mother worked as a house servant until the end of the Civil War. Dunbar, the only black in his class at Central High School in Dayton, achieved many honors while there. He published his first poems in 1888 and was class president, president of the literary club, and class poet, reading the class poem at his graduation in 1890. Dunbar longed to attend Harvard but could not do so, for lack of funds. Racial discrimination restricted him to menial jobs, and financial problems plagued him throughout his early life. Eventually, though, his poetry earned him international acclaim. His books include *Oak and Ivy* (1893), *Majors and Minors* (1895), and *Lyrics of Lowly Life* (1896), which became a best-seller. For much of his life he suffered from alcoholism; he died at the age of thirty-three in 1906.

TROY DUSTER directs the Institute for Social Change at the University of California at Berkeley. Duster, a grandson of Ida Wells Barnett, was born in Chicago in 1936 and received a B.S. (1957) and a Ph.D. (1962) from Northwestern. Since joining the sociology faculty at Berkeley in 1963, he has written *The Legislation of Morality* (1970) and *Back Door to Eugenics* (1990). He is one of the world's leading authorities on the social implications of scientific policies.

MICHAEL ERIC DYSON, born in Detroit in 1958, emerged in the early nineties as an important cultural critic. Dyson was one of five children born to a working-class inner-city family. After a bad experience in a private suburban high school, he returned to Detroit and finished high school. At an early age he married and served as a minister to several Baptist congregations. He journeyed south and enrolled at Knoxville College in 1979. He eventually transferred to Carson-Newman and earned his degree in philosophy magna cum laude. In Princeton's Department of Religion, he continued his study of philosophy and began to reflect on broader social and cultural questions. To reach a wider audience, Dyson wrote frequently for the popular press. After completing his doctorate at Princeton, he taught at Hartford and Chicago seminaries. He accepted a faculty position in Afro-American studies at Brown University. In 1994 he was named director of a research and cultural center at the University of North Carolina at Chapel Hill. His writings include *Reflecting Black* (1993) and a forthcoming book on the cultural significance of rap music.

GERALD EARLY, head of the Department of Afro-American Studies at Washington University, in St. Louis, was born in 1952 and grew up in Philadelphia. He received a B.A. from the University of Pennsylvania in 1974 and a Ph.D. in literature from Cornell in 1982. Since 1982 he has taught at Washington University. Among his books are *Tuxedo Junction* (1989), *Lure and Loathing* (1993), and *The Culture of Bruising* (1994), which won the National Book Critics Circle Award.

G. FRANKLIN EDWARDS, a sociologist, was born in Charleston, South Carolina, in 1915. He received a B.A. from Fisk University (1936) and a Ph.D. from the highly rated Department of Sociology at the University of Chicago (1953). After graduating from Fisk, Edwards worked with Charles Johnson researching patterns of race relations in the South. A student, and later a Howard University colleague, of E. Franklin Frazier, Edwards wrote *The Negro Professional Class* (1959) and edited *E. Franklin Frazier on Race Relations: Selected Papers* (1968).

RALPH ELLISON published one novel during his career, and it became a literary classic and one of the most important novels by an American writer of the twentieth century. Ellison was born in Oklahoma City in 1914. His father, an entrepreneur, died when Ellison was three, and his mother took on domestic work to support the family. He attended Tuskegee from 1933 to 1936, an experience he drew upon in writing *Invisible Man* (1952). He traveled to New York after his junior year to earn money for his senior year, but he never returned. In New York he became friends with Langston Hughes, who introduced him to Richard Wright. Wright urged Ellison to work at his writing, and in 1938 Ellison joined the Federal Writers'

Project, where he met Sterling Brown, its editor on Negro affairs. Ellison wrote reviews and short stories through the late forties and early fifties. *Invisible Man,* which won a National Book Award—and, later, *Shadow and Act* (1964), a collection of essays—garnered him many honors, both domestic and international, including a 1969 Presidential Medal of Freedom. Institutions at which he taught include Bard (1958–61), Rutgers (1962–69), the University of Chicago (1961), and New York University, where in 1970 he was named Albert Schweitzer Professor in the Humanities. A committed writer, he lectured widely and received many honorary degrees, among them one from Tuskegee (1963) and one from Harvard (1974). *Going to the Territory,* a collection of his speeches, essays, and reviews, appeared in 1968. He continued to work on a second novel from 1955 until the time of his death in New York in 1994.

RUDOLPH FISHER, a radiologist, a writer, and a musician, was born in 1897 in Washington, D.C., to the Reverend John W. and Glendora Fisher, and grew up in Providence, Rhode Island. Fisher received a B.A. from Brown in 1919, an M.A. from Brown in 1920, and an M.D. with highest honors from Howard in 1924. He became an important member of the Harlem Renaissance literati, noted for his use of humor as a way of shedding light on treacherous aspects of African American life. He was a fellow of the National Research Council at the Columbia University College of Physicians and Surgeons. Among his writings are short stories, children's books, and two novels, *Walls of Jericho* (1928) and *The Conjure Man Dies: A Mystery Tale of Dark Harlem* (1932). Fisher also compiled spirituals and performed with Paul Robeson. He died in New York City in 1934.

JOHN HOPE FRANKLIN, the dean of African American historians, was born in Rentiesville, Oklahoma, in 1915. His father, a lawyer, concluded that the family would be better off in Tulsa, and they moved to that city when John Hope was ten years old. Franklin attended Booker T. Washington High School in Tulsa and received a B.A. magna cum laude from Fisk (1935) and an M.A. (1936) and a Ph.D. (1941) from Harvard. He taught history at North Carolina College and at Fisk and was a member of a Howard University faculty that included E. Franklin Frazier, Rayford Logan, and Abram Harris. In 1956 he became the first African American to head a department in a major white university when he accepted an appointment as chair of the history department at Brooklyn College. In 1964 he assumed the same post at the University of Chicago. Franklin was also the first black to head two major professional associations, the Southern Historical Association and the American Historical Association. Ever conscious of broader obligations, he assisted in drafting the legal brief submitted by the NAACP in the 1954 *Brown* v. *Board of Education* case. His books include the seminal *From Slavery to Freedom* (1948), *The Militant South* (1956), and *George Washington Williams* (1985).

E. FRANKLIN FRAZIER was one of the most high-profile black sociologists of his era. He was born in 1894 in Baltimore, where his father was a bank messenger. Frazier graduated cum laude from Howard in 1916 and received a Ph.D. from the University of Chicago in 1931. Proficient in many disciplines, he taught math, French, English, and history at Tuskegee Institute. No other sociologist during the thirties and forties approached the volume and quality of his work on African Americans. Few cultural questions escaped his gaze; for instance, the scholarly exchanges with Melville Herskovits about the nature and significance of African culture among American blacks framed the debate for the next forty years. Frazier taught at Atlanta University and later chaired the sociology department at Howard from 1934 to 1959. When named president of the American Sociological Society in 1948, he became the first black to head a national academic association. His published works include *The Negro Family in America* (1939), *Race and Culture Contacts in the Modern World* (1957), and *Black Bourgeoisie* (1957), a thinly veiled exposé of the pretentiousness of his black middle-class cohorts. Frazier died in Washington, D.C., in 1962.

HENRY HIGHLAND GARNET, a minister and nationalist whose life closely paralleled that of his contemporary Alexander Crummell, was born into slavery in Maryland in 1815. His family escaped when he was nine, and he attended the African Free School, the New York Free School, and the High School for Colored Youth. Fearful of being captured and reenslaved, the family moved often. Like Crummell, Garnet attended the Noyes Academy in Canaan, New Hampshire, and the Oneida Institute in New York. After graduating from Oneida in 1839, he went on to become a militant abolitionist. He agitated for slave rebellion and launched two underfunded and short-lived newspapers in the 1840s. An advocate of black emigration, he founded the African Civilization Society, whose goal, in effect, was to Westernize Africa. Garnet was named general counsel to Liberia in 1881 and died there the following year.

MARCUS GARVEY, the political and intellectual leader of the largest mass organization in African American history, was born in St. Ann's Bay, Jamaica, in 1887. He left high school because of financial difficulties. A printer by training, he founded the United Negro Improvement Association (UNIA) in 1914, advocating unity of black people worldwide, international commercial activity, and colonization of Africa. Impressed by the ideas of Booker T. Washington and the potential of American blacks based in Harlem, he migrated to the United States. He soon achieved a widespread following and began publishing the *Negro World,* a black weekly. Despite the hostility of middle-class black leaders and government harassment, his appeal to self-help and racial pride resonated with less privileged blacks. He ranks as one of the most important black leaders of the early twentieth century; in spite of his deportation after being indicted for fraud in connection with his efforts to purchase a shipping line that would carry African Americans "back to Africa," his social and political impact on the period is indisputable. He died in London in 1940.

HENRY LOUIS GATES JR. was born in Keyser, West Virginia, in 1950 and received a B.A. summa cum laude from Yale in 1973. He earned an M.A. (1974) and a Ph.D. (1979) from Clare College in Cambridge, England, was a professor at Yale (1975–85), and is currently W. E. B. Du Bois Professor and chair of Afro-American studies at Harvard. One of the more prolific scholars of this generation, Gates

Harvard. One of the more prolific scholars of this generation, Gates also understands the importance of building and sustaining black cultural institutions. Since the 1980s he has helped revive the journal *Transitions,* brought out new editions of books by early black women writers, and continued the strengthening of African American studies at Harvard that began under the late Nathan Huggins. An articulate and personable advocate of literary analysis, Gates writes frequently on black cultural matters in publications such as *The New Yorker,* the *New York Times Book Review,* and *Emerge.* In 1981 he was awarded a MacArthur Fellowship, a high point in his career. Although widely acclaimed in American intellectual circles, Gates has been criticized for his championing of cultural and literary hierarchies—"canons"—and for what some view as excessive energy spent attacking unpopular targets such as blacks who are anti-Semites or extreme Afrocentrists. With his graduate students at Yale, he rediscovered Harriet Wilson's *Our Nig . . .* (reissued in 1983), now known as the first-ever novel by an African American woman. His *Signifying Monkey: A Theory of Afro-American Literary Criticism* (1988) won an American Book Award; a collection of his essays, *Loose Canons,* appeared in 1992.

HUGH GLOSTER, a literary critic and longtime president of Morehouse College, was born in Brownsville, Tennessee, in 1911. He received a B.A. from Morehouse in 1931, an M.A. from Atlanta University in 1933, and a Ph.D. from New York University in 1943. He helped found the College Language Association in 1937. He taught at LeMoyne College (1933–41) and at Hampton Institute (1946–67) before becoming president of Morehouse College (1967–87). His *Negro Voices in American Fiction* (1948) is a pioneering work in black literary criticism.

RICHARD GREENER, the first African American to graduate from Harvard, was born in Philadelphia in 1844. After finishing Harvard, Greener held numerous teaching and administrative positions, including principalships at the Institute for Colored Youth in Philadelphia and Sumner High School in Washington, D.C. He was a professor at the University of South Carolina during the Reconstruction period and, later, dean of law at Howard. Before his death in 1922 in Chicago, he served as U.S. consul in the Soviet Union and in India.

SUTTON GRIGGS, a prolific writer and vigorous proponent of black empowerment, denounced racist oppression and is considered an early black militant, though he grew more conservative later in life. He was born in Chatfield, Texas, in 1872, and at twenty-one completed theological course work at Richmond Theological Seminary. A Baptist preacher, he wrote numerous guides and "how to" books, as well as a host of novels. He spent his entire life in the South crusading against lynch mobs and slavery. In spite of his voluminous writings, he has been largely ignored by major black critics, with the notable exception of Hugh Gloster. Griggs died in Houston in 1930.

JUPITER HAMMON was the first black writer to be published in the Western Hemisphere. Born into slavery in Oyster Bay, Long Island, in 1711, Hammon and his father remained with the same slaveholding family all of their lives. Hammon's mother was sold when he was a child, and he had little formal education. He learned to write poetry. He died near the end of the eighteenth century in Oyster Bay.

VINCENT HARDING, a highly regarded historian, combined scholarship with political activism in the civil rights movement, working closely with Martin Luther King Jr. He was born in 1931 in New York and earned a B.A. from City College of New York (1952), an M.S. from Columbia (1953), and an M.A. (1956) and a Ph.D. (1965) from the University of Chicago. He was chair of sociology at Spelman from 1965 to 1969, when he became director of the Institute of the Black World at the Martin Luther King Memorial Center, in Atlanta. In 1981 he assumed a professorship at the University of Denver's Iliff School of Theology; that same year he was named chairman of the board of the King Center. He was a senior adviser to the acclaimed television series *Eyes on the Prize: America's Civil Rights Years* and author of *There Is a River: The Black Struggle for Freedom in America* (1981).

NATHAN HARE, a sociologist, is best known for his scathing critiques of the black middle class and his involvement in the movement for black studies in the late sixties. Hare is a native of Slick, Oklahoma, born in 1934. He earned a bachelor's degree from Langston University in 1954, before receiving advanced degrees from the University of Chicago. The intense Hare was recruited to the Howard faculty in 1961 but left in 1967 because of a clash with the campus administration over student activism. Students at San Francisco State, impressed by his militancy, lobbied successfully for his appointment as chair of the new black studies department in 1968. After a few years Hare resigned over conflicts about the nature of the black studies program. He helped found and publish *Black Scholar*, an important organ of black academic militancy. His books include *The Black Anglo-Saxons;* he has also written a number of works with his wife, Julia Hare.

FRANCES E. W. HARPER, an abolitionist, feminist, educator, and writer, was one of the earliest African American women to publish a novel. Born in 1825 in Baltimore, the only child of free parents, Harper published her first volume of poetry in the mid-1840s and in 1850 began teaching science at Union Seminary near Columbus, Ohio. Later she became the first woman teacher at the New School for Free Blacks, founded in 1847 by the African Methodist Episcopal church. She was active in the black women's club movements, and her novel *Iola Leroy; or, Shadows Uplifted* was published in 1892. She died in Philadelphia in 1911.

ABRAM HARRIS, a radical economist, advocated a class analysis when considering the status of black Americans. Born in Richmond, Virginia, in 1899, he was descended from slaves freed prior to the Civil War. Harris received a B.S. from Virginia Union University in 1922, an M.A. from the University of Pittsburgh in 1924, and a Ph.D. from Columbia in 1931. Most of his academic career was spent at Howard (1927–45) and the University of Chicago (1946–50). In the forties he frequently clashed with older black intellectuals who insisted on a strictly racial framework when focusing on black subordination. In 1961 he was awarded a Guggenheim Fellowship, which allowed him to earn an LL.D. from Virginia Union University that year. His books include *The Black Worker, the Negro & the Labor Movement* (1931) and *The Negro as Capitalist* (1936). He died in 1963.


WILLIAM HASTIE, a noted judge, was born in Knoxville, Tennessee, in 1904. After graduating from Amherst College in 1925, he went to Harvard and completed an LL.B. in 1930. He taught at Howard's law school for seven years. Franklin Roosevelt brought him into the New Deal administration as a solicitor in the Department of the Interior, where his work led to a 1937 appointment as judge of the U.S. District Court in the Virgin Islands. Hastie was the first black federal judge since Reconstruction. Uneasy with his role as judge, Hastie returned to Howard as law school dean in 1939 but was again drafted into high government service, this time as aide to Secretary of War Henry Stimson. When the executive branch failed to take steps to end segregation in the military, Hastie resigned. President Truman appointed him to the Federal Appeals Court in 1949, and he held that post until 1971. Hastie died in 1976.


DARLENE CLARK HINE, one of the foremost historians of black women, is John Hannah Professor of American History at Michigan State University. Hine was born in Morley, Missouri, in 1947 and earned a B.A. from Roosevelt University in 1968 and Ph.D. from Kent State in 1975. She edited *Black Women in America: An Historical Encyclopedia* and wrote *Black Women in White: Racial Conflict and Cooperation in the Nursing Profession, 1890–1950.* Before accepting the appointment at Michigan State, she taught at South Carolina State College and Purdue University.


PAULINE HOPKINS, born in Portland, Maine, in 1859, at age ten won a writing contest sponsored by the abolitionist William Wells Brown. Hopkins graduated from Girls' High School in Boston around 1875 and wrote her first play, *Slaves' Escape; or, The Underground Railroad,* in 1879. She joined the staff of *Colored America* magazine in 1900, the year she published her novel *Contending Forces: A Romance Illustrative of Negro Life North and South.* She died in her native Maine in 1930.

GERALD HORNE, a prolific historian, began his academic career in the public schools of St. Louis. After an academically impressive undergraduate career at Princeton University, Horne earned a law degree from the University of California at Berkeley in 1973. He then returned to the field of history and entered the Ph.D. program at Columbia. During this period he was active in many human rights and working-class movements. Awarded the Ph.D. in 1982, he began his teaching career at Sarah Lawrence College. In 1988 he joined the black studies department at the University of California at Santa Barbara, as chair. He published *Black and Red: W. E. B. Du Bois and the Afro-American Response to the Cold War, 1944–63* (1985) and *Communist Front: The Civil Rights Congress, 1946–1956* (1987). *The Fire This Time,* a scholarly treatment of the 1963 Watts uprising, appeared in 1995.

CHARLES HAMILTON HOUSTON preceded Thurgood Marshall as the most important black lawyer of the twentieth century. He was born in Washington, D.C., in 1895. Houston's father, a graduate of Howard University's law school, practiced law and taught at his alma mater. After completing M Street High (later Dunbar High School) in 1911, he entered Amherst College. In 1915 he graduated as valedictorian and Phi Beta Kappa, and returned to teach at Howard. In 1917 he enlisted in the armed forces, and served in World War I. After his discharge in 1919, he entered Harvard Law School, where he became the first black editor of the *Harvard Law Review*. He received his LL.B. in 1922 cum laude, and practiced law with his father from 1924 to 1950. He served as special counsel to the NAACP, becoming its first full-time, paid counsel while teaching and holding administrative positions at Howard. At Howard he was a mentor to Thurgood Marshall. Houston was a preeminent antidiscrimination lawyer whose efforts laid the legal groundwork for the *Brown* v. *Board of Education* ruling won by his protégé Marshall in 1954. Houston died in 1950 in Washington, D.C., and was posthumously awarded the NAACP's Spingarn Medal that same year.

LANGSTON HUGHES, one of the most published African American writers in history, was born in Joplin, Missouri, in 1902. His parents divorced while he was young. His mother was creative and wrote poems, and his father studied law, but racial discrimination kept him from taking the state bar examination. He eventually became bitter and left the United States for Mexico, where Hughes often visited him. On a train to Mexico in 1920, Hughes wrote his poem "The Negro Speaks of Rivers." He finished Central High School in Lincoln, Illinois, in 1920 and enrolled at Columbia the following year. The *Crisis* was the first journal to publish his work, in 1921. Alain Locke, the critic and talent broker, recognized Hughes's ability and carefully cultivated it. Hughes made many trips overseas, including one to the Soviet Union, and crossed paths with such luminaries as Carter G. Woodson, Zora Neale Hurston, James Weldon Johnson, and Carl Van Vechten. Hughes was quite unassuming and reveled in the folk culture of the black masses. He produced some fifty books— including his two-volume autobiography, *The Big Sea* (1940) and *I Wonder As I Wander* (1956)—more than a dozen plays, and a host of periodical articles. He also created the character Jesse B. Semple ("Simple") for a column in the *Chicago Defender,* around whom he wrote anecdotal short stories dealing with racism and related subjects. Hughes died in New York in 1967.


ZORA NEALE HURSTON was a prolific—and perhaps the most flamboyant—black woman writer between the Harlem Renaissance and the 1960s. She was born in 1871 in Eatonville, Florida, an all-black, self-governed township that helped her see the world from something of an Afrocentric perspective. Her schoolteacher mother died when she was thirteen, and her father, a carpenter, remarried a woman with whom Hurston had a rocky relationship. She attended Howard from 1919 to 1924 and received a B.A. from Barnard in 1928. In 1934–35 she studied at Columbia, where she worked with the anthropologist Franz Boas. In New York she participated in the Harlem Renaissance, referring sarcastically to its black writers as the "niggerati." She was an energetic and resourceful collector of folklore and a friend of Langston Hughes. In 1948 she was accused of molesting a ten-year-old boy, and although never convicted of any crime, she was devastated by the harsh treatment she received in the black press. She died in obscurity in Fort Pierce, Florida, in 1960. In the seventies Alice Walker and several other black women writers reawakened interest in her work.

BLYDEN JACKSON, a longtime literary critic and educator, was born in Paducah, Kentucky, in 1910 and earned a B.A. from Wilberforce University in Ohio (1930) and a Ph.D. from the University of Michigan (1952). Between 1945 and 1954 Jackson taught at Florida A&M University and Fisk University; from 1962 to 1969 he directed graduate studies at Southern University. Jackson left all-black Southern University to become professor of English at the University of North Carolina in 1969. During his long career he contributed to several scholarly journals, including the *College Language Association Journal,* the *Journal of Negro History,* and *Phylon.* He wrote, with Louis D. Rubin Jr., *Black Poetry in America: Two Essays in Historical Interpretation* (1974) and later published *Waiting Years: Essays in Historical Interpretation* (1976).

CHARLES JOHNSON, an influential black sociologist and an energetic opponent of racial discrimination and segregation, was born in Bristol, Virginia, in 1893. Johnson received a B.A. from Virginia Union University, in Richmond, in 1916 and pursued a Ph.D. at the University of Chicago, where he studied sociology with the famous Robert Park. Johnson adopted Park's belief that interracial relations were key to overcoming segregation, and during the Harlem Renaissance he facilitated interracial social gatherings. Johnson's personal style won him many friends in powerful white circles. He fought in World War I and survived the Chicago race riot of 1919, which further sparked his desire to improve race relations in America. He joined the staff of the Chicago Urban League around 1920 and founded *Opportunity* magazine with Eugene Jones. He reentered academe in 1928 to chair Fisk's sociology department. In 1947 he became Fisk's first black president and held that post until 1956. Black social scientists including St. Clair Drake considered Johnson a one-person clearing house for blacks seeking foundation support. Johnson received numerous awards and honors before his death in 1956 in Louisville, Kentucky.

JAMES WELDON JOHNSON, best known as the author of the classic *Autobiography of an Ex-Colored Man* (1912), was born in Jacksonville, Florida, in 1871. His self-educated father first worked as a waiter in New York, but achieved middle-class status as a headwaiter in Florida. His mother, of African, French, and English descent, was born in Nassau but grew up in New York. Johnson received a B.A. from Atlanta University in 1894 and attended Columbia from 1903 to 1906. He went on to many jobs, including those of teacher, songwriter, poet, journalist, and lawyer. He wrote numerous articles for various periodicals and anthologized many Harlem Renaissance writers as editor of *The Book of American Negro Poetry* (1922). His other works include *Black Manhattan* (1930) and *Along This Way* (1933). He was a major leader of the NAACP from 1916 to 1930, serving as its general secretary from 1920 to 1929. Johnson was U.S. consul in Venezuela from 1906 to 1910, and often clashed with younger black intellectuals. He taught creative literature at Fisk from 1930 until his death in a car accident in 1938.


EUGENE JONES, born in 1885, an energetic and important race relations activist of the early twentieth century, advocated interracial cooperation as a means for African Americans to gain socioeconomic parity. Jones's father, a former slave, was one of the first blacks in Virginia to graduate from college, and his mother was born free; both of his parents were teachers. Jones was raised in an interracial environment and learned much by watching his parents interact with their white colleagues. He received a B.A. from Virginia Union University in 1906 and an M.A. from Cornell in 1908. His teaching career included positions at State University and Central High School in Louisville, Kentucky. Jones worked for more than forty years with the National Urban League, where he was, among other things, executive secretary (1917–41) and general secretary (1941–50). With Charles Johnson, he founded *Opportunity: Journal of Negro Life* in 1923; it published writers such as Langston Hughes, Countee Cullen, and Claude McKay. A friend of Arthur A. Schomburg, Jones had a hand in establishing the New York Public Library's Schomburg Center for Research in Black Studies, in Harlem. He died in New York City in 1954.

JUNE JORDAN, a poet and activist, was born in 1936 in New York, to a Jamaican immigrant family. Jordon attended public elementary schools in New York City and enrolled in Midwood High School, where she was the only black in a student body of 3,000. In 1953 she matriculated at Barnard College while living at home. After attending Barnard sporadically, she dropped out in 1959 and began a career as a free-lance journalist, all the while raising a young son. Jordan worked at numberous writing-related jobs and in 1967 began a college teaching career at City College of New York. Her poetry and essays frequently address links between the personal and the political. Among her books are *Civil Wars, Naming Our Destiny: New and Selected Poems,* and *Kimakoo's Story.* In 1991 she joined the African American and women's studies faculty at the University of California at Berkeley.

ERNEST EVERETT JUST, a pioneer in the field of cell biology, was born in Charleston, South Carolina, in 1883. His father was a wharf builder, who died when Just was four; his mother taught school and worked in a phosphate quarry. She bought land on James Island and organized a small community there, but when Just was sixteen she encouraged him to go north. He went to Kimball Union Academy, in New Hampshire, and in 1903 enrolled at the newly opened Dartmouth College. In 1907 he graduated magna cum laude with a B.S. in biology and immediately joined the faculty of Howard, where in 1910 he took over the biology department. Six years later he received a Ph.D. from the University of Chicago. Delighting in the relative freedom that Europe provided, he spent as much time abroad as possible. The rise of fascism in Europe during the late thirties prompted his return to the United States. His two books, including *The Biology of the Cell Surface,* were published in 1939. He died at Howard in 1941.

ADRIENNE KENNEDY was born in Pittsburgh in 1931 and grew up in Cleveland. She received a B.A. from Ohio State University (1952) and did graduate work at Columbia. Her complex and surrealistic plays enjoyed an overdue surge of interest during the late eighties.

Kennedy has taught at Yale, the University of California at Berkeley, Princeton, and Brown. Her plays include *Funnyhouse of a Negro* (1962), *Sun: A Poem for Malcolm X Inspired by His Murder* (1968), *An Evening with Dead Essex* (1973), and *Black Children's Day* (1980).

JOHN MERCER LANGSTON was born in Louisa County, Virginia, in 1829 to a white father and a slave mother of Indian and African descent. From Oberlin College he received a B.A. in 1849 and an M.A. in 1852. He was the first black admitted to the Ohio bar, in 1854, and subsequently held numerous public offices, including the clerkship of Oberlin (1865–67) and the post of school inspector general of the Freedmen's Bureau. A professor of law and acting president of Howard from 1869 to 1876, Langston accepted the political post as U.S. minister to Haiti from 1877 to 1885, when he returned to head Virginia Normal and Collegiate Institute (now Virginia State University). He held a seat in the U.S. House of Representatives in 1890–91. The black town of Langston, Oklahoma, was named for him, and he was great uncle to the poet Langston Hughes. Langston died in Washington, D.C., in 1897.

NELLA LARSEN, a Harlem Renaissance writer whose novels were rediscovered and reexamined during the sixties rebirth of black arts and letters, was born in Chicago in 1891, to a Danish mother and a father of Caribbean descent. The young Nella eventually was alienated from her white family members, and her struggle to reconcile her own mixed heritage became a theme of her two major works, the novels *Quicksand* (1928) and *Passing* (1929). She attended Fisk's high school department for one year before traveling to Denmark and auditing courses at the University of Copenhagen from 1910 to 1912. She later studied nursing at Lincoln Hospital in New York City and worked for a while in city hospitals. After receiving a certificate from the school of the New York Public Library in 1923, she began to work as a librarian and to write fiction two years later. She married the prominent physicist Eugene Imes and, as his wife, became a leading Harlem socialite. Walter White of the NAACP, also a very fair-skinned African American, encouraged her writing and supplied important introductions to publishers and editors. W. E. B. Du Bois's positive review of *Quicksand* in the *Crisis* helped her enjoy fleeting success as a writer. Given to changing the spelling of her last name, her date of birth, and other biographical facts, Larsen spent the last half of her life avoiding public attention and worked as a nurse until the age of seventy-two, when she died in New York City.

SHELTON "SPIKE" LEE was born in Atlanta in 1957. His family moved to Brooklyn, but Spike eventually returned to Atlanta to attend Morehouse College. On graduating, in 1979, he went to New York University and earned an M.A. in film in 1983. He won the Student Director's Award from the Academy of Motion Picture Arts and Sciences, and a New Generation Award from the Los Angeles film critics. Throughout his career he has carefully cultivated not only his talent but also controversy, on the theory that the racial attitudes of white America force black filmmakers to take extra steps to draw attention to their work. Lee's films on interracial relationships (*Jungle Fever,* 1991) and urban racial tension (*Do the Right Thing,* 1989) tapped a reservoir of interest in the country. His other films include *She's Gotta Have It* (1986), *School Daze* (1988), and the epic *Malcolm X* (1992), based on the life of the nationalist activist. The diaries and screenplays for several of his films have appeared in book form.

DAVID LEVERING LEWIS, the Pulitzer Prize–winning biographer of W. E. B. Du Bois, was born in Little Rock, Arkansas, in 1936. Lewis received a B.A. from Fisk and a doctorate in French history from the London School of Economics. He has taught at the University of California at San Diego and currently holds the Martin Luther King Jr. chair in history at Rutgers. His other books include *When Harlem Was in Vogue* (1979) and *King: A Critical Biography* (1970).

ALAIN LOCKE, a leading black intellectual during the early twentieth century and an important elder of the Harlem Renaissance, was born in Philadelphia in 1886, to middle-class parents, both of whom were educators. He graduated from Harvard in 1907 and proceeded to go to Oxford as the first African American Rhodes Scholar. He received a B.A. from Oxford in 1910 and elected to stay in Europe and study philosophy at the University of Berlin. He returned to the States in 1912 to assume an assistant professorship at Howard. In 1916 he continued his education at Harvard, where he completed a Ph.D., and later resumed his career at Howard. His anthology *The New Negro*, dedicated to "The Younger Generation," was published in 1925. The resourceful Locke was especially close and helpful to the young writers Langston Hughes, Countee Cullen, Jean Toomer, and Rudolph Fisher. Somewhat paradoxically, he subscribed to Du Bois's Talented Tenth idea but also sought to remain connected to the "masses." He believed that the cultivation of more refined cultural tastes and production would bring black people the socioeconomic parity they sought. He died in New York City in 1954.

RAYFORD LOGAN, an African American historian, was born in Washington, D.C., in 1897. He received a B.A. (1917) and an M.A. (1929) from Williams College and a Ph.D. (1936) from Harvard. He taught at Virginia Union University (1925–30), Atlanta University (1933–38), and Howard (1938–65). He became chairman of Howard's history department in 1942 and, despite his prickly personality, guided it during the peak of its prominence. He is best known for his studies of Africa and African Americans. His writings include *Diplomatic Relations with the United States and Haiti* (1941), *The Negro and the Post-War World: A Primer* (1945), *The African Mandates in World Politics* (1948), *The Negro in American Life and Thought: The Nadir, 1877–1901* (1954), and the classic *Dictionary of American Negro Biography* (1982), coedited with Michael R. Winston. Logan retired from teaching in 1965 and died in 1982 in Washington, D.C.

AUDRE LORDE, a prolific poet and social activist whose work challenged social and racial oppression, was born in New York City in 1934 to West Indian immigrant parents. Her father, a real estate broker eager to see his children succeed, sent his seven daughters to parochial schools. Lorde began writing poetry in elementary school and received a B.A. from Hunter College (1959) and an M.L.S. from Columbia (1961). She later taught at the City College of New York (1968–70) and at Hunter (1987–92). In 1980 she cofounded Kitchen Table: Women of Color Press, which published such feminist anthologies as *Home Girls* and *This Bridge Called My Back*. Her personal battle with breast cancer, which took her life in 1992, led her to critique the U.S. health care system in her later works. Lorde's many books include *The Cancer Journals* (1984) and the now classic *Sister Outsider* (1984), which won the Manhattan President's Award for Literary Excellence in 1987 and a Walt Whitman Citation of Merit in 1991.

GLENN LOURY, one of many black intellectuals from Chicago, was born in 1948. His working-class parents stressed education, and young Glenn performed well in high school, graduating at sixteen. Loury married and started a family early. After working in entry-level jobs around Chicago, he won a scholarship to Northwestern University, where he finished as an outstanding student in economics. He completed a Ph.D. in economics at MIT in 1979 and began his teaching career at the University of Michigan. In 1982 he became a tenured professor at Harvard, where he started to write and speak critically of liberal social policies. As a critic of liberalism, he was attractive to the growing conservative movement and was considered for high government posts. Sidetracked by personal difficulties, he eventually returned to academic life at Boston University. Unlike some other black conservatives, he does not accept the virtual abandonment of urban black America by policymakers.

HAKI MADHUBUTI (formerly Don L. Lee), an influential poet, was born in Little Rock in 1942. Lee attended Roosevelt University, in Chicago (1966–67), and the University of Illinois. A proponent of the idea that blacks should control their art, he founded Third World Press in 1967 and the Institute for Positive Education in Chicago in 1969. His first book of poetry, *Think Black* (1967), was very well received, and he has published numerous books and essays, including *Black Men: Obsolete, Single, Dangerous?: Afrikan American Families in Transition* (1990). He edited *Why L.A. Happened: Implications of the '92 Los Angeles Rebellion* (1993). Madhubuti is currently professor of english and director of the Gwendolyn Brooks Center for Black Literature and Creative Writing at Chicago State University.

MANNING MARABLE, a historian, was born in 1950 and earned a Ph.D. in political science from the University of Maryland in 1976. Marable taught at Tuskegee, Purdue University, and the University of Colorado and is currently professor of history at Columbia. His published contributions to the dialogue about race and class in American life include *How Capitalism Underdeveloped Black America* (1983) and *Blackwater: Historical Studies in Race, Class Consciousness and Revolution* (1981).

THURGOOD MARSHALL, arguably the most important and influential black lawyer of the twentieth century, was born in segregated Baltimore in 1908. His father was a steward at a country club, and his mother taught elementary school; both instilled in him feelings of racial pride. Marshall attended Lincoln University and graduated at the top of his class from Howard's law school in 1933. He became a protégé of Charles Hamilton Houston's, adopting Houston's philosophy that law could be used in the fight against racism. He became assistant special counsel to the NAACP in 1936 and special counsel in 1938. Marshall was the key litigator who pressed the plaintiff's case in *Brown* v. *Board of Education*. He assumed a position on the U.S. Supreme Court in 1967, the first black to do so. He retired from the Supreme Court in 1991, two years before his death in Bethesda, Maryland.

BENJAMIN MAYS, president of Morehouse College from 1940 to 1967, was born in Epsworth, South Carolina, in 1895, to formerly enslaved parents. He earned a B.A. (1920) at Bates College, in Maine, and an M.A. (1925) and a Ph.D. (1935) from the University of Chicago. From 1921 to 1924 he taught at Morehouse and in 1934 became dean of Howard's school of religion. In 1940 he accepted the offer of the presidency of Morehouse, where in 1945 he introduced a studious undergraduate, Martin Luther King Jr., to the works and philosophy of Mahatma Gandhi. Mays's study *The Negro's God as Reflected in His Literature* (1938) was one of the first critical works by an African American writer that focused on black religion. In his later years Mays served on the Atlanta Board of Education and remained, until his death in 1984, an outspoken civil rights advocate.

CLAUDE MCKAY, one of the more militant and independent literary voices to emerge from the Harlem Renaissance, was born in Jamaica in 1889 to peasant parents. He came to the United States and enrolled at Tuskegee for about two months in 1912 and spent the next two years at Kansas State College. His poetry combined the British sonnet form and the content of black consciousness. "If We Must Die," perhaps his best-known poem, was written in 1919 in response to racial violence throughout the United States during the summer of that year. It earned him recognition among black people as an important poet. McKay for a while enjoyed good relations with prominent white cultural radicals in the first quarter of the century. Toward the end of his life, however, he became a Catholic and adopted more mainstream views. He died in Chicago in 1948.

KELLY MILLER, an important sociologist, was born in Winnsboro, North Carolina, in 1863. His father was probably a Confederate soldier and his mother a slave. He received a B.A. (1886), an M.A. (1901), and an LL.B. (1903) from Howard. He did postgraduate work at Johns Hopkins and began teaching in 1889 at a Washington, D.C., high school. In 1890 he joined the faculty of Howard and in 1907 became dean of its College of Arts and Sciences, a post he held until 1918. He filled various other academic roles at Howard until 1935. He was a founder of the American Negro Academy, a society of black intellectuals, and wrote a widely syndicated weekly newspaper column. His books include *Out of the House of Bondage* (1914). He died in 1939 in Washington, D.C.

TONI MORRISON, one of the most important American writers of the contemporary era, was born in Lorain, Ohio, in 1931, and grew up in that small steel mill town during the Great Depression. She received a B.A. from Howard (1953) and an M.A. from Cornell (1955). After teaching stints at Texas Southern University and Howard, she became a senior editor with Random House in 1965. In that capacity, she shepherded into print many works by black women during the late sixties and early seventies. Her own first novel, *The Bluest Eye,* was published in 1970. Since then, she has produced an award-winning body of work that includes the novels *Sula* (1974), *Song of Solomon* (1977), *Tar Baby* (1981), and the Pulitzer Prize–winning *Beloved* (1987). Among her nonfiction works are *Playing in the Dark: Whiteness and the Literary Imagination* (1992) and the anthology *Race*-ing *Justice,* En-*gender*ing *Power: Essays on Anita Hill, Clarence Thomas, and the Construction of Social Reality,* which she edited and introduced in 1992. In 1993 she was awarded the Nobel Prize in Literature. Morrison is currently a professor of English at Princeton.

WALTER MOSLEY is a novelist whose complex and imaginative accounts of the black urban community have gained him critical and popular acclaim in the 1990s. Among his titles are *Black Betty* and *Devil in a Blue Dress.*

WILSON J. MOSES, an expert on nineteenth-century black thought, was born in 1942 and grew up in Detroit and attended Catholic schools. After graduating from high school in 1959, Moses enrolled at Wayne State University and worked at a nearby automotive parts plant. After encountering the work of Du Bois, Moses decided to pursue African American Studies and enrolled in the graduate program in American Civilization at Brown, where he began his research on nineteenth-century black nationalism, particularly that of Alexander Crummell. Moses has held faculty appointments at Boston University, Brown, and Pennsylvania State University. His published works include *The Golden Age of Black Nationalism* (1978) and *Alexander Crummell* (1989).

ALBERT MURRAY, an educator and writer, was born in Nokomis, Alabama, in 1916 and attended Tuskegee Institute at the same time as Ellison. Murray received an M.A. in literature from New York University (1948). Prior to beginning a full-time career as a writer, he taught at a number of universities, including Tuskegee, Colgate, and Emory. A truly independent thinker, he criticizes many of the intellectual and cultural staples of the past twenty-five years. His writings include *The Omni-Americans: New Perspectives on Black Experience and American Culture* (1970), *Stomping the Blues* (1977), *Good Morning Blues: The Autobiography of Count Basie As Told to Albert Murray* (1986), and *The Spyglass Tree* (1991).

CHANDLER OWEN, a close friend and associate of A. Philip Randolph's, was born in Warrentown, North Carolina, in 1889 and graduated from Virginia Union University in 1913. Later, while a student at Columbia, he befriended Randolph, and the two joined the Socialist Party in 1916 and founded the *Messenger,* a Marxist journal, in 1917. While Owen was running for the New York assembly in 1920, he and Randolph were jailed and harassed for their Socialist affiliations. Owen grew disillusioned with socialism and became managing editor of the *Chicago Bee* and in that capacity supported Randolph's effort to unionize Pullman porters. In the late 1920s he became a Republican, running unsuccessfully for a House seat and working primarily in public relations—speech writing and the like—for the remainder of his life. He died in 1967.

NELL IRVIN PAINTER, Edwards Professor of History at Princeton University, was born in 1942 and grew up in Oakland, California. She did her undergraduate work at the University of California at Berkeley. In 1974 she a received a Ph.D. in American history from Harvard. Before joining the faculty at Princeton in 1988, she taught at the University of North Carolina at Chapel Hill. Her books include *The Narrative of Hosea Hudson: His Life as a Negro Communist in the South* and *Standing at Armageddon: The United States, 1877–1919*. In 1996 she published *Sojourner Truth: A Life, A Symbol*. She is a frequent contributor to the field of black women's studies.

ROBERT PURVIS, a rarity as a wealthy black antislavery crusader, was born in Charleston, South Carolina, in 1810, to a freeborn mother and a white Englishman—a cotton broker who left Purvis $120,000 upon his death in 1826. Before his father's death, Purvis attended a private school in Philadelphia; with the security of his inheritance, he became an abolitionist. In 1830 he met William Lloyd Garrison; the two became longtime friends and founded the American Anti-Slavery Society in 1833. Purvis was known for his staunch opposition to all organizations and movements that appeared racially exclusive. A founder of the American Moral Reform Society, he firmly held out hope for a world where race did not matter. From 1845 to 1850 he was president of the Pennsylvania Anti-Slavery Society. His son, Charles Purvis, was a professor at Howard's medical school from 1868 to 1907. Robert Purvis died in Philadelphia in 1898.

BENJAMIN QUARLES, historian, was born in Boston in 1904. He received a B.A. from Shaw University (1931) and an M.A. (1933) and a Ph.D. (1940) from the University of Wisconsin. Quarles taught at Shaw and at Dillard University before becoming a professor of history at Morgan State College. He served on several important boards, including the editorial board of the *Journal of Negro History*. His books include *Frederick Douglass* (1948), *The Negro in the Civil War* (1948), *The Negro in the American Revolution* (1961), and *Blacks on John Brown* (1972).

A. PHILIP RANDOLPH, the most influential black labor organizer of the twentieth century, was born in Crescent City, Florida, in 1889. His father, a tailor and itinerant minister, wanted his son to be a clergyman, but Randolph became a labor organizer instead. After high school he went to New York and took classes at City College of New York. In 1925 he became a Socialist and, with Chandler Owen, organized the Brotherhood of Sleeping Car Porters. It took ten years and several strikes for the Pullman Company to recognize the union. Randolph threatened a mass march in Washington, and the specter of such a march led President Roosevelt to establish the Fair Employment Practices Commission (FEPC). Recipient of an honorary LL.D. from Howard in 1941 and the Spingarn Medal from the NAACP in 1942, Randolph was elected the first black vice-president of the AFL-CIO. During World War II he fought for the desegregation of the U.S. armed forces, which President Truman mandated after much resistance from the military. He died in 1979 in New York City.

REVERDY RANSOM, an African Methodist Episcopal bishop, was born in Flushing, Ohio, in 1861 and attended Wilberforce University, earning a bachelor of divinity degree in 1886, a D.D. in 1898, and an LL.D. in 1912. Ordained in 1887, he served as pastor of various AME churches in Ohio, Pennsylvania, Illinois, Massachusetts, and New York. A shrewd church politician, he was elected bishop in 1924. He died in Wilberforce, Ohio, in 1959 at age ninety-eight.

CHARLES RAY, an abolitionist and journalist, was born in Falmouth, Massachusetts, in 1807. Aided by abolitionists, Ray studied at Wesleyan Seminary in Wilbraham, Massachusetts. He went on to Wesleyan University, in Middletown, Connecticut, but could not cope with the racism there. In 1832 he settled in New York and opened a shoe and boot store, joining the American Anti-Slavery Society a year later. In 1837 he was ordained and that same year became general agent of the *Colored American,* a black newspaper, in which he disseminated his political opinions. A year later he bought this weekly and from 1839 until its demise in 1842 was its sole editor. In 1845 he became pastor of Bethesda Congregational Church in New York. He died in 1886.

CHARLES REASON, an abolitionist and advocate of black suffrage, was born in 1818 in New York City to Caribbean émigrés. He attended the favored New York African Free School and became an instructor there at age fourteen. He hoped to go to the General Theology Seminary in New York, but was denied entrance on the basis of race. In 1849–50 he was a professor at New York Central College, in McGrawsville, New York, and in 1852–55 he headed the Institute for Colored Youth in Philadelphia. From 1855 to 1892 he taught and was a principal at a number of New York schools. He remained an eloquent champion of black rights until his death in 1893.

J. SAUNDERS REDDING, a literary critic and scholar, was born in 1906 to middle-class parents in Wilmington, Delaware. Redding enrolled at Brown and, despite the alienation described in his semi-autobiographical account *No Day of Triumph* (1942), persisted and earned a B.A. (1928) and an M.A. (1932). He began teaching at Morehouse 1928, but was fired because of critical comments made in *No Day of Triumph*. He spent most of his academic career at Hampton Institute (1943–66) and stayed active in many national humanities organizations. His other books include *To Make a Poet Black* (1939), *They Came in Chains: Americans from Africa* (1950), and *The Negro* (1967). Redding died in Ithaca, New York, in 1988.

ISHMAEL REED, an innovative black novelist, was born in Chattanooga in 1938. He graduated from East High School in Buffalo in 1956. The shy Reed's work got the attention of several English professors who encouraged him, but he dropped out of the State University at Buffalo in 1960, for lack of funds. He moved to New York City and in 1962 began his professional writing career as a journalist. He was very active in New York's cultural scene through 1967, when he moved to Berkeley. His work is frequently described as some of the most imaginative writing of the seventies. Since the seventies he has published several hard-hitting collections of essays. Few persons have provided more publication opportunities for Third World writers than Reed. Despite his penchant for career-enhancing controversy, he remains a force in American writing. In 1976 he established the Before Columbus Foundation, to promote cultural diversity in literature. His books include *Mumbo Jumbo* (1972), *Flight to Canada* (1976), and *Airing Dirty Laundry* (1993). He continues to teach at UC Berkeley.

PAUL ROBESON, an internationally renowned singer, actor, and human rights activist, was born in Princeton, New Jersey, in 1898. He received an A.B. with honors from Rutgers in 1919 and an LL.B. from Columbia in 1923. He never hesitated to speak out for the rights of people all over the world. Throughout his life he relished the chance to sing folk material that reflected struggles for freedom. An avowed socialist, he never formally joined the Communist Party, but he did praise the Soviet social system. When his activities prompted the House Un-American Activities Committee to call him to testify, Robeson remained undaunted. He acted in *Simon the Cyrenian* in 1921 and went on to appear in numerous other plays, including *All God's Chillun Got Wings* (1924) and *Othello* (1930 and 1943). Among his film credits are *Body and Soul* (1924), *Emperor Jones* (1933), and *Show Boat* (1936). He died in Philadelphia in 1976.

ARMISTEAD ROBINSON was born in New Orleans in 1947 and finished high school in Memphis. As an undergraduate at Yale, Robinson led the push for an academically respectable African American studies program. He edited *Black Studies in the University* (1969), one of the first books on black studies. After earning a Ph.D. in history from Rochester University, he taught at UCLA. In 1980 he joined the University of Virginia and as professor of history proceeded to build its Carter G. Woodson Institute into one of the premier research centers in the South. He died in 1995.

CEDRIC ROBINSON, a California native, finished studies at the University of California at Berkeley in 1963 and in 1975 received a Ph.D.

in political science from Stanford. After a five-year stint at SUNY Binghamton, Robinson returned to California as director of the black studies center and professor in the political science department at the University of California at Santa Barbara. He now chairs the black studies department there. His most influential work is *Black Marxism* (1983).


BAYARD RUSTIN, a political activist and organizer during the civil rights movement and close associate of Martin Luther King Jr., was born in 1910 in West Chester, Pennsylvania. His parents were unmarried at the time of his birth, and his father left his mother shortly thereafter. Rustin grew up believing that his grandparents were his parents; his mother lived with them, but posed as his sister. He attended Wilberforce in 1930–31, Cheyney State Normal School (now Cheyney State College) in 1931–33, and City College of New York in 1933–35. Rustin was a member of the Communist Party and an organizer with the Young Communist League from 1936 until 1941, when he left the party. He was cofounder and field secretary of the Congress of Racial Equality (CORE), cofounder of the Southern Christian Leadership Conference (SCLC), and a co-organizer of the 1963 March on Washington. He also was executive director of the A. Philip Randolph Institute in New York from 1964 to 1979. During the sixties he frequently challenged the Black Power activists, encouraging instead coalition politics. His writings include *Down the Line: The Collected Writings of Bayard Rustin* (1971) and *Strategies for Freedom: The Changing Patterns of Black Protest* (1976). Rustin died in New York City in 1987.


GEORGE SCHUYLER, an iconoclastic thinker, was born in Providence, Rhode Island, in 1895. After high school he spent eight years in the U.S. Army before becoming a civil service clerk. From 1923 to 1928 he worked as a staff member on the *Messenger,* and in 1924 started to write for the *Pittsburgh Courier,* where he stayed for twenty-five years. From 1937 to 1944 he also was business manager of the NAACP's *Crisis.* He emerged as an outspoken critic of liberal approaches to race relations. His books include *Black No More*

(1931) and an autobiography, *Black and Conservative* (1966). Schuyler died in 1977.

ROBERT SMITH, a widely published political scientist, was born in Benton, Louisiana, in 1947. He earned a B.A. from the University of California at Berkeley in 1970 and a Ph.D. in political science from Howard in 1976. After holding faculty appointments at SUNY at Purchase (1976–80) and at Howard (1980–89), he joined the political science department at San Francisco State University. He is an editor of a series on black political science for the State University of New York Press.

THOMAS SOWELL, an economist and challenger of many liberal assumptions, was born in Gastonia, North Carolina, in 1930 and moved to Harlem at age eight. Ranked near the top of his class, he dropped out of school in the ninth grade to work; eventually he finished high school at night and went on to Howard. He ultimately transferred to Harvard, where he received a B.A. in 1958. He later earned an M.A. from Columbia (1959) and a Ph.D. in economics from the University of Chicago (1966). He has taught at Howard, Brandeis, and UCLA and is currently a fellow at Stanford's Hoover Institute. He is best known as an opponent of affirmative action, minimum wage, and government assistance programs, and in 1981 *Newsweek* called him "the fountainhead of black conservatives." His books include *Economics: Analysis and Issues* (1971), *Black Education: Myths and Tragedies* (1972), and *Race and Economics* (1973).

SHELBY STEELE was born in 1946, grew up on the outskirts of Chicago, and attended Coe College, in Iowa, where he joined black activist movements. After graduation he taught high school in East St. Louis, Illinois. In 1970 he enrolled in the University of Utah's graduate program in English and earned a Ph.D. His book *The Content of Our Character* (1990) argues for a less collective approach to racial dilemmas. He also writes persuasively of the anxiety experienced by many blacks who are not viewed as individuals. Steele is professor of English at California State University at San Jose.

MARY CHURCH TERRELL, an energetic suffragist and a leader in the black women's club movement, was born in Memphis in 1863. Her father was a self-educated former slave who achieved great wealth as an entrepreneur, and her mother owned a successful chain of hair salons. Terrell received a B.A. from Oberlin in 1884 and taught at the Preparatory School for Colored Youth in Washington, D.C., until 1886, when she traveled to Europe to study. She married Robert Terrell, who was later appointed to the bench in Washington, D.C. In 1896 she became the first president of the National Association of Colored Women (NACW), and from 1895 to 1901 she was a member of the board of trustees of the District of Columbia public school system. She was active in the Washington branch of the NAACP in 1913 and became increasingly militant later in life. Her autobiography, *A Colored Woman in a White World* (1940), provides insights into black middle-class perspectives. From 1950 to 1953 she fought successfully to desegregate public eating places in Washington, D.C. She died in 1954 in Annapolis.

MICHAEL THELWELL, an author and educator, was born in 1942. He received a B.A. from Howard University (1964) and an M.F.A. from the University of Massachusetts at Amherst (1969). He worked with the Student Nonviolent Coordinating Committee (SNCC) and the Mississippi Freedom Democratic Party. He was chairman of the University of Massachusetts at Amherst's W. E. B. Du Bois Department of African American Studies, where he has taught since 1980. He received a National Endowment for the Arts Writers Fellowship and was a senior adviser to the PBS civil rights documentary television series *Eyes on the Prize II*. A collection of his essays, *Duties, Pleasures, and Conflicts*, was published in 1987.

WALLACE THURMAN, a writer who exemplified the potential and contradictions of the Harlem Renaissance, was born in Salt Lake City in 1902. He attended the University of Utah for a while but, attracted by the more liberal reputation of California, moved to Los Angeles and studied at the University of Southern California during 1922–25. He found work in the post office and wrote for a local black weekly. The idea of flowering and innovative black cultural expression fascinated Thurman, and he tried in Los Angeles to set in motion what was happening in Harlem. He failed, moved to New York in 1925, and plunged into the hectic world of Harlem's black artistic community. He edited the critically praised, but short-lived, journal *Fire!* Slowly he became disillusioned with the quality and originality of the art produced by Harlem's writers. Though he never had a steady income, he was able to complete his first novel, *The Blacker the Berry* in 1928, and three years later he published *Infants of the Spring,* a scathing commentary on the Harlem literary scene. Thurman was always a somewhat sickly man, and the fast pace of New York took its toll. He died there of tuberculosis in 1934.

JEAN TOOMER, a writer who avoided racial themes, was born in Washington, D.C., in 1894. His father had been a Georgia planter and his maternal grandfather a Louisiana politician, and Toomer enjoyed a thoroughly upper-middle-class upbringing in one of the largest mansions in Washington. Although he attended six different colleges—among them the University of Wisconsin, the University of Chicago, and New York University—the easily bored Toomer never received a college degree. In 1919 he decided to become a writer, and his landmark *Cane,* which some critics of Harlem Renaissance–era literature have called the finest work of that period, appeared in 1923. Toomer shunned discussions of race, writing in his autobiographical essay "On Being an American" that "Scotch, Welsh, German, English, French, Dutch, Spanish, [and] some dark blood" coursed through his veins. He was a member, he insisted, of the American race, neither black nor white. Shortly after the publication of *Cane,* Toomer submerged himself in the spiritual world of Gurdjieff, where he all but disappeared. Toomer died in 1967 in Doylestown, Pennsylvania.

DARWIN TURNER, a writer and educator, was born in 1931. He spent his early years in Cincinnati and received a B.A. (1947) and an M.A.

(1949) in English from the University of Cincinnati. Turner taught at Clark College in Atlanta and at Morgan State in Maryland before receiving a Ph.D. from the University of Chicago in 1956. From 1957–59 he chaired the English department at Florida A&M University; later he was the first chair of English and then dean of the graduate school at North Carolina A&T University, in Greensboro. He finished his academic career at the University of Iowa, where he was professor of English and chair of African American studies from 1972 until his death in 1991. A volume of his own poetry, *Katharsis*, was published in 1964, and he wrote extensively on the works of Jean Toomer. *In a Minor Chord: Three African American Writers and Their Search for Identity* (1971) examined Toomer's writings along with those of Zora Neale Hurston and Countee Cullen. His other writings include *Black American Literature: Essays, Poetry, Fiction, Drama* and *Black Drama in America: an Anthology*, both published in 1970.

CLARENCE WALKER, a historian, was born in 1946. He attended Berkeley, California, schools while they were in the throes of voluntary integration and remained in the Bay Area, graduating from San Francisco State with a degree in history and then pursuing graduate studies at UC Berkeley. Walker took advantage of the formidable talent in Berkeley's history department, studying with Kenneth Stampp, Leon Litwack, Winthrop Jordan, and Lawrence Levine. He taught at Wesleyan University from 1981 to 1990, and accepted an appointment as professor of history at the University of California at Davis in 1986. His first book, *A Rock in a Weary Land* (1982), examined the history of the African Methodist Episcopal church. A collection of essays, *Deromanticizing Black History*, was published in 1991.

DAVID WALKER, an abolitionist, was born to a free mother and a slave father in 1785 in Wilmington, North Carolina. Walker eventually settled in Boston and taught himself to read and write. By 1826 he had become an uncompromising advocate of revolution for black people, and he wrote one of the earliest pieces of abolitionist literature, *Walker's Appeal in Four Articles: Together with a Preamble to the Colored Citizens of the World* (1829). A vigorous indictment of slavery, the pamphlet encouraged free blacks in the North to unite with enslaved blacks in the South to overthrow the slavocracy. Unsuccessful attempts were made to ban *Walker's Appeal* in the South, and two years after its publication came Nat Turner's bloody revolt in Virginia. Walker never learned of Turner's rebellion, though, for he died under mysterious circumstances—in retaliation for his revolutionary agitating, some have speculated—in Boston in 1830.

MARGARET WALKER, author and editor, was born in Birmingham, Alabama, in 1915. She received a B.A. from Northwestern University in 1935 and an M.A. (1940) and a Ph.D. (1965) from the University of Iowa. Her early, carefully crafted poems were published in the *Crisis* and *Opportunity,* and her first volume of poetry, *For My People,* appeared in 1942. Walker taught at Livingston College in North Carolina and West Virginia State College before beginning a career at Jackson State University in 1949. There she assumed the chair of black studies until her retirement in 1979. During a long career, Walker received many awards and honors, including Rosenwald, Ford, and Houghton Mifflin fellowships. Her novel *Jubilee,* set in the slavery period, was a best-seller, and in 1985 she published *Daemonic Genius,* a biography of her old friend Richard Wright.

RONALD WALTERS, a political scientist, was born in 1938 in Wichita, Kansas. He earned a B.A. from Fisk in 1963 and a Ph.D. in political science from American University in 1971. After serving in the Afro-American studies department at Brandeis from 1969 to 1971, he joined the political science faculty at Howard. He played a key advisory role in the 1984 presidential campaign of Jesse Jackson. During the eighties he also helped mobilize opinion against the white regime in South Africa. In 1984 he received the Black Scholar/Activist Award from *Black Scholar* magazine. He currently chairs Howard's political science department.

BOOKER T. WASHINGTON, a powerful champion of practical education for African Americans, was born in rural Virginia in 1856 to an unknown white father and an enslaved mother. In 1875 he graduated with honors from the Hampton Normal and Agricultural Institute. A subsequent, frustrating stint at a more academically oriented seminary school persuaded him that vocational training was the most valuable education for black people during that time. In 1881 he was recommended to head Tuskegee Institute, a school conceived but poorly funded by the Alabama state legislature, to train black teachers. His emphasis on educating blacks in the trades precipitated a long-standing philosophical conflict with W. E. B. Du Bois. In spite of, or because of, his controversial position vis-à-vis black education and his accommodationist political stance, Washington was the most powerful black man in the United States at the turn of the century and wielded considerable influence in governmental circles. He died in 1915 at Tuskegee.

IDA B. WELLS BARNETT, one of the first African American women journalists and an unwavering antilynching crusader and activist in the black women's club movement, was born in Holly Springs, Mississippi, in 1862. Her father was the son of his master and a carpenter; her mother, a cook. A yellow fever epidemic killed her parents in 1878, leaving the sixteen-year-old Wells to raise six siblings. In spite of her weighty family responsibilities, she became editor of two black newspapers, the *Evening Star* and *Living Way*. Under the pen name Iola she wrote a weekly column that reached a large audience. In 1889 she bought a one-third share in the Memphis *Free Speech and Headlight*. In 1892 three black businessmen, friends of hers, were lynched because their grocery store was competing with a white-owned enterprise. That incident ignited her passionate antilynching activism—she wrote and spoke across the country not only denouncing the violent act but debunking the myth of the black rapist that was frequently used to justify lynchings. In 1909 she was among those who supported the founding of the NAACP, and in 1913 she helped organize the first black women's suffrage club in Chicago. She advocated protest and activism as means of achieving change and had little patience with the more moderate proponents of civil rights for blacks. She died in Chicago in 1931.

CORNEL WEST, a philosopher and social writer, was born in 1953 and grew up in Sacramento. At Harvard he excelled in the classroom and achieved recognition as a student leader. He subsequently earned a Ph.D. from Princeton and then taught at Union Theological Seminary. After five years as head of Princeton's Afro-American studies program, he left and joined Afro-American studies at Harvard in 1994. He wrote the best-selling *Race Matters* in 1993 and emerged as an articulate and forceful advocate for progressive causes.

DOROTHY WEST, a Harlem Renaissance writer, was born in 1907 in Boston, to a formerly enslaved father who became a well-to-do Boston businessman. West graduated from high school in 1923, and took courses at Boston University and Columbia University School of Journalism. Having written her first short story at the age of seven and won her first literary prize at ten, she began in her twenties submitting material to *Opportunity,* and she moved to New York to join a circle of friends that included Wallace Thurman, Countee Cullen, Langston Hughes, Zora Neale Hurston, and Claude McKay. Though West worked in Harlem as an actress and social work investigator, the white literary patron Carl Van Vechten encouraged her to write. West traveled to the Soviet Union in the early thirties and published her first novel, *The Living Is Easy,* in 1948. Her short stories appeared in Langston Hughes's *The Best Short Stories of Negro Writers* (1967), and her second novel, *The Wedding,* was finally published in 1994. West died in 1995.

PHILLIS WHEATLEY, the first black woman poet to be published in the United States, was born in Gambia, Africa, around 1753. She was purchased by a white man as company for his wife, who taught young Phillis how to read and write. When she was thirteen, she began writing poetry that appeared in various New England newspapers. Her poem "On the Death of the Reverend Mr. George Whitefield, 1770" made her famous at age seventeen. She traveled to London in 1773 and published her only book, *Poems on Various Subjects, Religious and Moral,* that same year. Wheatley's popularity was largely the result of curiosity about the Christianized African-born slave-poet, and she faded into relative obscurity after her death in Boston in 1784.

WILLIAM WHIPPER, an entrepreneur and founder of the American Moral Reform Society (1853), was born around 1804 in Little Britain Township, in Pennsylvania. Starting in the late 1820s he was an entrepreneur in Philadelphia, and from 1830 to 1835 he actively participated in the annual Convention of Free People of Color. He joined Robert Purvis in protesting all-black movements. Whipper continued as a businessman in Philadelphia until his death there in 1876.

WALTER WHITE, a writer and journalist, was born in Atlanta in 1893. White was a fair-haired, blue-eyed African American who earned a B.A. from Atlanta University in 1916 and two years later, passing as a white man, began work for the NAACP as an undercover reporter on lynchings. White supported Alain Locke's "New Negro" philosophy; James Weldon Johnson was his mentor, and White in turn inspired a host of young Renaissance writers, including Claude McKay, Countee Cullen, Langston Hughes, Rudolph Fisher, Zora Neale Hurston, and Nella Larsen. His *Rope and Faggot: A Biography of Judge Lynch* (1929) was the first formal attempt to examine the causes of lynching. He published scores of periodical articles, such as "The American Negro and His Problems" and "The Negro's Contributions to American Culture" (both 1927), and wrote a weekly column for the *Chicago Defender*. His awards and honors include the 1937 Spingarn Medal from the NAACP and an honorary doctor of laws degree from Howard. White died in New York in 1955.

JOHN EDGAR WIDEMAN, a novelist, was born in Washington, D.C., in 1941 and grew up in Pittsburgh, where his great-great-great-grandmother, a fugitive slave, had settled in the mid-nineteenth century. Wideman, the eldest of five children, was an honor student and star athlete in high school. He attended the University of Pennsylvania, where he received his B.A. and became a Rhodes Scholar in 1963. He taught at the University of Pennsylvania (1966–74) and chaired its African American studies department; he also taught at the University of Wyoming and the University of Massachusetts at

Amherst. His many books include *A Glance Away* (1967), *Hurry Home* (1970), *The Lynchers* (1973), *Brothers and Keepers* (1984), *Fever* (1989), *Philadelphia Fire* (1992), and *FatherAlong* (1994).

CHARLES WILLIE, a sociologist, was born in 1927 in Dallas. He received a B.A. from Morehouse College (1948), an M.A. from Atlanta University (1949), and a Ph.D. from Syracuse University (1957). Willie taught at Syracuse, where he chaired the sociology department from 1967 to 1971. He became vice-president of student affairs in 1972, but left Syracuse to teach at Harvard University in 1974. Willie's research focuses on the impact of American racism on the personality, education, and family life of blacks. His writings include *Church Action in the World* (1969), *The Family Life of Black People* (1970), *Black Students and White Colleges* (1972), and *Racism and Mental Health* (1973).

AUGUST WILSON, America's premier playwright, was born in 1945 and grew up in Pittsburgh, one of six children. Wilson's mother and his German immigrant father never married. Young August survived poverty and the racism of Pittsburgh's parochial schools and spent time listening to storytellers in the bars and shops of black Pittsburgh. After a short and unpleasant stint in the military, Wilson settled in Cleveland and became active in local community theater groups. In 1970 he moved to St. Paul, Minnesota, where he "found his voice." His play *Ma Rainey's Black Bottom* received rave reviews and had a long run on Broadway. It was followed by *Joe Turner's Come and Gone* (1986). *Fences* (1987) won a Pulitzer Prize, as did *The Piano Lesson* (1990).

CARTER G. WOODSON, often called the Father of Negro History, for his own work and for inspiring others, was born into a large, poor family in Buckingham County, Virginia, in 1875. His parents were former slaves who became farmers. He was basically self-educated until the age of seventeen, when the family moved to Fayette, West Virginia. His educational career then took off. He studied at Berea

College, in Kentucky, earned a B.A. from the University of Chicago in 1908, and completed a Ph.D. at Harvard in 1912. While doing graduate research, Woodson taught (1909–18) at Washington's M Street Dunbar High School. He helped found the Association for the Study of Negro Life and History in 1912; four years later he established the *Journal of Negro History*. Named dean of the faculty at Howard in 1919, Woodson had difficulty with the administrative environment there and left after one year. In 1921 the resourceful devotee of black history organized Associated Publishers, a black-owned company, to bring into print scholarship dealing with blacks. Throughout his career he worked to demonstrate the importance of historical research in combatting the prejudices of white Americans. His writings include *The History of the Negro Church* (1921) and *The Miseducation of the Negro* (1933). He died in Maryland in 1950.

RICHARD WRIGHT, author of *Black Boy* (1945) and *Native Son,* was born in Natchez, Mississippi, in 1908. Wright's father abandoned the family, and his mother, who was very ill, barely supported Wright and his siblings with the assistance of various relatives. After finishing the ninth grade in 1925, he went to Memphis. There he worked at various jobs and struggled to maintain his reading habit, borrowing library cards from white associates and surreptitiously checking out books under the guise of a runner. Like thousands of other black southerners, Wright left the South in search of greater political freedom and economic opportunity. In depression-era Chicago, he worked at the post office and became part of the Federal Writers' Project. Disillusioned and bitter about racial discrimination, he joined the Communist Party in 1933. The publication and commercial success of *Native Son,* in 1940, gave him more options. He severed ties with the Communists, believing that they did not genuinely respect the interests of black people and that they held restrictive views about art. Wright exiled himself to France in 1947 and spent the rest of his life there. He continued to write and aid younger writers, including Ralph Ellison, Chester Himes, and James Baldwin. Among his later books are *The Outsider* (1953) and *The Long Dream* (1958). He died in Paris of a heart attack in 1960.

# NOTES «««

PREFACE

1. Richard Hofstadter, *Anti-Intellectualism in American Life* (New York: Vintage Books, 1963), 25.


1: LAYING THE FOUNDATIONS

1. Joseph E. Inikori and Stanley L. Engerman, eds., *The Atlantic Slave Trade* (Durham: Duke University Press, 1992), 6.
2. Deborah Gray White, *Ain't I a Woman?* (New York: W. W. Norton, 1985).
3. Respondent, "There Ain't No Conjurers," in *The American Slave: A Composite Autobiography,* ed. George Rawick, vol. 19, *God Struck Me Dead* (Westport, Conn.: Greenwood Press, 1972), 75.
4. "Autobiography of Susan Snow, Meridian, Mississippi," in *The American Slave: A Composite Autobiography,* ed. George Rawick, suppl., ser. 1, vol. 10, *Mississippi Narratives, Part 5* (Westport, Conn.: Greenwood Press, 1977), 2012.
5. Albert Rabateau, *Slave Religion* (New York: Oxford University Press, 1978); Charles Joyner, *Down by the Riverside: A South Carolina Slave Community* (Chicago: University of Illinois Press, 1984), 170.
6. B. A. Botkin, ed., *Lay My Burden Down: A Folk History of Slavery* (Athens: University of Georgia Press, 1989), 26.
7. John W. Blassingame, "Status and Social Structure in the Slave Community: Evidence from New Sources," in *Perspectives and Irony in American Slavery,* ed. Harry Owens (Jackson: University Press of Mississippi, 1976), 137–51; Eugene D. Genovese, *Roll, Jordan, Roll: The World the Slaves Made* (New York: 1974).
8. "Eighteenth Century Slaves as Advertised by Their Masters," *Journal of Negro History* 1 (1916): 177.
9. Thomas Johnson, *Twenty-eight Years a Slave; or, The Story of My Life on Three Continents,* 7th ed. (Bournemouth, England: W. Mate, 1909), reprinted in Margaret Branson and Edward France, *The Human Side of Afro-American History* (Lexington, Mass.: Ginn, 1972), 51.
10. John Duff and Peter M. Mitchell, eds., *The Nat Turner Rebellion: The Historical Event and the Modern Controversy* (New York: Harper & Row, 1971).
11. Earle West, ed., *The Black American and Education* (Columbus, Ohio: Charles E. Merrill, 1972), 35.
12. Sherman Savage, "Abolitionist Literature in the Mails," *Journal of Negro History* 13 (1928): 156–57.

13. Kenneth M. Stampp, *The Peculiar Institution: Slavery in the Ante-Bellum South* (New York: Alfred A. Knopf, 1967), 208.

14. Horace Mann Bond, *The Education of the Negro in the American Social Order* (New York: Octagon Books, 1966).

15. Meyer Weinberg, *A Chance to Learn: The History of Race and Education in the United States* (Cambridge: Cambridge University Press, 1977), 23.

16. Richard Hofstadter, W. Miller, David Aaron, and Winthrop Jordan, *The United States: Conquering a Continent* (Englewood Cliffs, N.J.: Prentice-Hall, 1976), 251.

17. Weinberg, *Chance to Learn*, 18.

18. Bond, *Education of the Negro*, 371.

19. Phillip Foner and George Walker, eds., *Proceedings of the Black State Conventions, 1840–1865,* 2 vols. (Philadelphia: Temple University Press, 1979–80), 2:86.

20. Leonard Curry, *The Free Black in Urban America, 1800–1856* (Chicago: University of Chicago Press, 1981), 171–72.

21. Leon Litwack, *North of Slavery: The Negro in the Free States, 1790–1860* (Chicago: University of Chicago Press, 1961), 70–71.

22. Carter G. Woodson, *The Education of the Negro People to 1861* (Washington, D.C.: Associated Publishers, 1919), 228.

23. John Mercer Langston, *Selected Letters and Addresses* (Washington, D.C., 1883), 135, quoted in Benjamin Quarles, *Black Abolitionists* (New York: Oxford University Press, 1969), 69.

24. Quarles, *Black Abolitionists*, 68.

25. *Freedom's Journal,* March 16, 1827. This paper, published weekly until March 28, 1929, is indexed in Donald M. Jacobs, ed., *Antebellum Black Newspapers* (Westport, Conn.: Greenwood Press, 1976).

26. Benjamin Quarles, *Allies for Freedom: Blacks and John Brown* (New York: Oxford University Press, 1974).

27. Foner and Walker, eds., *Black State Conventions* 1:88.

28. Ibid., 191–92.

29. Bert Loewenberg and Ruth Bogin, eds., *Black Women in Nineteenth-Century American Life* (University Park: Pennsylvania State University Press, 1976), 86.

30. Stanley Austin Ransom Jr., ed., *America's First Negro Poet: The Complete Works of Jupiter Hammon of Long Island* (Port Washington, N.Y.: Kennikat Press, 1970), 112.

31. Vernon Loggins, *The Negro Author: His Development in America to 1900* (Port Washington, N.Y.: Kennikat Press, 1964), 20, synthesizing the "Memoir" by a descendant in Phillis Wheatley, *Memoir and Poems of Phillis Wheatley, a Native African and a Slave* (Boston: Isaac Knapp, 1838; reprint, Miami, Fla.: Mnemosyne, 1969), 11–35.

32. J. Saunders Redding, "The Forerunners," in *Black Expression: Essays by and about Black Americans in the Creative Arts,* ed. Addison Hoyle (New York: Weybright and Talley, 1969), 65.

33. Othello, "What the Negro Was Thinking during the Eighteenth Century," *Journal of Negro History* 1 (1916): 61.

## 2: Black Thinkers in a White Movement

1. Bertram Wyatt-Brown, "Proslavery and Antislavery Intellectuals: Class Concepts and Polemical Struggle," in *Anti-Slavery Reconsidered: New Perspectives on the Abolitionists,* ed. Lewis Perry (Baton Rouge: Louisiana State University Press, 1979), 314.
2. Robert Allen, *Reluctant Reformers: Racism and Social Reform Movements in the United States* (Garden City, N.Y.: Anchor Books, 1975), 18.
3. Frederick Douglass, *Life and Times of Frederick Douglass, Written by Himself,* reprinted from the revised edition of 1892 (London: Collier Books, 1962), 217.
4. Ibid., 218.
5. Jane H. Pease and William H. Pease, *They Who Would Be Free: Blacks' Search for Freedom, 1830–1861* (New York: Atheneum, 1974), 146.
6. *Liberator,* February 6, 1850, quoted ibid., 148.
7. "Robert W. Purvis," in Philip S. Foner, ed., *The Voice of Black America: Major Speeches by Negroes in the United States, 1797–1971* (New York: Simon and Schuster, 1976), 227.
8. Robert Purvis, *Colored National Convention* (Philadelphia, 1855), 11.
9. Pease and Pease, *They Who Would Be Free,* 139.
10. *Frederick Douglass' Paper,* July 29, 1853.
11. *Liberator,* August 1, 1835, in *Minutes of the Fifth Annual Convention of the Free People of Colour,* 1835 (reprint, New York: Arno Press, New York Times, 1969), 15.
12. *Colored American,* August 26, 1837, 2. This journal, published weekly from March 4, 1837, to December 25, 1841, is indexed in Donald M. Jacobs, ed., *Antebellum Black Newspapers* (Westport, Conn.: Greenwood Press, 1976).
13. *Freedom's Journal* (New York), March 28, 1829.
14. Douglass, *Life and Times,* 286.
15. Ibid.
16. Pease and Pease, *They Who Would Be Free,* 268.
17. Martin Delany, *The Condition, Elevation, Emigration and Destiny of the Colored People of the United States,* reprinted from 1852 edition (New York: Arno Press, New York Times, 1969); Alexander Crummell, *The Relations and Duties of Free Colored Men to Africa* (Hartford: Case, Lockwood, 1861).
18. Martin Delany, "The Condition, Elevation, Emigration, and Destiny of the Colored People of the United States," in *Negro Social and Political Thought, 1850–1920: Representative Texts,* ed. Howard Brotz (New York: Basic Books, 1966), 39.
19. Marcia Stewart, "Lecture at the African Masonic Hall, 1833," in *We Are Your Sisters,* ed. Dorothy Sterling (New York: W. W. Norton, 1984), 157.
20. Adrienne Koch and William Peden, eds., *The Life and Selected Writing of Thomas Jefferson* (New York: Modern Library, 1944), 256–62.

## 3: The Black Intellectual Infrastructure

1. J. W. Alvord, *A Report Submitted to the Bureau of Refugees, Freedmen, and Abandoned Lands, Joint Committee on Reconstruction,* January 1, 1866, 39th Cong., 1st sess., 253.

2. Horace Mann Bond, *Negro Education in Alabama: A Study in Cotton and Steel* (New York: Atheneum, 1969), 99.

3. Alvord, *Report,* 15.

4. Horace Mann Bond, *The Education of the Negro in the American Social Order* (New York: Octagon Books, 1966), 86–88.

5. Earle West, ed., *The Black American and Education* (Columbus, Ohio: Charles E. Merrill, 1972), 73.

6. Ronald E. Butchart, *Northern Schools, Southern Blacks, and Reconstruction: Freedmen's Education, 1862–1875* (Westport, Conn.: Greenwood Press, 1980); Jacqueline Jones, *Soldiers of Light and Love: Northern Teachers and Georgia Blacks, 1865–1873* (Chapel Hill: University of North Carolina Press, 1980).

7. Dorothy Sterling, ed., *We Are Your Sisters* (New York: W. W. Norton, 1984), 263.

8. Ibid., 301.

9. "Reports of the Baptist Home Mission Board, 1866," in Walter Lynwood Fleming, ed., *Documentary History of Reconstruction, Political, Military, Social, Religious, Educational and Industrial,* 2 vols. (Cleveland: A. H. Clark, 1906–7), 2:248.

10. James D. Anderson, *The Education of Blacks in the South, 1860–1935* (Chapel Hill: University of North Carolina Press, 1988).

11. Ibid., 110–47.

12. Bond, *Education of the Negro,* 153.

13. C. Eric Lincoln and Lawrence Mamiya, *The Black Church in the African American Experience* (Durham: Duke University Press, 1990), chaps. 2–3.

14. Monroe N. Work, ed., *The Negro Year Book, 1931–1932* (Tuskegee, Ala.: Tuskegee Institute Press, 1931), 293.

15. Wyn Craig Wade, *The Fiery Cross: The Ku Klux Klan in America* (New York: Simon and Schuster, 1987), 71.

16. David Levering Lewis, *W. E. B. Du Bois: Biography of a Race, 1868–1819* (New York: Henry Holt, 1994).

17. Samuel Armstrong, "Normal School among the Freedmen," in *Proceedings of the National Education Association* (Boston, 1872).

18. Booker T. Washington, *Up from Slavery* (New York: Doubleday, 1902; reprint, New York: Bantam Pathfinder, 1963), 61.

19. Louis R. Harlan, *Booker T. Washington: The Wizard of Tuskegee, 1901–1915* (New York: Oxford University Press, 1983).

20. Bond, *Negro Education in Alabama,* 206.

21. Howard Brotz, ed., *Negro Social and Political Thought, 1850–1920* (New York: Basic Books, 1966), 333.

22. Testimony of A. D. Candler, in *Report of the Industrial Commission,* vol. 7 (Washington, D.C.: Government Printing Office, 1901), 539.

23. W. E. B. Du Bois, "The Talented Tenth," in *The Negro Problem* (New York: James Pott, 1903), 60.

24. Herbert Aptheker, ed., *The Correspondence of W. E. B. Du Bois, vol. 1, Selections, 1877–1934* (Amherst: University of Massachusetts Press, 1973), 216.

25. Harlan, *Booker T. Washington.*

26. Benjamin Mays, *Born to Rebel: An Autobiography* (Athens: University of Georgia Press, 1987), 40.

27. Meyer Weinberg, *A Chance to Learn: The History of Race and Education in the United States* (Cambridge: Cambridge University Press, 1977), 271.

28. Langston Hughes, "Cowards from the Colleges," *Crisis* 41 (1934): 226–28.

29. Louis R. Harlan et al., eds., *Booker T. Washington Papers,* 13 vols. (Urbana: University of Illinois Press, 1972–84), 9:561.

30. Ibid., 7:194–95.

31. Ibid., 432.

32. W. E. B. Du Bois, ed., *The College-Bred Negro* (Atlanta: Atlanta University Press, 1900), 29–30.

33. Ibid., 17.

34. Ibid., 18.

35. Ibid., 63.

36. Mary Church Terrell, "History of the High School for Negroes in Washington," *Journal of Negro History* 2 (1917): 253.

37. James D. Anderson, "Northern Philanthropy and the Training of the Black Leadership: Fisk University, a Case Study, 1915–1930," in *New Perspectives on Black Educational History,* ed. V. P. Franklin and James D. Anderson (Boston: G. K. Hall, 1978), 121.

38. Morehouse, quoted in *Independent,* April 29, 1896, in James M. McPherson, *The Abolitionist Legacy from Reconstruction to the NAACP* (Princeton: Princeton University Press, 1975), 222.

39. W. E. B. Du Bois, "The Talented Tenth," in *The Seventh Son: The Thought and Writing of W. E. B. Du Bois,* ed. Julius Lester, vol. 1 (New York: Vintage Books, 1971), 403.

## 4: Slowly Making Their Mark

1. Vernon Loggins, *The Negro Author* (Port Washington, N.Y.: Kennikat Press, 1964), 313–17.

2. *The Complete Poems of Paul Lawrence Dunbar* (New York: Dodd, Mead, 1980), 138.

3. Richard Bardolph, *The Negro Vanguard* (New York: Vintage Books, 1959), 126.

4. Wallace Thurman, "Negro Poets and Their Poetry," in *Black Expression,* ed. Addison Gayle (New York: Weybright and Talley, 1969), 75.

5. Russell Ames, "Social Realism in Charles W. Chesnutt," in *The Black Novelist,* ed. Robert Hemenway (Columbus, Ohio: Charles E. Merrill, 1970), 27–28.

6. Francis Richardson Keller, *An American Crusader: The Life of Charles Waddell Chesnutt* (Provo, Utah: Brigham Young University Press, 1978), 110.

7. Richard H. Brodhead, ed., *The Conjure Woman and Other Conjure Tales [by] Charles W. Chesnutt* (Durham: Duke University Press, 1993).

8. Richard Wright, "The Literature of the Negro in the United States," in *Black Expression,* 209.

9. John Hope Franklin, *George Washington Williams: A Biography* (Chicago: University of Chicago Press, 1985), 104.

10. Dorothy Sterling, ed., *We Are Your Sisters* (New York: W. W. Norton, 1984), 461.

11. Ibid., 436.

12. Darryl Pinckney, "Professionals," *New York Review of Books,* April 20, 1995, 34.
13. Abby Johnson and Ronald Johnson, *Propaganda and Aesthetics: The Literary Politics of Afro-American Magazines in the Twentieth Century* (Amherst: University of Massachusetts Press, 1979).
14. Pinckney, "Professionals," 34.
15. Joel Williamson, *The Crucible of Race: Black-White Relations in the American South since Emancipation* (New York: Oxford University Press, 1984).
16. Louis R. Harlan, *Booker T. Washington* (New York: Oxford University Press, 1983).
17. W. E. B. Du Bois, *Dusk of Dawn* (New York: Harcourt, Brace, 1940; reprint, New York: Schocken Books, 1968), 70–72.
18. Herbert Aptheker, ed., *The Correspondence of W. E. B. Du Bois,* vol. 1 (Amherst: University of Massachusetts Press, 1973), 216.
19. Du Bois, *Dusk of Dawn,* 82–83.
20. Hugh Gloster, "Race and the Negro Writer," *Phylon* 11 (1950): 369–71.
21. Wilson Jeremiah Moses, *Alexander Crummell: A Study of Civilization and Discontent* (New York: Oxford University Press, 1989).
22. Alfred Moss, *The American Negro Academy* (Baton Rouge: Louisiana State University Press, 1981), 291.
23. Horace Mann Bond, *Black American Scholars: A Study of Their Beginnings* (Detroit: Balamp, 1972), 18–20.
24. Rayford Logan, *The Negro in American Life and Thought: The Nadir, 1877–1901* (New York: Dial, 1954).
25. Paul Robeson, *Here I Stand* (New York: Othello Associates, 1955), 26.
26. Horace Cayton, *Long Old Road* (New York: Trident Press, 1965), 34.
27. Louis R. Harlan, et al., eds., *Booker T. Washington Papers,* 13 vols. (Urbana: University of Illinois Press, 1972–84), 4:194.
28. Jarena Lee, *Religious Experience and Journal of Mrs Jarena Lee, Giving an Account of Her Call to Preach the Gospel* (Philadelphia, 1849), in *Black Women in Nineteenth-Century American Life,* ed. Bert Loewenberg and Ruth Bogin (University Park: Pennsylvania State University Press, 1976), 139.
29. Elizabeth Cady Stanton, Susan B. Anthony, and Matilda Gage, *History of Woman Suffrage,* vol. 2 (New York: Fowler and Wells, 1881), 215.
30. Loewenberg and Bogin, eds., *Black Women,* 246.
31. Mary Church Terrell, "What Role Is the Educated Negro Woman to Play in the Uplifting of the Race?" in *Twentieth Century Negro Literature,* ed. D. W. Culp (Naperville, Ill.: J. L. Nichols, 1902), 175.
32. Robert Allen, *Reluctant Reformers: Racism and Social Reform Movements in the United States* (Garden City, N.Y.: Anchor Books, 1975), 172.
33. James Weldon Johnson, *Along This Way: An Autobiography of James Weldon Johnson* (New York: Viking Compass, 1968), 66.
34. Alexis de Tocqueville, *Democracy in America,* trans. Henry Reeve, introd. by John Stuart Mill (1835; reprint, New York: Schocken Books, 1964), 341.
35. Ibid., 342.
36. W. E. B. Du Bois, "Of Our Spiritual Strivings," in *The Souls of Black Folk* (1903; reprint with a new introd. by Du Bois, New York: Blue Heron Press, 1953), 1–12.

37. W. E. B. Du Bois, *The College-Bred Negro* (Atlanta: Atlanta University Press, 1900), 94.
38. Herbert Aptheker, ed., *The Autobiography of W. E. B. Du Bois* (New York: International Publishers, 1968), 123.

5: PROSPERITY, CHANGE, AND MORE OF THE SAME

1. Florette Henri, *Movement North, 1900–1920: The Road from Myth to Man* (Garden City, N.Y.: Anchor Books, 1976); Alferdteen Harrison, ed., *Black Exodus: The Great Migration from the American South* (Jackson: University Press of Mississippi, 1991).
2. Horace R. Cayton and George S. Mitchell, *Black Workers and the New Unions* (Chapel Hill: University of North Carolina Press, 1939); William H. Harris, *The Harder We Run: Black Workers since the Civil War* (New York: Oxford University Press, 1982), chaps. 2–3.
3. Horace Mann Bond, *Black American Scholars* (Detroit: Balamp, 1972), 26–27.
4. Ruth Edmond Hill, ed., *The Black Women Oral History Project: From the Arthur and Elizabeth Schlesinger Library on the History of Women in America,* vol. 4 (Westport, Conn.: Meckler, 1991), 237.
5. Kenneth Manning, *Black Apollo of Science: The Life of Ernest Everett Just* (New York: Oxford University Press, 1983), 206.
6. Linda O. McMurry, *George Washington Carver: Scientist and Symbol* (New York: Oxford University Press, 1981), 52–70.
7. Philip Rieff, introd. to Kelly Miller, *Radicals and Conservatives and Other Essays on the Negro in America* (New York: Schocken Books, 1968).
8. John Bracy, August Meier, and Elliott Rudwick, *The Black Sociologists: The First Half-Century* (Belmont, Calif.: Wadsworth, 1971), 3–4.
9. Frederick L. Hoffman, *Race Traits and Tendencies of the American Negro* (New York: Macmillan, 1896).
10. Kenneth Bock, "Theories of Progress, Development, Evolution," in *A History of Sociological Analysis,* ed. Thomas Bottomore and Robert Nisbet (New York: Basic Books, 1978), 39–80.
11. W. E. B. Du Bois, *The Philadelphia Negro* (Philadelphia: University of Pennsylvania, 1899).
12. Gunnar Myrdal, *An American Dilemma* (New York: Harper, 1944), 1132.
13. Chicago Commission on Race Relations, *The Negro in Chicago: A Study of Race Relations and a Riot* (Chicago: University of Chicago Press, 1978), 39–79.
14. Mary Church Terrell, *A Colored Woman in a White World* (1940; reprint, New York: Arno Press, New York Times, 1980), 224.
15. Abby Johnson and Ronald Johnson, *Propaganda and Aesthetics* (Amherst: University of Massachusetts Press, 1979), 151.
16. Roi Ottley, *New World A-Coming: Inside Black America* (Boston: Houghton Mifflin, 1943), 277.
17. Charles Flint Kellogg, *NAACP: A History of the National Association for the Advancement of Colored People,* vol. 1, *1909–1920* (Baltimore: Johns Hopkins University Press, 1967), 52–53.

18. W. E. B. Du Bois, in *Crisis* 18 (5, 1919): 231.

19. Herbert Aptheker, ed., *The Correspondence of W. E. B. Du Bois,* vol. 1 (Amherst: University of Massachusetts Press, 1973), 168–69.

20. Johnson and Johnson, *Propaganda and Aesthetics,* 49.

21. Cary D. Wintz, *Black Culture and the Harlem Renaissance* (Houston: Rice University Press, 1988), 124.

22. Johnson and Johnson, *Propaganda and Aesthetics,* preface.

23. Ottley, *New World A-Coming,* 272.

24. W. E. B. Du Bois, "The Class Struggle," *Crisis* 22 (1921): 151–52.

25. Chandler Owen, editorial, in *Messenger* 3 (1921): 247.

26. Nathan I. Huggins, *Harlem Renaissance* (New York: Oxford University Press, 1971), 221–27, 239–43.

27. Countee Cullen, *Color* (new York: Harper, 1925), 8. 28. Darwin T. Turner, ed., *The Wayward and the Seeking: A Collection of Writings by Jean Toomer* (Washington, D.C.: Howard University Press, 1980); Therman B. O'Daniel, ed., *Jean Toomer; A Critical Evaluation* (Washington, D.C.: Howard University Press, 1988).

29. Jean Toomer, *Cane* (New York: W. W. Norton, 1988).

30. Alain Locke, ed., *The New Negro: An Interpretation* (New York: A & C Boni, 1925).

31. Turner, ed., *The Wayward and the Seeking,* 4. Also of note is the publication of Toomer's privately published poems, *Essentials,* with a foreword by Rudolph P. Ayrd (Athens: University of Georgia Press, 1991).

32. Malcolm Cowley, *Exile's Return* (New York: Compass Books, 1951), 77.

33. Harold Cruse, *The Crisis of the Negro Intellectual: A Historical Analysis of the Failure of Black Leadership* (New York: William Morrow, 1967); Huggins, *Harlem Renaissance.*

34. DuBose Heyward, *Porgy and Bess,* music by George Gershwin (New York: Gershwin Publishing, 1935).

35. Wintz, *Black Culture,* 126–27.

36. David Levering Lewis, *When Harlem Was in Vogue* (New York: Alfred A. Knopf, 1981), 120.

37. Ibid.

38. Langston Hughes, *The Big Sea* (New York: Hill and Wang, 1963), 325.

39. Robert Hemenway, *Zora Neale Hurston: A Literary Biography* (Urbana: University of Illinois Press, 1977), 110.

40. Otto Klineberg, *Negro Intelligence and Selective Migration* (New York: Columbia University Press, 1933).

41. Hemenway, *Zora Neale Hurston,* 239.

42. Hughes, *Big Sea,* 238–39.

43. Hemenway, *Zora Neale Hurston,* 286–87.

44. Alice Walker, foreword, ibid., xvi.

45. Lewis, *When Harlem Was in Vogue,* 154.

46. Hill, ed., *Black Women Oral History Project,* 4:169.

47. J. Saunders Redding, *They Came in Chains* (Philadelphia: Lippincott, 1950), 122.

48. Hughes, *Big Sea,* 229.

49. Wallace Thurman, "Negro Poets and Their Poetry," in *Black Expression,* ed. Addison Gayle (New York: Weybright and Talley, 1969), 70–82.

50. Wintz, *Black Culture*, 159–160.
51. W. E. B. Du Bois, "Criteria of Negro Art", in *Crisis* 32 (1926): 296.
52. Wallace Thurman, *Infants of the Spring* (New York: MacCauley, 1932; reprint, Carbondale: Southern Illinois University Press, 1979), 219.
53. Ibid., 91.
54. Ibid., 62.
55. Huggins, *Harlem Renaissance*, 240.
56. Du Bois, "Criteria of Negro Art," 297.
57. Ibid., 290.
58. Harold Cruse, interview by the author.

6: Beyond Incubation: A Talented But Trapped Tenth

1. Rudolph Fisher, *The Conjure-Man Dies* (New York: Arno Press, New York Times, 1971); *The Walls of Jericho* (New York: Arno Press, New York Times, 1969).
2. Horace Mann Bond, *Black American Scholars* (Detroit: Balamp, 1972), 27.
3. Ibid., 27.
4. Ibid., 114–16.
5. Horace Mann Bond, *The Education of the Negro in the American Social Order* (New York: Octagon Books, 1966), 278.
6. Ibid., 276. See also Fred McCuistion, *The South's Negro Teaching Force* (Nashville: Julius Rosenwald Fund, 1932).
7. Henry Allen Bullock, *A History of Negro Education in the South: From 1619 to the Present* (Cambridge: Harvard University Press, 1967).
8. J. Saunders Redding, *On Being Negro in America* (Indianapolis: Bobbs-Merrill, 1951), 91.
9. Horace Cayton, *Long Old Road* (New York: Trident Press, 1965), 192.
10. St. Clair Drake, lecture in graduate sociology department, University of California at Berkeley, spring 1985.
11. Raymond Wolters, *The New Negro on Campus: Black College Rebellions of the 1920s* (Princeton: Princeton University Press, 1975), 51–61.
12. Ibid., 130–34.
13. Meyer Weinberg, *A Chance to Learn* (Cambridge: Cambridge University Press, 1977), 286.
14. Kenneth Manning, *Black Apollo of Science* (New York: Oxford University Press, 1981), 206.
15. Benjamin Quarles, "The Breach between Douglass and Garrison," *Journal of Negro History* 23 (1938): 144–54.
16. Harold Cruse, interview by the author.
17. Algernon B. Jackson, "A Criticism of the Negro Professional," *Journal of Negro History* 18 (1933): 54.
18. Weinberg, *Chance to Learn*, 294.
19. Henry Allen Bullock, *A History of Negro Education* (New York: Praeger, 1970), 175.
20. Doug McAdam, *Political Process and the Development of Black Insurgency* (Chicago: University of Chicago Press, 1982), 103.
21. Rayford Logan, commencement address at Miner Teachers College, Washington, D.C., June, 22, 1939, RL(H)-II, box 21, "Addresses."

22. E. Franklin Frazier, "Graduate Education in Negro Colleges and Universities," *Journal of Negro Education* 2 (1933): 329–41.
23. Cedric Robinson, *Black Marxism* (London: Zed Press, 1983), 306.
24. E. Franklin Frazier, "The Status of the Negro in the American Social Order," *Journal of Negro Education* 4 (1935): 307.
25. Abby Johnson and Ronald Johnson, *Propaganda and Aesthetics* (Amherst: University of Massachusetts Press, 1979), 120.
26. Claude McKay, *A Long Way from Home* (New York: Harcourt, Brace & World, 1970), 228.
27. Ibid., 229.
28. Wilson Record, *Race and Radicalism: The NAACP and the Communist Party in Conflict* (Ithaca: Cornell University Press, 1964); Mark Naison, *Communists in Harlem during the Depression* (Urbana: University of Illinois Press, 1983).
29. Theodore Vincent, *Black Power and the Garvey Movement* (San Francisco: Ramparts Press, 1972).
30. Naison, *Communists in Harlem,* 8–9.
31. Robinson, *Black Marxism,* 311.
32. Naison, *Communists in Harlem,* 16.
33. W. E. B. DuBois, "Negro and Socialism," *Horizon* 1, no. 2 (1907): 7.
34. Raymond Wolters, *Negroes and the Great Depression* (Westport, Conn.: Greenwood Press, 1970), 230–65.
35. Ralph Bunche, "The Programs of Organizations Devoted to the Improvement of the Status of the Negro," *Journal of Negro Education* 8 (1939): 539–40.
36. William H. Harris, *The Harder We Run: Black Workers since the Civil War* (New York: Oxford University Press, 1982), esp. chap. 5.
37. Wolters, *Negroes and the Great Depression,* 353–81.
38. William Julius Wilson, *The Declining Significance of Race: Blacks and Changing American Institutions* (Chicago: University of Chicago Press, 1978).
39. Drake, lecture, 1985.
40. Jerre Mangione, *The Dream and the Deal: The Federal Writers' Project, 1935–1943* (Boston: Little, Brown, 1972).
41. Writers' Program (Va.), *The Negro in Virginia, Compiled by Workers of the Writers Program of the Work Projects Administration in the State of New York* (New York: Hastings House, 1940).
42. Algren, quoted in Mangione, *The Dream and the Deal,* 121.
43. Ibid., 255–56.
44. James McCune Smith, "Freedom and Slavery for Africans," *Liberator,* February 16 and 23, 1844.
45. Robert Guthrie, *Even the Rat Was White: A Historical View of Psychology* (New York: Harper & Row, 1976).
46. Otto Klineberg, *Negro Intelligence and Selective Migration* (New York: Columbia University Press, 1935).
47. Herman G. Canady, "The Effect of 'Rapport' on the I.Q.: A New Approach to the Problem of Racial Psychology," *Journal of Negro Education* 5 (1936): 209–19.
48. Martin D. Jenkins, "A Socio-Psychological Study of Negro Children of Superior Intelligence," *Journal of Negro Education* 5 (1936): 175–90.
49. Arthur Goren, *The American Jews* (Cambridge: Belknap Press, Harvard University Press, 1982).

50. Naison, *Communists in Harlem,* 174–75.
51. Walter White, *A Man Called White* (Bloomington: Indiana University Press, 1948), 228.
52. "World War II and Negro Higher Education," special issue of *Journal of Negro Education* 11 (1942): 241–434.
53. Clayton Kopps and Gregory Brooks, "Blacks, Loyalty and Motion Picture Propaganda in World War II," *Journal of American History* 73 (1986): 383–87.
54. John Hope Franklin, "Their War and Mine," *Journal of American History* 77 (1990): 577–78.
55. John B. Kirby, *Black Americans in the Roosevelt Era: Liberalism and Race* (Knoxville: University of Tennessee Press, 1980), 151.
56. Wolters, *Negroes and the Great Depression,* 219–29.
57. Edwin R. Embree to Clark Foreman, June 19, 1933, Julius Rosenwald Fund Archives, Fisk University, box 412.
58. Will Alexander to Aubrey Williams, January 16, 25, 1934, Civil Work, Administration, National Archives, box 83.
59. Ibid., 140.
60. Kirby, *Black Americans in the Roosevelt Era,* 111–21.
61. Roi Ottley, *New World A-Coming* (Boston: Houghton Mifflin, 1943), 258.
62. Genna Rae McNeil, *Groundwork: Charles Hamilton Houston and the Struggle for Civil Rights* (Philadelphia: University of Pennsylvania Press, 1983), 213–24.

## 7: Not a Lull, Not a Storm

1. Richard Pells, *The Liberal Mind in a Conservative Age* (New York: Harper & Row, 1985), 183–249.
2. Martin B. Duberman, *Paul Robeson* (1988; reprint, New York: Ballantine Books, 1990), 360–61.
3. "Copy of Transcript: State Department Information Program Senate Permanent Subcommittee on Investigations of the Subcommittee on Government Operation," Washington, D.C., March 26, 1953.
4. Arnold Rampersad, *The Life of Langston Hughes,* vol. 2 (New York: Oxford University Press, 1988), 93.
5. Ibid., 219.
6. Gerald Horne, *Black and Red: W. E. B. Du Bois and the Afro-American Response to the Cold War, 1944–1963* (Albany: State University of New York Press, 1986), 180.
7. C. Wright Mills, *The Power Elite* (New York: Oxford University Press, 1956).
8. Arthur Goren, *The American Jews* (Cambridge: Belknap Press, Harvard University Press, 1982), 83.
9. Meyer Weinberg, *A Chance to Learn* (Cambridge: Cambridge University Press, 1977), 288.
10. Hugh Graham, *The Civil Rights Era* (New York: Oxford University Press, 1990), 11–14.
11. Doug McAdams, *Political Process and the Development of Black Insurgency, 1930–1970* (Chicago: University of Chicago Press, 1982), 103.
12. Richard Kluger, *Simple Justice* (New York: Random House, 1975).
13. Ibid., 714.
14. J. Saunders Redding, *No Day of Triumph* (New York: Harper, 1942), 34.

15. Clayborne Carson, interview by the author.
16. Horace Mann Bond, *Black American Scholars* (Detroit: Balamp, 1972), 61–63.
17. Henry Louis Gates Jr., interview by the author.
18. Janice Willis, interview by the author.
19. Douglas Daniels, interview by the author.
20. Willis interview.
21. William Russell Ellis, interview by the author.
22. Ishmael Reed, interview by the author.
23. Richard Yarborough, interview by the author.
24. Gwendolyn Brooks, *Report from Part One: An Autobiography* (Detroit: Broadside Press, 1972), 177.
25. Troy Duster, interview by the author.
26. Ibid.
27. Gates interview.
28. Joseph Himes, interview by the author.
29. Bond, *Black American Scholars,* 73.
30. *From Slavery to Freedom* is now in its 7th textbook ed. (New York: McGraw-Hill, 1994). Alfred A. Moss Jr. is the coauthor of the more recent editions.
31. Hugh M. Gloster, "Race and the Negro Writer," *Phylon* 11 (1950): 369.
32. J. Saunders Redding, "American Negro Literature," in *Black Expression,* ed. Addison Gayle (New York: Weybright and Talley, 1969), 239.
33. Abby Johnson and Ronald Johnson, *Propaganda and Aesthetics* (Amherst: University of Massachusetts Press, 1979), 126.
34. Howard Schuman, Charlotte Steeh, and Lawrence BoBo, *Racial Attitudes in America* (Cambridge: Harvard University Press, 1988), chap. 6.
35. Martin Luther King Jr., "Letter from Birmingham Jail," in *Why We Can't Wait* (New York: Harper & Row, 1963), 79–80.
36. Ralph Ellison, *"An American Dilemma:* A Review," in *Shadow and Act* (New York: New American Library, 1964), 300.
37. Martin Luther King Jr., "Letter from Birmingham Jail" (1963), in *A Testament of Hope: The Essential Writings of Martin Luther King, Jr.,* ed. James Washington (San Francisco: Harper & Row, 1986), 302.
38. James Baldwin, *The Fire Next Time* (1963; reprint, New York: Dell, 1985), 128.
39. Reed interview.
40. Eldridge Cleaver, *Soul on Ice* (New York: McGraw-Hill, 1967); Michael Thelwell, "Black Studies: A Political Perspective," in *Duties, Pleasures, and Conflicts* (Amherst: University of Massachusetts Press, 1987), 3–29; Vincent Harding, "The Vocation of the Black Scholar and the Struggles of the Black Community," in *Education and Black Struggle,* ed. Institute of the Black World, Harvard Educational Review Monograph Series, no. 2 (Cambridge: Harvard Educational Review, 1974).
41. James Baldwin, *Notes of a Native Son* (Boston: Beacon Press, 1955), 165.
42. Ellison, *"American Dilemma,"* 302.
43. E. Franklin Frazier, "The Failure of the Negro Intellectual," *Negro Digest,* February 1962, 34.
44. Sally Belfrage, *Freedom Summer* (Charlottesville: University Press of Virginia, 1990); Clayborne Carson, *In Struggle: SNCC and the Black Awakening of the 1960s* (Cambridge: Harvard University Press, 1980).

45. Clayborne Carson, David Garrow, et al., eds., *The Eyes on the Prize Reader* (New York: Penguin Books, 1991), 164.

46. David Garrow, *Bearing the Cross: Martin Luther King and the Southern Leadership Conference* (New York: William Morrow, 1986), 281–83.

47. Harold Cruse, *The Crisis of the Negro Intellectual* (New York: William Morrow, 1984); Amiri Baraka, *Blues People: Negro Music in White America* (New York: Morrow Quill, 1963).

48. Brooks, *Report from Part One*, 177.

49. Amiri Baraka, *Black Magic Poetry* (New York: Bobbs-Merrill, 1967); Gwendolyn Brooks, *Jump Bad: A New Chicago Anthology* (Detroit: Broadside Press, 1971); Don L. Lee, *Dynamite Voices: Black Poets of the 1960s* (New York: Broadside Press, 1971).

50. David Caute, *The Illusion: An Essay on Politics, Theatre and the Novel* (London: Andre-Deutsch, 1971), 63.

51. Ralph Ellison, interview in *The Black American Writer*, vol. 1, ed. C. W. E. Bigsby (Baltimore: Penguin Books, 1971), 165.

## 8: STANDING AT THE CROSSROADS

1. Department of Commerce, *Statistical Abstract of the United States* (Washington, D.C.: Government Printing Office, 1970), 369.

2. Harvard Sitkoff, *The Struggle for Black Equality, 1954–1980* (New York: Hill and Wang, 1981), 229.

3. C. Eric Lincoln, ed., *Is Anybody Listening to Black America?* (New York: Seabury Press, 1968).

4. Kenneth B. Clark, introd. to *The Negro American*, ed. Talcott Parsons and Kenneth B. Clark (Boston: Beacon Press, 1967), xvii.

5. Malcolm X, "The Ballot or the Bullet," in *The Voice of Black America*, ed. Phillip Foner (New York: Simon and Schuster, 1972), 992.

6. Elijah Muhammad, in Louis Lomax, *When the Word Is Given* (New York: Signet, 1964), 56.

7. Ibid., 123.

8. Malcolm X, in *Malcolm X Speaks*, ed. George Breitman (New York: Grove Press, 1965), 213.

9. Roy Wilkins, with Tom Mathews, *The Autobiography of Roy Wilkins* (New York: Penguin Books, 1984), 317–19.

10. C. Eric Lincoln, "The Muslim Mission in the Context of American Social History," in *African American Religious Studies*, ed. Gayraud Wilmore (Durham: Duke University Press, 1989), 349.

11. William Brink and Lewis Harris, *Black and White: A Study of U.S. Racial Attitudes Today* (New York: Simon and Schuster, 1966), 120.

12. Kwame Ture (formerly Stokely Carmichael) and Charles V. Hamilton, *Black Power: The Politics of Liberation* (1968; reprint, New York: Vintage Books, 1992), 53.

13. Orlando Patterson, "The Moral Crisis of the Black American," *Public Interest*, no. 32 (Summer 1973): 43–69.

14. Clark, introd. to *Negro American*, xvii.

15. Roy Wilkins, *Standing Fast* (New York: Penguin Books, 1984), 309–27; Nancy

Weiss, *Whitney Young, Jr. and the Struggle for Civil Rights* (Princeton: Princeton University Press, 1989), 175–90.

16. Edward W. Blyden, "The Call of Providence to the Descendants of Africa in America," in *Negro Social and Political Thought: 1850–1920,* ed. Howard Brotz (New York: Basic Books, 1966), 117.

17. Ralph Ellison, *"An American Dilemma:* A Review," in *Shadow and Act* (New York: New American Library, 1964), 301.

18. Bayard Rustin, "Black Power and Coalition Politics," in *Down the Line: The Collected Writings of Bayard Rustin* (Chicago: Quadrangle Books, 1971), 154–54.

19. Harold Cruse, *Rebellion or Revolution* (New York: William Morrow, 1968).

20. Bayard Rustin, quoted in *New York Times,* December 15, 1963.

21. Martin Luther King Jr., *Where Do We Go from Here: Chaos or Community?* (New York: Harper & Row, 1967), 119–25.

22. Fern Marja Eckman, *The Furious Passage of James Baldwin* (New York: Popular Library, 1966), 195.

23. "Ideological Statement of the Congress of African Peoples," in *African Congress: A Documentary of the First Modern Pan-African Congress* (New York: William Morrow, 1972), 109.

24. Interview with Kwame Ture (formerly Stokely Carmichael), in Henry Hampton and Steve Fayer, with Sarah Flynn, *Voices of Freedom: An Oral History of the Civil Rights Movement from the 1950s through the 1980s* (New York: Bantam Books, 1990), 289–91.

25. Ralph Ellison, in "Conference Transcripts," *The Negro American,* ed. Parsons and Clark, 409.

26. Frantz Fanon, *The Wretched of the Earth* (New York: Grove Press, 1966), 176.

27. Ibid., 179.

28. Stokely Carmichael, "The Dialectics of Liberation," in *Stokely Speaks* (New York: Vintage Books, 1971), 77–99.

29. Larry Neal, "The Black Contribution to American Letters: Part II," in *Black American Reference Book,* ed. Mabel Smythe (Englewood Cliffs, N.J.: Prentice-Hall, 1976), 775.

30. Karl Mannheim, *Ideology and Utopia: An Introduction to the Sociology of Knowledge,* trans. Louis Wirth and Edward Shils (New York: Harcourt, Brace, 1936), 131.

31. Henry Louis Gates Jr., interview by the author.

32. James Washington, ed., *A Testament of Hope: The Essential Writings of Martin Luther King, Jr.* (San Francisco: Harper & Row, 1986), 374–75.

33. Whitney Young, in *Voice of Black America,* ed. Foner, 967; Baynard Rustin, "A Way Out of the Exploding Ghetto," ibid., 1078.

34. Clayborne Carson, interview by the author.

35. Richard Yarborough, interview by the author.

36. Carson interview.

37. Gates interview.

38. Harold Cruse, *Crisis of the Negro Intellectual* (New York: William Morrow, 1968); St. Clair Drake, "Studies of the African Diaspora: The Work and Reflections of St. Clair Drake" (based on interviews with Benjamin Bowser), *Sage Race Relations Abstracts* 14, no. 3 (August 1989): 3–29; Vincent Harding, "The

Vocation of the Black Scholar and the Struggles of the Black Community," in *Education and Black Struggle,* ed. Institute of the Black World, Harvard Educational Review Monograph Series, no. 2 (Cambridge: Harvard Educational Review, 1974).

## 9: CAPTURING THE DEFINITION

1. Henry Louis Gates Jr., interview by the author.
2. John Edgar Wideman, *Brothers and Keepers* (New York: Holt, Rinehart & Winston, 1984), 114.
3. Armstead Robinson, quoted in *Yale Alumni Magazine,* reprinted in *The University Crisis Reader,* ed. Immanuel Wallerstein and Paul Starr, vol. 1 (New York: Vintage Books, 1971), 378.
4. Glenn E. deChabert, quoted ibid, 384.
5. Nathan Hare, "The Case for Separatism: Black Perspective," in *Black Power and Student Rebellion,* ed. James McEway and Abraham Miller (Belmont, Calif.: Wadsworth, 1969), 233.
6. Gates interview.
7. Richard Yarborough,interview by the author.
8. Adolph Reed, "The Black Revolution and the Reconstruction of Domination," in *Race, Politics, and Culture: Critical Essays on the Radicalism of the Sixties,* ed. Adolph Reed (Westport, Conn.: Greenwood Press, 1986), 61–95.
9. Clayborne Carson, interview by the author.
10. Troy Duster, interview by the author.
11. Frantz Fanon, *The Wretched of the Earth,* trans. Constance Farrington (New York: Grove Press, 1963), 211–27.
12. Angela Davis, *An Autobiography* (New York: Random House, 1974; reprint, New York: International Publishers, 1988).
13. Gates interview.
14. Bayard Rustin, *Down the Line* (Chicago: Quadrangle Books, 1971), 226.
15. Thomas Sowell, "Patterns of Black Excellence," in *Public Interest,* no. 43 (September 1976): 26–58.
16. Vincent Harding, "The Vocation of the Black Scholar and the Struggles of the Black Community," in *Education and Black Struggle,* ed. Institute of the Black World, Harvard Educational Review Monograph Series, no. 2 (Cambridge: Harvard Educational Review, 1974).
17. Thomas Sowell, *Markets and Minorities* (New York: Basic Books, 1971), 103–24.
18. Duster interview.
19. Halford Fairchild, interview by the author.
20. Lee Rainwater and William L. Yancey, *The Moynihan Report and the Politics of Controversy* (Cambridge: MIT Press, 1967).
21. Herbert Gutman, *The Black Family in Slavery and Freedom, 1750–1925* (New York: Pantheon Books, 1976).
22. Carol B. Stack, *All Our Kin: Strategies for Survival in a Black Community* (New York: Harper & Row, 1974).
23. Ron Karenga, "Black Cultural Nationalism," *Negro Digest,* January 1968, 5–9.
24. Gates interview.

10: RUDE AWAKENINGS

1. Halford Fairchild, interview by the author.
2. William Exum, "Climbing the Crystal Stair: Values, Affirmative Action, and Minority Faculty," *Social Problems* 30 (1983): 383–99.
3. George Napper, *Blacker Than Thou* (Grand Rapids: William Eerdmans, 1973), 113.
4. Nathan Hare, "The Case for Separatism," *Newsweek,* February 10, 1969, 56.
5. Benjamin Quarles, interview by the author.
6. Ronald Taylor, interview by the author.
7. Robert Cummings, interview by the author.
8. Nell Irvin Painter, interview by the author.
9. Albert Rabateau, interview by the author.
10. Douglas Daniels, interview by the author.
11. Michael Thelwell, "Black Studies and White Universities," *Duties, Pleasures, and Conflicts: Essays in Struggle* (Amherst: University of Massachusetts Press, 1987), 138.
12. Richard Yarborough, interview by the author.
13. Clayborne Carson, interview by the author.
14. Yarborough interview.
15. Carson interview.
16. Thomas Sowell, *Affirmative Action Reconsidered: Was It Necessary in Academia?* (Washington, D.C.: American Enterprise Institute, 1975), 17.
17. John Hope Franklin, interview by the author.
18. Nell Irvin Painter, "Hers," *New York Times,* December 10, 1981, 22.
19. Norris Johnson, interview by the author.
20. Duster interview.
21. J. Saunders Redding, *On Being Negro in America* (Indianapolis: Bobbs-Merrill, 1951), 43–44.
22. Taylor interview.
23. Ibid.
24. Hare, "Case for Separatism," 233.
25. Michael Thelwell, "From San Francisco State & Cornell: Two Black Radicals Report on Their Campus Struggles," *Ramparts,* July 1969, 50.
26. Robert Merton, "Insiders and Outsiders: A Chapter in the Sociology of Knowledge," *American Journal of Sociology* 78 (1972): 11.
27. Ibid., 27.
28. David Southern, *Gunnar Myrdal and Black-White Relations: The Use and Abuse of "An American Dilemma," 1944–1969* (Baton Rouge: Louisiana State University Press, 1987), 20–25.
29. John Blassingame, *New Perspectives in Black Studies* (Urbana: University of Illinois Press, 1971), 164.
30. Anthony DePalma, "Hard-won Acceptance Spawns New Conflicts around Ethnic Studies," *New York Times,* January 2, 1991, B7.
31. Blassingame, *New Perspectives,* 153.
32. Raymond Nunn, member of the Black Student Alliance at Yale, quoted in *Yale Alumni Magazine,* May 1969, reprinted in *The University Crisis Reader,* ed. Immanuel Wallerstein and Paul Starr, vol. 1 (New York: Vintage Books, 1971), 381.

33. Amiri Baraka, "A Reply to Saunders Reddings' 'The Black Revolution in American Studies,' " in Amiri Baraka, ed., *Daggers and Javelins* (New York: Quill, 1984), 282.
34. Allan Sindler, *Bakke, Defunis and Minority Admissions: The Quest for Equal Opportunity* (New York: Longman, 1978).
35. Arthur Goren, *The American Jews* (Cambridge: Belknap Press, Harvard University Press, 1982).
36. Stephen Steinberg, *The Ethnic Myth: Race, Ethnicity, and Class in America* (New York: Atheneum, 1981).
37. Neil Jumonville, *Critical Crossings: The New York Intellectuals in Postwar America* (Berkeley: University of California Press, 1991), 118; Irving Howe, *World of Our Fathers* (New York: Simon and Schuster, 1976), 412.
38. Lewis Feuer, "The Stages of Social History of Jewish Professions in American Colleges and Universities," *American Jewish History* 71 (1982): 432–65.
39. Steinberg, *Ethnic Myth,* 250.
40. Goren, *American Jews,* 94.
41. Bernard Rosenberg and Irving Howe, "Are American Jews Turning to the Right?" in *The New Conservatives: A Critique from the Left,* ed. Lewis Coser and Irving Howe (New York: Quadrangle Books, 1974), 72.
42. Interview by the author.
43. Duster interview.
44. Painter interview.
45. Peter Novick, *That Noble Dream* (Cambridge: Cambridge University Press, 1988), 479; interview by the author.
46. Cummings interview.
47. Painter interview.

11: IMAGINING FOR THE PEOPLE

1. Larry Neal, "The Black Arts Movement," in *The Black Aesthetic,* ed. Addison Gayle (Garden City, N.Y.: Doubleday, 1971), 272.
2. Ron Karenga, "Black Cultural Nationalism," *Negro Digest,* January 1968, 8.
3. Richard Wright, "Blueprint for Negro Writing," in *Amistad 2,* ed. John A. Williams and Charles Harris (New York: Vintage Books, 1981), 11.
4. LeRoi Jones, "Black Art," *Liberator* 6, no. 1 (January 1966): 18.
5. Ralph Ellison, "Some Questions and Some Answers," in *Shadow and Act* (New York: New American Library, 1964), 254–55.
6. "Transcript of the American Academy Conference on the Negro American— May 14–15, 1965," *Daedalus,* 95, no. 1 (Winter 1966): 436–37.
7. Albert Murray, *The Omni-Americans* (1970; New York: Avon, 1971), 14.
8. Ibid.
9. Nathan Huggins, *Black Odyssey* (New York: Random House, 1977).
10. Larry Neal, quoted in Hoyt W. Fuller, "A Survey: Black Writers Views on Literary Lions and Values," *Negro Digest,* January 1968, 35.
11. Jennifer Jordan, "Cultural Nationalism in the Sixties: Politics and Poetry," in *Race, Politics, and Culture* ed. Adolph Reed (Westport, Conn.: Greenwood Press, 1986), 29–60.
12. George Schuyler, "The Negro Art Hokum," *Nation* 122 (June 26, 1926): 662–63.

13. J. Saunders Redding, quoted in Fuller, "Survey," 12.

14. Robert W. Hayden, quoted ibid., 84.

15. Richard Gilman, "White Standards and Negro Writing," *New Republic,* March 9, 1968, 25.

16. Ibid., 28.

17. Richard Gilman, "More on Negro Writing," *New Republic* April 13, 1968, 27.

18. Theodore Gross, "Our Mutual Estate: The Literature of the American Negro," *Antioch Review* 28 (Fall 1968): 293–303.

19. "American Academy Conference on the Negro American," 436.

20. Ishmael Reed, ed., *19 Necromancers from Now* (Garden City, N.Y.: Doubleday, 1970), xiii.

21. Harold Cruse, *The Crisis of the Negro Intellectual* (New York: William Morrow, 1967).

22. Alice Walker, interview in John O'Brien, ed., *Interviews with Black Writers* (New York: Liveright, 1973), 184–211.

23. John Wideman, interview ibid., 212–23.

24. Robert Merton, "Role of the Intellectual in Public Bureaucracy," *Social Forces* 23 (1945): 405–15.

25. Nathan I. Huggins, *Harlem Renaissance* (New York: Oxford University Press, 1971), 199.

26. Adrienne Kennedy, interview by the author.

27. Romare Bearden, "The Negro Artist and Modern Art," *Journal of Negro Life,* December 1934, 371.

28. Darwin Turner, "Afro-American Literary Critics: An Introduction," in *Black Aesthetic,* 59–33.

29. Arnold Rampersad, *The Life of Langston Hughes,* 2 vols. (New York: Oxford University Press, 1986–88); Robert O'Mealy, *The Craft of Ralph Ellison* (Cambridge: Harvard University Press, 1980); Gerald Early, *Tuxedo Junction: Essays on American Culture* (New York: Echo Press, 1989); Barbara Christian, *Black Women Novelists* (Westport, Conn.: Greenwood Press, 1980); Henry Louis Gates, *The Signifying Monkey: A Theory of Afro-American Literary Criticism* (New York: Oxford University Press, 1988); Trudier Harris, *From Mammies to Militants: Domestics in Black American Literature* (Philadelphia: Temple University Press, 1982).

30. Audre Lorde, interview in Claudia Tate, ed., *Black Women Writers at Work* (New York: Continuum, 1983), 107.

31. Stanley Crouch, *Notes of a Hanging Judge* (New York: Oxford University Press, 1990).

32. Ibid., xi.

33. Ishmael Reed, interview in O'Brien, ed., *Interviews with Black Writers,* 179.

34. Ishmael Reed, *Yellow Back Radio Broke-Down* (Garden City, N.Y.: Doubleday, 1969), 35.

35. Larry Neal, "The Black Contribution to American Letters: Part II," in *Black American Reference Book,* ed. Mabel Smythe (Englewood Cliffs, N.J.: Prentice-Hall, 1976), 774.

36. Charles Wright, *The Messenger* (New York: Farrar, Straus, 1963); idem, *The Wig: A Mirror Image* (New York: Farrar, Straus & Giroux, 1966); John Edgar Wideman, *Hurry Home* (New York: Harcourt Brace Jovanovich, 1970); idem,

*The Lynchers* (New York: Harcourt Brace Jovanovich, 1973); Carlene Hatcher Polite, *The Flagellants* (New York: Farrar, Straus & Giroux, 1967).

37. Kennedy interview.
38. Russell Ross, *Bird Lives* (London: Quartet Books, 1973), 173.
39. Leo Steinberg, "Contemporary Art and the Plight of Its Public," in *Sociology of Art and Literature,* ed. Milton Albrecht, James Barnett, and Mason Triff (New York: Praeger, 1970), 519.
40. LeRoi Jones, *Black Music* (New York: William Morrow, 1970), 15.
41. Ibid., 17.
42. Neal, "Black Contribution to American Letters," 784.
43. Toni Morrison, interview in Claudia Tate, ed., *Black Women Writers at Work* (New York: Continuum, 1983), 121.
44. Wynton Marsalis, quoted in Nat Hentoff, "New Horn from New Orleans," *Progressive,* April 1982, 52.
45. Ralph Ellison, "The Golden Age, Time Past," in *Shadow and Act,* 211–12.
46. Marsalis, quoted in Hentoff, "New Horn from New Orleans," 52.
47. Playthell Benjamin, "Spike Lee: Bearing the Cross," *Emerge,* November 1991, 31.
48. Ibid., 32.
49. *Transition,* no. 56 (1992): 188.
50. August Wilson, "I Want a Black Director," *New York Times,* September 26, 1990.
51. Randall Kennedy, "Making It," *Reconstruction* 1 (Spring 1990): 66–67.
52. *Transition: An International Journal* began its new series with issue no. 55 (1992).
53. Ron Karenga, "Black Cultural Nationalism," in *Black Aesthetic,* 34.
54. Henry Louis Gates, *Loose Canons* (New York: Oxford University Press, 1992), 3–42.
55. Hazel Carby, "The Multicultural Wars," in *Black Popular Culture,* ed. Gina Dent (Seattle: Bay Press, 1992), 197.
56. Trey Ellis, "The New Black Aesthetic," *Callaloo* 12 (1989): 233–43.
57. Ishmael Reed, "Integration or Cultural Exchange," *Yardbird Reader* 5 (1976): 3.
58. Ellis, "New Black Aesthetic," 235.
59. Eric Lott, "Response to Trey Ellis's 'The New Black Aesthetic,' " *Callaloo* 12 (1989): 244.
60. Crouch, *Notes of a Hanging Judge,* 206.
61. Susan Willis, "Eruptions of Funk: Historicizing Toni Morrison," in *Black Literature and Literary Theory,* ed. Henry Louis Gates (New York: Methuen, 1984), 270.

## 12: WHAT SHALL I RENDER?

1. Karl Mannheim, *Ideology and Utopia,* trans. Louis Wirth and Edward Shils (New York: Harcourt, Brace, 1936), 155.
2. Richard Yarborough, interview by the author.
3. Clarence Walker, interview by the author.
4. Troy Duster, interview by the author.

5. J. Saunders Redding, *On Being Negro in America* (Indianapolis: Bobbs-Merrill, 1951), 26.

6. Alain Locke, "Spiritual Truancy," in *Voices from the Harlem Renaissance,* ed. Nathan I. Huggins (New York: Oxford University Press, 1976), 406.

7. John Hope Franklin, "The Dilemma of the American Negro Scholar," in *Soon, One Morning: New Writing by American Negroes, 1940–1962,* ed. Herbert Hill (New York: Alfred A. Knopf, 1963), 73.

8. F. M. Dostoevsky, *Notes from Underground* (New York: Dutton, 1960), 10.

9. Henry Louis Gates Jr., interview by the author.

10. W. Russell Ellis, interview by the author.

11. Duster interview.

12. Jane Pease and William Pease, *They Who Would Be Free* (New York: Atheneum, 1974).

13. Amy Jacques Garvey, *The Philosophy and Opinions of Marcus Garvey* (1925; reprint, London: Frank Cass, 1967); August Meier, *Negro Thought in America, 1880–1915* (Ann Arbor: University of Michigan Press, 1963).

14. John Brown Childs, *Leadership, Conflict and Cooperation in Afro-American Social Thought* (Philadelphia: Temple University Press, 1989).

15. Nathan I. Huggins, *Harlem Renaissance* (New York: Oxford University Press, 1971); Arnold Rampersad, *The Life of Langston Hughes,* 2 vols. (New York: Oxford University Press, 1986–88).

16. Wayne Cooper, *Claude McKay: Rebel Sojourner in the Harlem Renaissance* (Baton Rouge: Louisiana State University Press, 1987), chap. 10.

17. Milton Friedman, foreword to Thomas Sowell, *Markets and Minorities* (New York: Basic Books, 1981), vii–viii.

18. Thomas Sowell, *Black Education: Myths and Tragedies* (New York: David McKay, 1972), *Affirmative Action Reconsidered: Was It Necessary in Academia?* (Washington, D.C.: American Enterprise Institute, 1975), and *Markets and Minorities.*

19. Thomas Sowell, *Ethnic America* (New York: Basic Books, 1981).

20. Thomas Sowell, "Blacker Than Thou," *Washington Post,* February 14, 1983, 23.

21. Christopher Lasch, "Discrimination and Thomas Sowell," in *New York Review of Books,* March 3, 1983, 19; Ronald Takaki, "Is Race Surmountable? Thomas Sowell's Celebration of Japanese-American 'Success,' " in *Ethnicity and the Work Force,* ed. Winston Van Horne (Madison: University of Wisconsin Press, 1985), 208–22; Troy Duster, "The Ideological Frame of 'Benign Neglect,' " *Journal of Contemporary Studies* 4 (1981): 80–91.

22. William Julius Wilson, *The Declining Significance of Race* (Chicago: University of Chicago Press, 1978).

23. G. Franklin Edwards, interview by the author.

24. Charles V. Willie, "The Inclining Significance of Race," *Society* 15, no. 5 (1979): 10, 12–15.

25. Gates interview.

26. Duster interview.

27. Kenneth Robert Janken, *Rayford W. Logan and the Dilemma of the African-American Intellectual* (Amherst: University of Massachusetts Press, 1993), 232.

28. Rampersad, *Life of Langston Hughes,* 2:402.

29. Mack Jones, interview by the author.
30. Harold Cruse, *The Crisis of the Negro Intellectual* (New York: William Morrow, 1984), 476–97.
31. J. Saunders Redding went from Hampton to George Washington University; Darwin Turner, from North Carolina A&T to Iowa; Samuel DuBois Cook, from Atlanta University to Duke; and Blyden Jackson, from Southern University to Louisiana State University.
32. Henry Lee Allen, "The Mobility of Black Collegiate Faculty Resisted: Whatever Happened to the 'Brain Drain'?" *Journal of Negro Education* 60 (1991): 107.
33. Patricia Williams, *The Alchemy of Race and Rights* (Cambridge: Harvard University Press, 1991), 120.
34. Andrew Hacker, *Two Nations* (New York: Scribner's, 1992); Ellis Cose, *The Rage of a Privileged Class* (New York: HarperCollins, 1993).
35. Edward C. Banfield, *The Unheavenly City: The Nature and Future of Our Urban Crisis* (Boston: Little, Brown, 1970).
36. Cornel West, "The Dilemma of the Black Intellectual," *Cultural Critique* 1 (Fall 1985): 122.
37. Edward Shils, "Color, the Universal Intellectual Community, and the Afro-Asian Intellectual," *Daedalus* 96, no. 2 (Spring 1967): 279–95; Milton Gordon, *Assimilation in American Life* (New York: Oxford University Press, 1964).
38. Antonio Gramsci, *Selections from the Prison Notebooks,* ed. and trans. Quintin Hoare and Geoffrey N. Smith (New York: International Publishers, 1977).
39. Cornel West, *Race Matters* (Boston: Beacon Press, 1993).
40. Robert Boynton, "The New Intellectuals," *Atlantic Monthly,* March 1995, 53–70; Michael Alan Bérubé, "Public Academy," *New Yorker,* January 9, 1995, 73–80; Jervis Anderson, "The Public Intellectual," *New Yorker,* January 17, 1994, 39ff.
41. Adolph Reed, "The Current Crisis of the Black Intellectual," *Village Voice,* April 11, 1995, 31–36.
42. Ibid., 32.
43. Adolph Reed, *The Jesse Jackson Phenomenon: The Crisis of Purpose in Afro-American Politics* (New Haven: Yale University Press, 1986), 123–36.
44. Reed, "Current Crisis," 33.
45. Ibid., 35.
46. Ibid.
47. Martin Kilson, "Anatomy of Black Conservatism," *Transitions* no. 59 (1993): 4–19; Derrick Bell, *Faces at the Bottom of the Well: The Permanence of Racism* (New York: Basic Books, 1992), 114–16.
48. Stephen Carter, *Confessions of an Affirmative Action Baby* (New York: Basic Books, 1991).
49. Glenn Loury, "Comments on Stephen Carter's Reflections of an Affirmative Action Baby," *Reconstruction* 1, no. 4 (1992): 119.
50. Shelby Steele, "I'm Black, You're White, Who's Innocent?" *Harper's Magazine,* June 1988, 45–53.
51. Walter Mosley, *Devil in a Blue Dress* (New York: Pocket Books, 1991), 153.
52. Martin Luther King, "Letter From Birmingham Jail"; Bayard Rustin, *Down the Line* (Chicago: Quadrangle Books, 1971), 238.

Epilogue

1. Al Young, "Statement on Aesthetics, Poetics and Kinetics," in *New Black Voices*, ed. Abraham Chapman (Bridgeport, N.J.: Mentor, 1972), 554.
2. Jerry G. Watts, "Dilemmas of Black Intellectuals," *Dissent* 36 (Fall 1989): 507.
3. Douglas Massey and Nancy Denton, *American Apartheid: Segregation and the Making of the Underclass* (Cambridge: Harvard University Press, 1993); Shelby Steele, *The Content of Our Character* (New York: HarperCollins, 1991).

# INDEX